NUCLEAR TERROR SURVIVAL HANDBOOK
Part 2 – Beyond One Mile

With this knowledge you can survive.

Vern Blanchette

Rev 1   1711041

Areli Books

Test Shot "Buster Dog" 1951 viewed from 6 miles[1].
With this knowledge you can survive, just as these men did.

---

[1] Government photograph in the public domain, available at many websites and nuclear weapons historical museums.

This book is the second of the two-part *Nuclear Terror Survival Handbook*. Readers are encouraged to begin reading *The Nuclear Terror Survival Handbook Part 1 – Within One Mile* because some of the topics discussed in Part 1, such as the effects of heat, light, blast, and radiation, as they relate to the experiences of the 11 citizens discussed in Part 1, will aid in understanding the scenarios of the 11 citizens spotlighted in Part 2.

Preface

A stark white light suddenly filled the room, and over Tessie's shoulder Rob could see through their picture window what appeared to be a white-hot star rising from Yorksberg's downtown district across the river. Its brilliance kept him from looking directly at it. For a second he hesitated, and then he saw it - a circle of disturbance spreading rapidly toward them across the river. Recognizing the spreading circle as evidence of a blast wave coming from the explosion, he grabbed Tessie's arm and pulled her out from in front of the window.

"Rob! You hurt my elbow!" she said just before the window shattered into the living room and the house shuddered under a singular, loud boom. A strong, cold wind briefly blew in along with a distant, deep, horrible rumble, like continuous thunder coming from across the Taconic River.

"What happened?" she said.

"That was close." Rob shook a piece of broken glass off his shoe. His heart raced and his hands trembled from their close call.

"My fish!" Tessie wailed at the sight of their broken fish tank.

"Ten gallons of water on the rug and dying fish are nothing compared to what the folks over there are going through," he said, pointing out the window. "Forget the fish babe. Yorksberg has just been nuked."

"Nuked? You mean that was a nuclear explosion?" Tessie turned from the fish and looked at the mushroom-shaped cloud rising from the distant city. She grabbed his arm. "Rob, what do we do?"

That is the question, isn't it? What would you do? Clean up the broken glass? Save the fish? Fix the window? Pack and leave?

We will rejoin Rob and his wife in one of the stories in this book and find out what they do, but for now consider that you are living in or visiting a large metropolitan area when a terrorist organization explodes a nuclear bomb in the city. You have survived the nuclear explosion; now what will you do to survive the aftermath?

> **What you do, or fail to do, may determine whether you live or die.**

If you live in a suburb, a small town, or far from a city, don't make the mistake of thinking you are safe. In fact, you and your family could be in grave danger even if you survive the explosion.

What must you do to assure that you and your loved ones survive? This is what this survival handbook is about. Using a mixture of fiction and fact, this handbook will present you with the knowledge you need to help you survive a terrorist's nuclear attack in a city.

Note: Topics covered in this two-part handbook are listed in Appendix E1 of Part 1.

TABLE OF CONTENTS
(Note: Chapters 1 through 11 are contained in Part 1 of this Handbook)

Introduction

The section below is a recap of some of the introductory information for those who have not read the Nuclear Terror Survival Handbook Part 1. Those who have read part 1 may choose to skip to Chapter 12 and meet Yorksberg citizen Lamar Henderson. Events in this cold December day will change his life.

Civil Defense educational material tends to be boring, so in order to engage the reader's interest the author has created a fictional city (Yorksberg) populated with fictional people who undergo a nuclear attack. The bomb's explosion is seen over and over again in the lives of twenty-two fictional citizens, each given their own chapter, with the bomb's effects correlated to the person's location and technical details of the effects ferreted out of Glasstone and Dolan's epic "The Effects of Nuclear Weapons". The reader will "experience" the nuclear attack from the point of view of these twenty-two fictional lives. The stories of several people a long distance from the attacked city are included to allow discussion of the effect of the bomb at distant locations.

If you will read all twenty-two short stories, carefully consider what the analysis section says about each story, and try your hand at the self-check questions at the end of each chapter, you will be more nuclear street-smart and your chances of surviving a nuclear attack will improve.[2]

At the end of each short story an analysis will walk you through the details of what just happened in the story. This will help you understand the effects of the bomb and the consequences of the choices made by the people in the stories. Your ability to survive the coming attack will improve as you read and learn.

Believing that there is nothing you can do to survive is a self-fulfilling prophesy. Throw away that stinking thinking. You can improve your survival chances. You can survive a nuclear attack.

---

[2] Read the footnotes, like this one. References, technical data and knowledge enriching content will be included as footnotes.

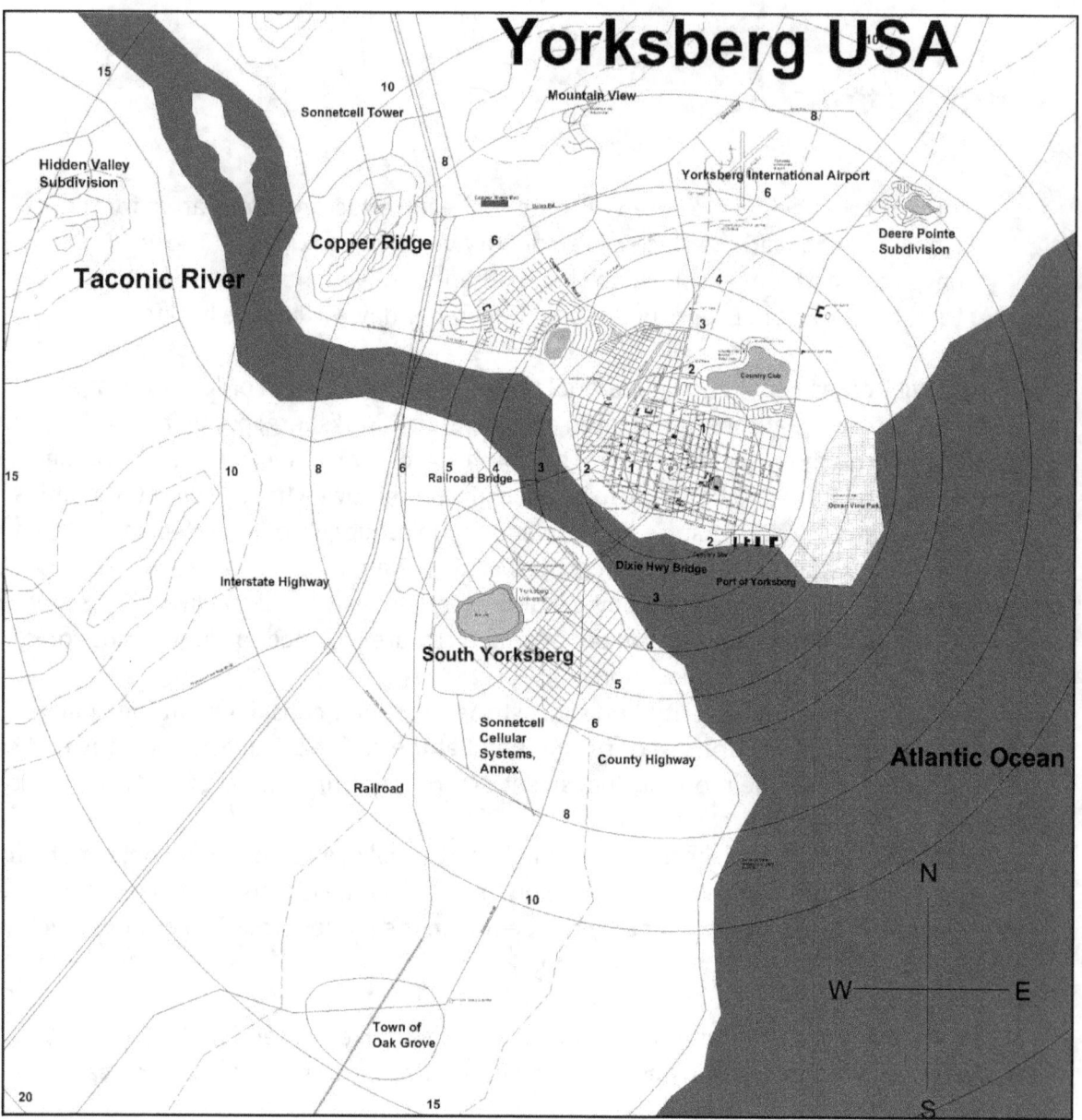

Wide View of the Yorksberg Area

Setting the Scene

Before visiting our first Yorksberg citizen, let's bring our fictional city of Yorksberg to life. The *Wide View of the Yorksberg Area* is a map of Yorksberg showing features within fifteen miles of the city. Other maps of Yorksberg associated with each chapter will help you follow the stories as you read.

While some of the details in this first map may appear too small to see, they will be zoomed in on subsequent maps to reveal important details. The circular rings are centered on the location where the bomb explodes, and the rings are marked off in miles.

Note on this general view of Yorksberg that the city sits at the mouth of the Taconic River and on the Atlantic Ocean. Many of the city streets are visible as fine black lines. The double line is the interstate highway, which runs generally north to south as it passes a local elevated feature called Copper Ridge and then crosses the river into South Yorksberg. Elevations are roughly indicated by faint, dashed, contour lines.

You are encouraged to follow each story using the maps provided because distances from where the bomb explodes are critically important, and at times the fictional characters will move within the city.

The downtown Yorksberg area is shown in more detail in the map below.

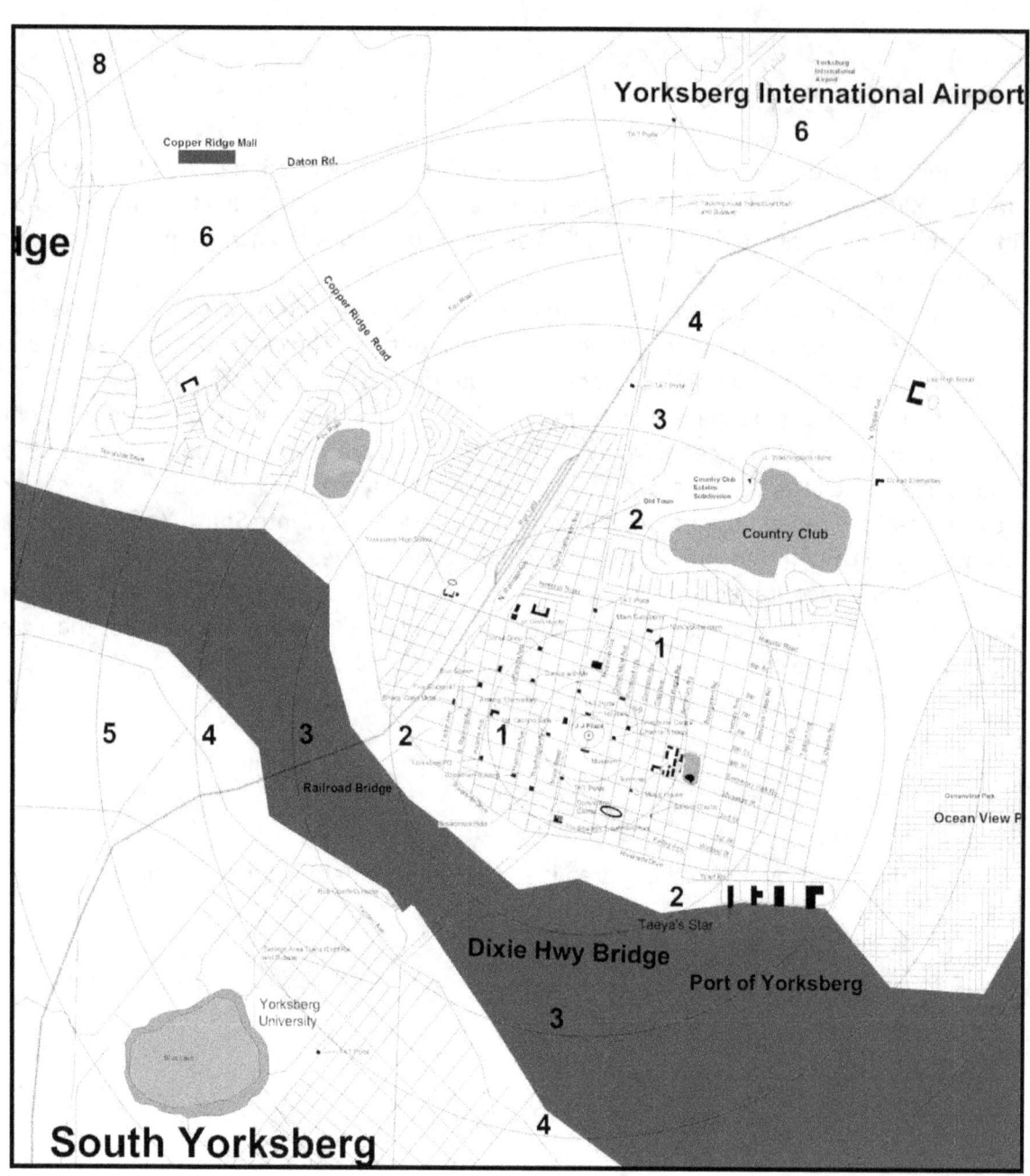

The City of Yorksberg

In this view we are looking at an area of the city within 5 to 6 miles of the bomb's explosion. The names of the major streets are now resolved, although still difficult to read at this scale. A railroad line crosses the Taconic River on the first bridge downstream of the interstate highway bridge. You can follow it up into the city to the railyards.

The second bridge downstream of the interstate highway carries the "Dixie Highway." This is the older state highway that carried traffic prior to the building of the interstate.

There is also a light rail subway called the Taconic Area Transit that citizens refer to as the TAT. You can see it as a dashed line next to the Dixie Highway Bridge. Follow it with your eyes as it runs from South Yorksberg under the river and then under the city up to the airport. It plays an important part in one of the stories.

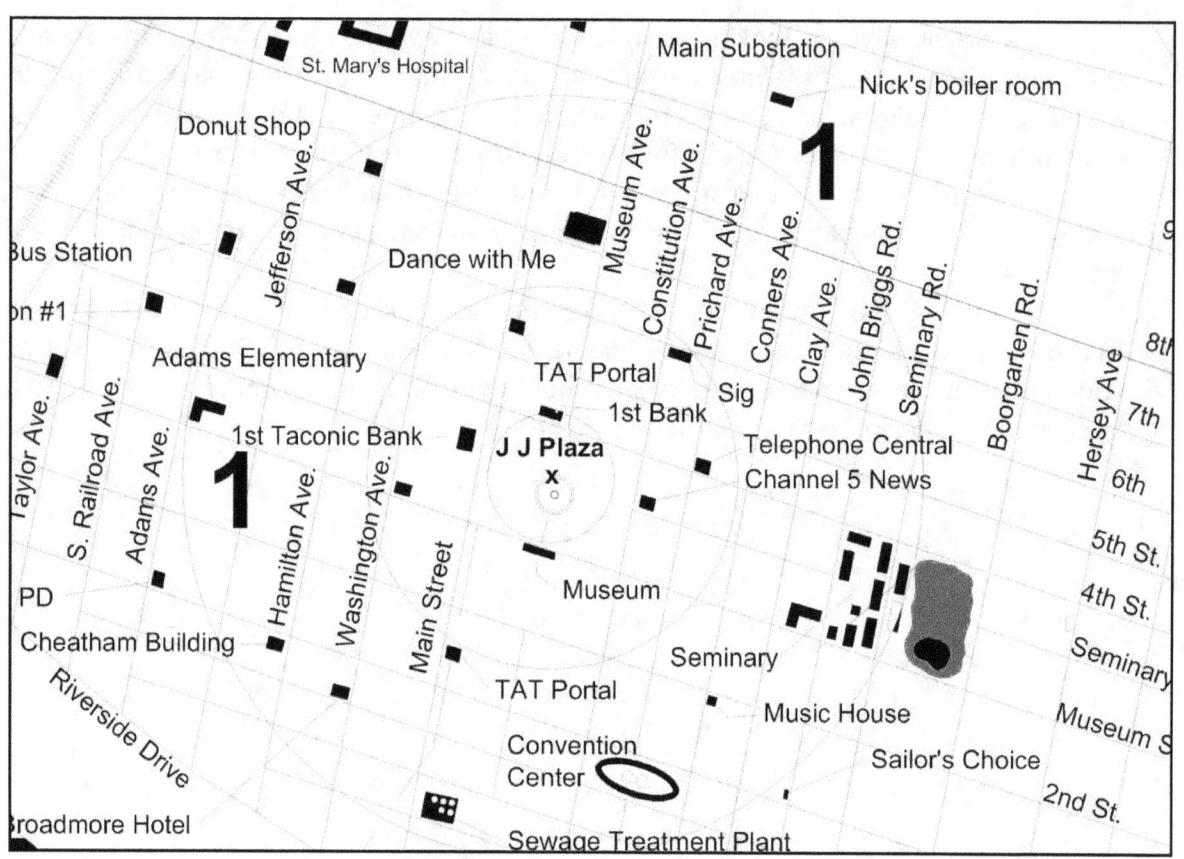

Downtown Yorksberg

Downtown Yorksberg

The map of the heart of downtown Yorksberg shows John Jay Plaza. At the center of the plaza is a fountain (the smallest circle) ringed by a circular driveway. The small "x" on the north side of the circular driveway is the location of the truck containing the nuclear bomb when it explodes.

The next larger light gray circle that almost touches the museum is the approximate diameter of the white-hot fireball the bomb creates. Just to the left of the big numeral "1" is a light gray ring one mile from the explosion. The light gray ring between this one-mile ring and J J Plaza is one-half mile from the bomb.

The small rectangles are various buildings in the city. Not all buildings and streets are shown, but most of the ones with labels will play a part in one or more of the short stories.

Look at the Downtown Yorksberg map and see if you can spot the location of the action in these chapters:

Chapter 1 – The Museum
Chapter 2 – Sigmund Johanson's (Sig's) Apartment
Chapter 3 – Sailor's Choice Restaurant
Chapter 4 – Music House
Chapter 5 – Broadmore Hotel
Chapter 6 – "Dance with Me" dance studio
Chapter 7 – Convention Center
Chapter 8 – Cheatham Building Construction Site
Chapter 9 – Donut Shop
Chapter 10 – Seminary
Chapter 11 – Adams Elementary School
Chapter 14 – St. Mary's Hospital

Throughout the narratives of each of the lives discussed in these short stories, the author has tried to keep the effect of the bomb and scale of destruction accurate to the energy released (19 kt)[3].

Ready or Not!

It is a cold December afternoon, about 35 °F, with a visibility of 10+ miles and no cloud ceiling. Ground-level winds are out of the south-southwest at a fairly steady 15 mph. The roads are clear of snow, but patches of melting snow still linger along some roadways and on the north-facing slopes of hills. Winds at high altitudes, 30,000 to 50,000 feet, where the

---

[3] 19 kt means 19,000 tons of TNT equivalent. TNT is an abbreviation for the chemical explosive TriNitroToluene.

heat from the explosion will carry much of the radioactive material, trend generally toward the north.[4]

In Part 1 we answered the question "Can anyone survive two tenths of a mile (322 meters) from the bomb?" and now we ask "Is there anything to worry about if you are more than a mile away?" Or better yet, "How far away is safe?"

To begin answering these questions, let's visit a not-so-nice man waiting for a phone call a little more than a mile from ground zero.[5]

---

[4] Our bad guys have picked this day because of the weather. They have chosen a day when the upper-level winds will carry radioactive materials across as many other major cities as possible.
[5] Ground zero is where the bomb is on the ground, or the point on the ground directly below the bomb when it explodes up above the ground.

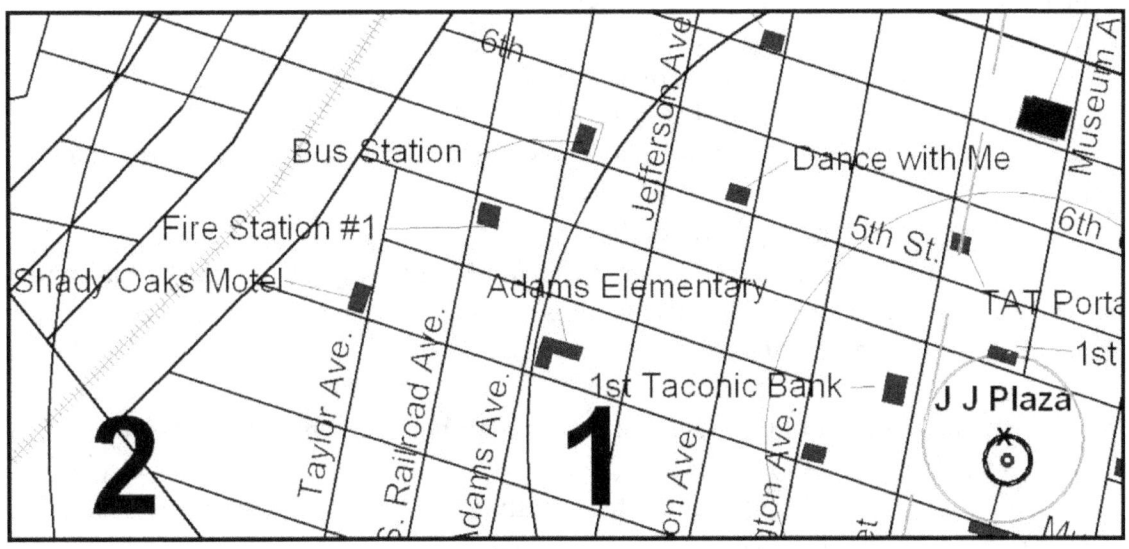

Yorksberg and Lamar's Neighborhood

12 - Lamar Henderson – Waiting for a Call (1.1 miles)

His mind had replayed the death of his buddy J.P. Flagg at least fifty times. Hell, he dreamed that death. Even as he waited his memories played again the whole sorry attempt to rob a convenience store as seen from his vantage point as the get-a-way driver.

That girl behind the counter; now that was some woman! She handed Flagg the entire cash register drawer, and while he was balancing it and trying to shoot her at the same time, she pulled out a dang forty-five and popped him three times in his chest. Flagg got daisies growing on him and I got eight years. Eight damn wasted years just for sitting in a freakin' car.

He felt around in his coat pockets for a light, the cold cigarette dangling from his beard-scruffy face, needing a flame and smelling good. Finding no matches, he walked out to the corner of 5th and Adams Avenue where he could look downtown for Rock's car while dialing Dallas on his cell phone.

"Hello," his mother said. The connection made her sound far away.

"Howdy, Ma."

"Lamar Bergin Henderson! Is that you?"

"Who else would it be, Ma?" He moved behind a USPO curbside mailbox, attempting to get out of the cold wind. There was little traffic and no sign of Rocks.

"I hope you aren't calling for money, you no-good son of mine. Why did you break your parole?"

"Calm down, Ma; I got a job. You'll get your money."

"You got a job? Where are you at?"

"I'm working as a dishwasher on night shift, and you don't need to know where. I'm making a new life here, just like I promised."

"They are looking for you, Lamar."

This made him pause. He looked at his watch. It was almost time for Rocks to call.

I wonder if they can trace this call.

"I gotta go now. I'll call you again soon. I just wanted you to know I am doing better."

"Wait, don't hang up," she said as he hung up.

He walked back over to the bus station and out of the cold wind. The idea of walking back to the Shady Oak Motel for his matches came to him, but that wind was just too cold.

Damn I need a cigarette.

Lamar glanced at his nine-dollar watch. Another ten minutes had passed.

Almost 2:30 and no call yet.

"C'mon, Rocks," he said under his breath in frustration. "How are my customers going to have a good day if you don't do your part?"

Back at the mail box at the curb he dialed Rocks' number, unconsciously feeling in his pockets again for that missing book of matches. He put the cigarette in the corner of his mouth so he could keep one hand warm in a coat pocket.

In an instant the world went brilliant white and the skin on Lamar's exposed cheek and hand began to hurt. Reflexively he shut his eyes and turned his back to the light, bending over in surprise and pain. His now-lit cigarette falling out of his half-open mouth as he uttered a common street expression that starts with "What the...!" He could smell burning coat and with his eyes shut he could see a bright afterimage shaped roughly like a mail box.

An instant later a huge blast of wind and flying debris whammed into him, flinging him over a small concrete curb and into the ditch along the east side of Adams Avenue.

Stunned, he lay flat on his back in eight inches of icy-cold snowmelt that covered the bottom of the ditch, along with several beer bottles, six empty plastic water bottles, a soggy gray mass that was once somebody's sweater, and the decaying remains of a Big Mac nestled inside a paper bag. The ice-cold water felt good on his burned hand and face, but the cold water, which instantly soaked into his clothing and against his body, took his breath away.

Sputtering and cursing, he righted himself and looked up into the sky, his eyes widening in amazement at the sight of an orange and white, roiling, toroid-shaped mass of brilliant light rising majestically into the sky, pulling behind it a thick column of dark, orange-tinged smoke and dust. He watched it dim as it rose, first decreasing to bright orange pocketed with brilliant white, and then fading out into red patches hidden by the swirling clouds of dark dust. He stared wide-eyed in a fog of disbelief and wonder until the cold of the water brought him back to reality.

"You okay, Mister? I saw you tumble into the ditch," said a man in the uniform of a bus station attendant; the name sewn on the front said "Finch." The man held out his hand.

"I guess so," he said, grabbing Mr. Finch's hand. "What the hell was that?" he said with Finch pulling him up, dripping wet, and leading him into the bus station lobby.

"We been bombed," the uniformed man said. "Probably Al-Qaeda again. Osama may be dead, but his boys are alive and kicking."

Realizing something more important than a bomb was at stake; Lamar put his hand into his right coat pocket and groped around for his stash of pot and OxyContin tablets. They were still there, but had become a sopping-wet, unsellable mass of melting pills and ground-up Mary Jane. "Damn, this sucks."

"Yah. This is really bad," Mr. Finch said. "I'm sure glad we weren't downtown. They caught hell down there. I don't see how anybody could have survived."

"Damn," Lamar said, repeating one of his most-used words. One side of his face was hurting like hell; the wet clothing in the freezing air made him shiver; and worst of all, Rocks had been downtown.

Damn! Maybe the deal with Rocks is off.[6]

Mr. Finch held the restroom door open for him.

"I'll get some rags for you to dry off with, and a set of coveralls. Use the driver's shower. I'll be right back."

Lamar walked in and the door shut behind him with a bang.

Damn! It's darker than Carlsbad Caverns at midnight.

Angry and fumbling, he found the door and walked back out. Leaning against the wall, he surveyed the pink back of his burnt hand.

"Hurts like hell," he said to no one in particular.

The kindly station attendant returned with some old towels.

"Hey, there ain't no lights in there," Lamar said. "What kind of a bus station is this?"

"Right," Mr. Finch said, "I should have known. Power's off. That means no hot water either. Let's just prop open the door. That will let some light in. You go in and strip, dry off, and put on the coveralls."

Walking out of the bus station several minutes later, wearing the clothes the kind bus station attendant had loaned him, he found a small group of walking wounded assembled in the parking lot. He could see blood from cuts and abrasions on heads, arms, and legs; missing pieces of clothing; burns of various types; one person with a missing shoe; and a half-naked woman lying in a heap where someone had dragged her. Her soft crying, more like a dog whimpering, the awful-looking gash on her head, and her hair matted with her own blood, deeply bothered him.

He leaned over her and saw red burns on her face and neck, like those on the back of his hand. Oddly, the burn on her neck included a small unburned area that clearly spelled "Susan."

Damn, branded by her necklace. Poor woman.

---

[6] Yep, the deal is off. Rocks was lifted by nuclear elevator to the pearly gates. When asked why he should be allowed in, he offered three ounces of crystal meth, the latest cop-killer rap CD, and a stolen Rolex watch. That didn't work.

"Hey, Mister, help us here," a man said as Lamar began walking away.

"Can't do it," Lamar said. "Ain't got nothing on under these coveralls and I am freezing my butt off." He held out a sodden pile of his wet clothing, then pointed down at his wet shoes on his damp, sockless feet.

"Help us carry this lady inside. She's hurt pretty bad," the man pleaded.

Looking straight ahead, he just kept walking. *Got to get to my motel room… get some warm clothes and my other jacket.*

"Hey, Mister!" someone called one last time.

A few minutes later, at the corner of 4th and Taylor, he could see home; the old Shady Oaks Motel, built to resemble an out-of-place and out-of-time Spanish hacienda, and turned south toward it. Off in the distance a siren was wailing, and he could hear a helicopter flying high overhead.

Chilled to the bone, he finally reached unit 14. *Home sweet home.* Setting all the wet clothes down, except his pants, he dug into his cold and damp pocket for the room key. Entering the room, he flipped on the light switch and stood there a second or two while his mind caught up to the fact here the power was off too. This disappointment was quickly forgotten because the room was warm after a long walk in the cold wind, and it felt so good. Stripping off the bus station's coveralls, he put on some of his own dry clothing and then went into the bathroom.

The small bathroom window provided enough light for him to get a look at his face in the mirror. It reminded him of a movie he had seen where an alien spaceship had shone a bright light at a man and burned his face.

I've got regular alien sunburn. He smiled at his humor, and looking himself over, he could see the back of one hand and a small part of one cheek had small water-filled blisters forming. These burns are uncomfortable and he suspects they should be treated, but he has nothing to put on them. He considers walking the eight blocks to a pharmacy to get something for the burns, but decides not to go just then. He is hungry and shaking a bit from his experience, so he recovers a half-empty bottle of whisky from his dresser drawer. A few sips and he feels much better, warm all over.

Before falling asleep, he wound up his alarm clock, pleased with himself for remembering, and set it to wake him up in time to get to work at the Taconic Inn's steakhouse for the evening shift.[7] The bed is warm and comfortable and soon he was asleep.

A noise wakes him up. It sounds like a low-flying helicopter. Angry at the pilot for constantly flying around, he gets up, stumbles over his wet shoes, goes to the door, and flips on the useless light switch. He curses again. It is very cold in his dark room.

Pulling back the curtains, he stands there wondering why it is so dark outside. The motel's sign is usually flashing its friendly "Vacancy" in neon orange. Shoeless, he steps outside and can't believe his eyes. He sees several aircraft circling overhead with bright

---

[7] The Taconic Inn is a nice joint. You would like it. Unfortunately what is left of it will burn to the ground by morning.

lights beaming down into the dark city. He counts four… no, five, maybe six huge fires burning off in the distance, mostly downtown, and oddly, no traffic is visible. Cold, he goes back in and gets under the covers. His head hurts and under the covers is the only warm place in the room.

Mushing up through a fog of warm, alcoholic slumber, Lamar realizes someone is pounding on his motel room door.

Cursing the freezing temperature, the darkness, and the pounding on the door, he opens it to find the motel manager. The man does not look happy.

"You gotta get out of here," he said.

Overhead a voice from a helicopter drones on. "This is an emergency. You must leave the city immediately. Buses are waiting to evacuate you. Proceed to Riverside and Fox Road, or the Interstate and Dayton Road. This is an emergency…."

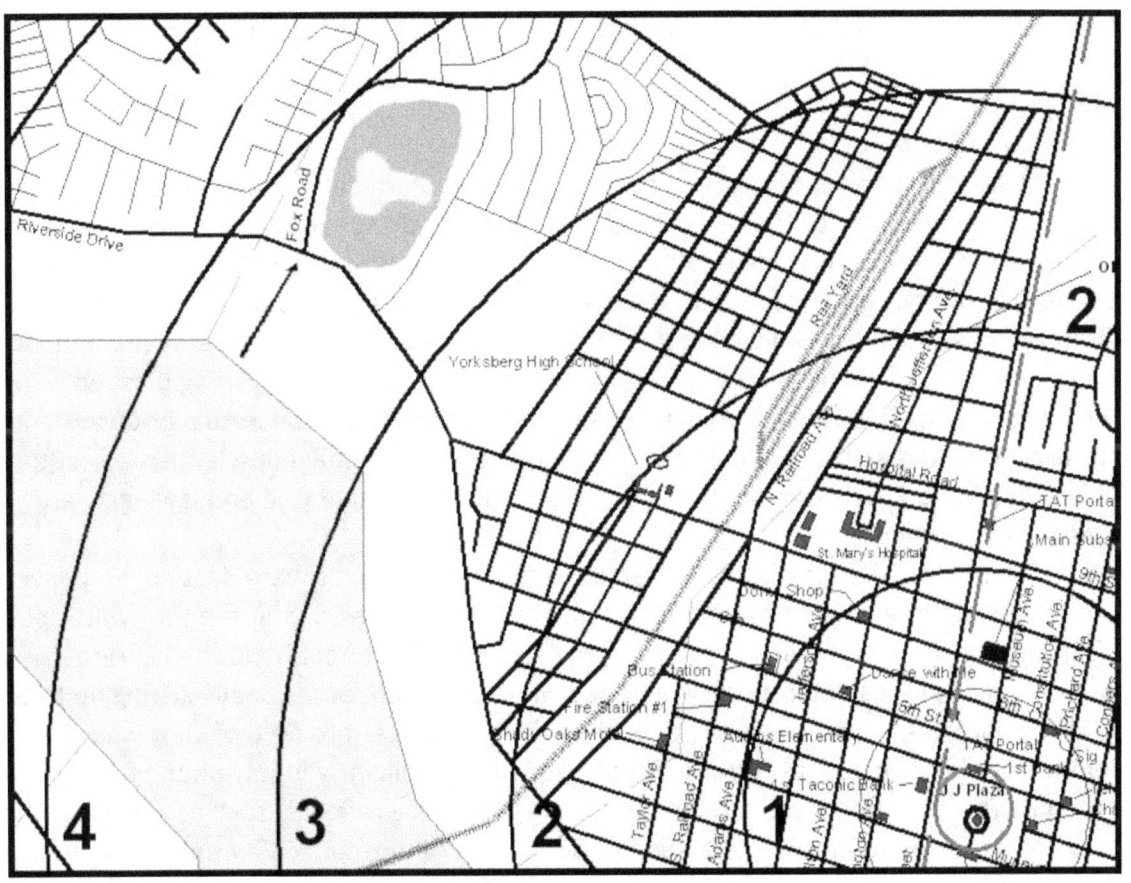

Trace Lamar's Route to the Buses

After a brief argument, Lamar puts on his wet shoes and joins hundreds of cold, tired people streaming west up Riverside Drive in the dark. Far up the road he can see the lights of police cars and buses. The sight of the police disturbs him, but he is tired and cold, and decides they are too busy to be looking for him. So he continues walking with the crowd.

As he reaches the police cars where the line of people is bunching up, he sees a man in a white suit with a yellow box in his hand waving it over each person. He waits in line and watches as the man then directs each person onto one of several yellow school buses that say "Hamilton County School System" in black letters on their sides.

Finally it is his turn. The space-suited man waves the yellow box over him.

"Damn, this one is clean," he says to a cop standing nearby. "You get on bus number four... it's that one." He points. "But leave the shoes here."

"Leave my shoes?" Lamar whines, "Hell if I'm going to take my shoes off. It's cold out here." But before he can finish he is practically lifted off his feet by a large policeman with a very short temper.

"Take your shoes off, buddy, and don't give us any crap," the man says into Lamar's face before setting him back down. "Your shoes are radioactive. You can't take them on the clean bus."

"You will get clean shoes later," someone nearby says.

Lamar leaves his shoes and climbs barefoot into the mostly empty bus and sits down. His feet are cold and his burns hurt, but at least it is not freezing cold in the bus.

Analysis of Chapter 12

One of the points of this section is even the ignorant can survive, but it does take a bit of luck, providence, or the helping hand of others to do so when one is clueless.

Lamar was just outside one mile of the bomb's explosion point. You can locate the bus station on the corner of 5th and Adams. At that distance we would expect overpressures of above 2 psi and blast-wave wind gust of as much as 120 mph. Had he stayed on the west side of the bus station he would not have been touched by the diminishing blast wave or the intense light. The bus station was constructed of reinforced concrete block walls and suffered little damage. Only the sheet metal bus shed was damaged. A large piece of the metal was peeled back and is hanging in the air, still attached at one end, swinging and twisting in the wind.

Note that when the bomb's flash occurred, Lamar's eyes were dazzled. You have seen the same effect when someone takes a flash picture of you. You see this white spot afterimage in your eyes, which fades in a few seconds. This effect happened in Hiroshima where "--many cases of temporary blindness were reported, occasionally lasting up to two or three hours, --."[8] Instead of one tiny white dot, Lamar's entire field of view was temporarily blinded. He saw only an afterimage of the brilliantly lit pay phone for a few seconds. This flash blindness can inhibit normal protective reflexes, such as trying to quickly move to a safe location to try to avoid the blast wave of pressurized air moving toward you at the speed of sound.

The heat radiated from the explosion was intense enough to give Lamar first-degree burns on parts of his exposed skin, with second-degree burns in spots. The amount of

---

[8] *The Effects of Nuclear Weapons*, Samuel Glasstone and Philip J. Dolan, United States Department of Defense, 1977, section 12.79, "Effects of Thermal Radiation on the Eyes."

damage from burning depends on the intensity of the heat radiation, the presence or absence of protective clothing, and the length of time of exposure. Note that the parts of Lamar covered by clothing, even clothing that charred before the blast wave arrived, did not receive burns. This should be attributed to the thickness of the winter clothing Lamar wore. There were incidents reported in Hiroshima where bomb-heated clothing in direct contact with skin did result in burns.

Do not confuse heat radiation with nuclear radiation or with radioactivity. Heat radiation is just light in the infrared portion of the spectrum. Your stove gives off heat radiation. It can't make you radioactive, but it can burn you.

The weather the day the bad guys attacked is important. If it is rainy or foggy, the radiant heat energy will not spread as far or burn as quickly as on a clear day. They have picked a cold day to make survival more difficult for those injured or trapped in the wreckage. Don't expect utilities such as electricity, water, and heating gas to be available after such an attack. If you live in a northern city and the attack occurs on a day with subzero temperatures, the cold and wind will place tens of thousands of survivors in extreme peril. This danger is easy to handle if you plan ahead.

What will you do to stay warm?

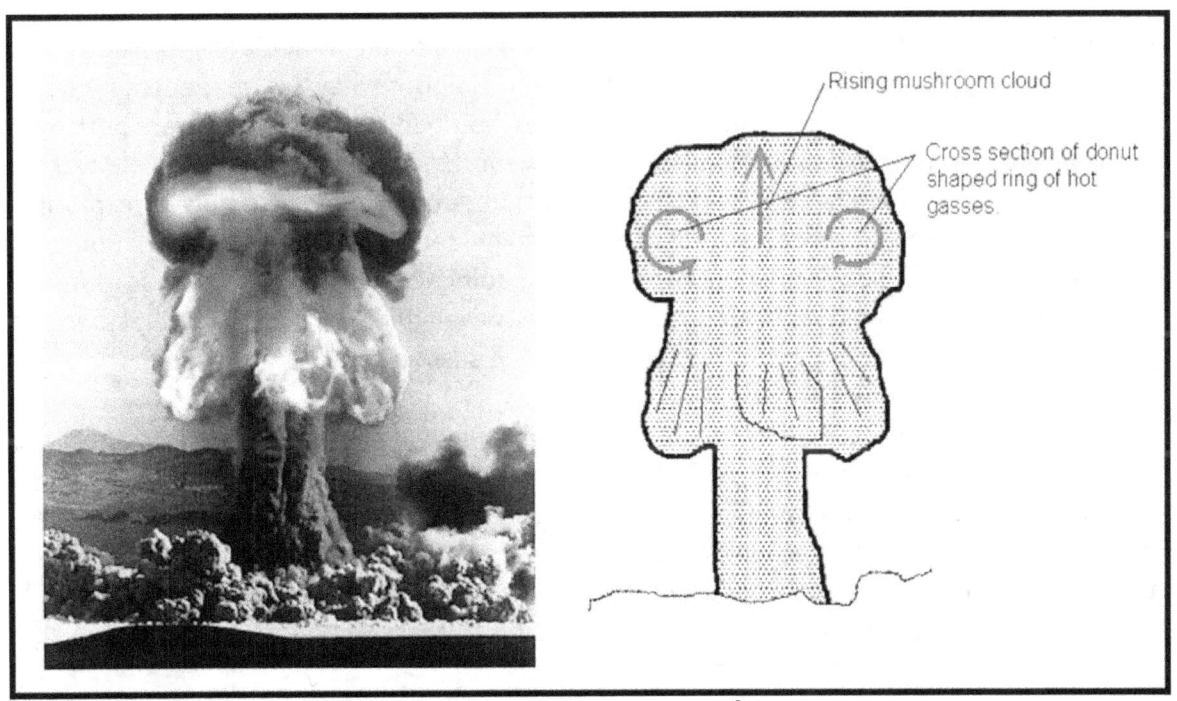

Motion in the Rising Cloud[9]

The toroid shape of the fireball Lamar saw is a characteristic of some nuclear explosions. It occurs when the hotter center of the fireball, perhaps assisted by ground

---

[9] This photo is available in many World War II and national archives. Test shot "Easy" in the Nevada desert.

reflection of the shockwave, rises faster than the edges. This results in a donut-shaped ring of hot gasses that rises while rotating with the inside edge of the donut moving up and the outside edges moving relatively down. This ring can be clearly seen in the nuclear test shot shown above.

The white-hot gasses shown in this picture are the source of much of the burn-causing heat radiation. You can protect yourself from this by simply putting something between you and the glowing gasses.

The hot gasses are cooling and rapidly rising away from the ground, so the rising fireball of a Yorksberg-sized bomb can cause burns only within the first thirty seconds of the explosion.

Heat burns can also be caused by the initial burst of light from the explosion. These are called flash burns and can occur up to several miles away from the explosion, particularly when the explosion occurs high in the air on a clear day.

Lamar might have resisted the blast wave at his location if he had been prepared for it. As it was, he had not been prepared and the blast wave knocked him into a ditch. The peak winds occur with the front of the blast wave and then drop to zero a few seconds later.

Lamar had the misfortune of being pushed into a ditch of water, which later contributed to infections occurring where his burn blisters were broken. The lack of electric power and prompt treatment were also factors in his burns becoming infected. This will be typical of many injuries in your city where the lack of electric power after the explosion may stop public water system pumps, and where first aid will not be immediately available.

Perhaps you noticed that Lamar seems clueless about what has happened. He does not even respond to Mr. Finch when told "We been bombed." This is an accurate portrayal of many adults in our society, particularly if they went through school after the cold war abated. They quite literally have never been taught about nuclear war or nuclear explosions and their effects. Lamar treated school as a joke, so he does not know about radiation, and many other subjects. Besides, when told about the bomb, at that moment he was more concerned with what he truly valued, the drugs he carried in his pocket. He understands an inkling of what has happened only when he begins to suspect he might not see his drug contact "Rocks" as he had hoped.[10]

The bus station manager is typical of many city dwellers, good at heart and ready to help someone in need. They often don't show it until the chips are down, and then it comes out. Both the manager and Lamar are not fully connected with the magnitude of the event, as evidenced by their slow recognition of the lack of power and its consequences. They are those who plan to fill their car tanks before evacuating the city, not connecting the flow of gasoline from the pump with the need for electricity. This lack of understanding may hinder

---

[10] For those who have to know, Rocks was downtown a few blocks from ground zero and not wearing his seatbelt, as usual. The blast accelerated his heavy, tail-finned car down the street at such a rate that it expelled him through the back window. If he had not been killed when he hit the pavement, the damage to his lungs from the huge blast overpressure at his location probably would have killed him. Remember that Rocks is human too. He was not downtown making drug deals; he was actually there to pick up some food from Parrots-Are-Us for his tropical bird "Lady," which he kept in his apartment.

your escape during the real event too if your tank is dry, or if a car in front of you runs out of gas in the traffic jam exiting the city. Always plan ahead.

The walking wounded gathering at the bus station after the blast only scratches the surface of the problem of the tens of thousands of injured people who will survive the initial explosion, clueless about the radiation, but needing help of some kind. As time passes, many more wounded will make it out of the zone of survivable destruction to less-damaged parts of the city, many of them badly contaminated and many seriously hurt. This radioactive contamination will make them an invisible hazard to others around them as the radioactive material in their hair, on their shoes, and on their clothing irradiates anyone standing nearby. Quite a few of them will have received a lethal dose of radiation before they make it out to places like the bus station, and some will come out carrying others too hurt to make it themselves.

Note that people who receive a lethal dose of radiation seldom die instantly. Usually they last for a few hours, days, or even weeks as their damaged bodies try to heal. It is usually infections due to the damaged immune system, or damage to the radiation-sensitive intestinal tract or blood cells that kills them. Many will die due to lack of immediate first aid, such as the crying woman with the word "Susan" burned on her neck. She, by the way, died of internal bleeding about thirty minutes after Lamar departed for his motel. She had been downtown with her daughter and a friend for some shopping when the attack came. You met her in Part 1, Chapter 6, "Dance with Me"; you learned the fate of her daughter in Chapter 7, "Caring for Others"; and you will see how the bomb affects her husband in Chapter 14, "Medical Mayhem."

It is likely that several hours after such an attack, uncontrolled fires will be burning all over the city, started by the intense heat of the atomic explosion. This is because there is no water pressure, blast damage to buildings that had been normally designed for fire-safety, debris blocking fire-fighter access to the fires, lack of personnel and equipment, and the presence of dangerous levels of radiation.

Big cities often store their hook-and-ladder engines in the downtown fire houses so the fire departments can respond more quickly to fires in the tall buildings. City fire administrators might consider positioning some ladder engines in a more survivable location, betting on the assumption the bad guys will opt for a downtown shot. Keep in mind the most critical time for fighting and controlling small fires near you will be in the first thirty minutes following the blast, before those fires enlarge. During that time, little can actually be done by fire department personnel near the blast zone because of two serious difficulties. First, fire fighters will be inhibited by the large amount of radioactivity in the area, and second, access will be inhibited by the huge debris field in the vicinity (~3/4 of a mile for a 19-kt weapon) of the blast center. Early after the blast, it is more likely that fires some distance (miles) from the center of the blast will be engaged by the fire department.

You would expect helicopters and other aircraft to be in the area soon after such an event. Many will be media personnel trying to get the best photos of the destruction, but there is an issue of radioactive contamination such people might consider. Even after the mushroom cloud is gone, prevailing fires can transport radioactive materials from the burning structures into the atmosphere above the city. The pilots and film crews may not receive lethal doses of radiation, but they could be damaged by it and may return to their home airport to find their contaminated helicopter quarantined by the civil defense or military authorities. They will do well to stay high and far up-wind of the city.

Several hours after the blast, our story has the first organized response showing up in force, in the form of helicopters with loudspeakers, trying to get survivors to move out of the city. Many people will be gone by then, but thousands may remain. Transportation will have to be provided for people and their destinations organized to control the spread of radioactive contamination. Initial screening (the guy in the white suit with the radiation detector, placing folks in different buses based on their levels of contamination) is one possibility.

Lamar was clean because he was inside the bus station when most of the fallout fell in that area, and because he changed clothes. By chance and wind, the fallout on the motel was light, and because the cheap motel had been built with concrete walls and 8-inch-thick concrete roof panels, both on the second floor and between the second floor and Lamar's room, his radiation exposure was relatively small. Lamar's body received more than 50 rem[11] of radiation damage, but not enough to make him sick. Many of the others that remained at the bus station received much higher doses and some of them exhibited evidence of radiation poisoning[12] weeks later.

Rapidly moving survivors out of a fallout zone cannot be emphasized enough. This is something most cities are totally unprepared for. They have not prepared a plan that includes which vehicles to use, how to determine assembly points, how to communicate with the public at large without radio or TV, how to screen the clean from the contaminated, and which destinations can be used for contaminated people (the latter may require written agreements between neighboring cities and counties).

The following day, in a city several hundred miles from Yorksberg, Lamar happened upon an interview with a national news organization when his red and blistered face was spotted by a camera crew. They broadcast his face and injuries all over the world as he told his story about how he "got blowed into ice water" by the atom bomb. Unfortunately for him, his new celebrity status was seen in Dallas and he was identified, re-arrested for a parole violation, and sent back to Texas. He became a star attraction at the Dallas county jail, displaying his red badges of courage to anyone interested.

We will end the tale of Lamar Hendricks by saying the notoriety of his experience changed him. He gained a degree of self-confidence, and after learning the details of what had really happened that night, confessed "the man upstairs was looking after me." After doing his time, he never went back to jail, married a nice Ft. Worth country-western dance

---

[11] See the *Nuclear Terror Survival Handbook Part 1*, Chapter 1, analysis for a discussion of radiation-dose size and its effect on humans.

[12] The words "radiation poisoning" do not really mean anything. Radiation is not a poison like arsenic or radiator fluid. It kills by damaging cells in our bodies by striking those cells with tiny fast-moving particles. If you get hit by enough of these tiny particles, you will become ill, just as if you were poisoned. "Radiation poisoning" may mean you got sick from the damage radiation did to you, or may indicate the damage you received can be seen in changes detectable by testing your blood.

instructor, and ten years later has a home, three kids, and a good job selling and repairing air conditioners.

Quiz on Chapter 12   (Answers are in Appendix A2)

1.   Walking wounded people will walk out of the more seriously damaged portions of the city into the less-damaged areas. Many will have received significant radiation exposure. Is this a significant problem? Why?

2.   Can news helicopters and sightseeing light planes flying over the city become contaminated?

3.   In planning for possible nuclear terrorism, what is one possible problem with the way most large cities locate fire stations, police stations, and the radio dispatchers and antennas for these departments?

4.   What caused Lamar to fall into the ditch?

5.   Lamar was burned by the rising mushroom cloud. Were his burns radioactive?

Can you sleep through a nuclear explosion? Our next Yorksberg citizen does, with the help of a liquid friend. You'll read about him in the next chapter and learn if he lives or dies.

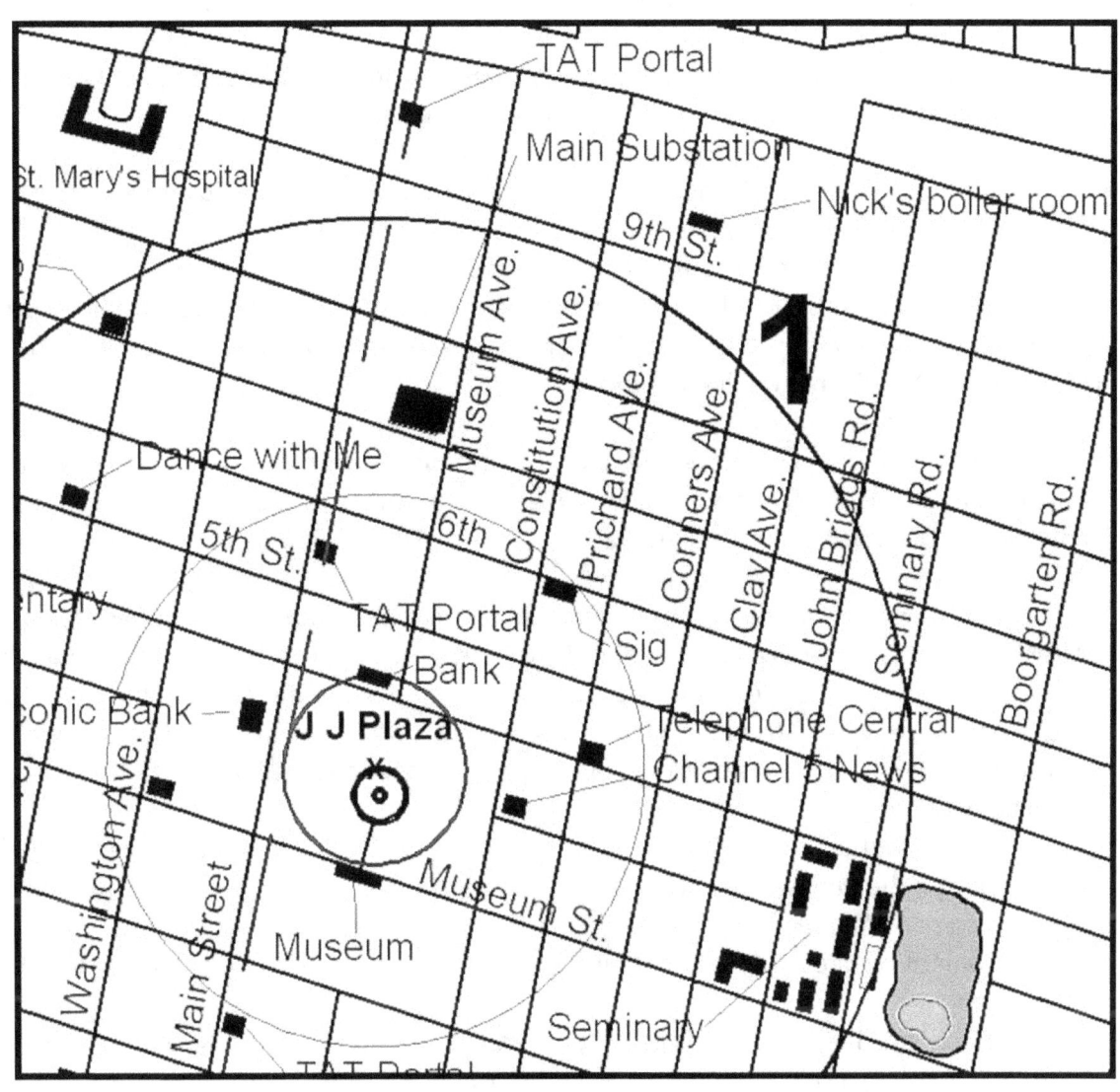

Nick Allison's Wanderings

13 - Nick Allison – Fallen into Disrepair (1.2 miles)

In his dream Nick saw himself dying today, and that it would not be booze that killed him. He cursed the darkness as he sat up on his soiled mattress, heart racing, in the boiler-room basement of an abandoned building on Prichard Avenue. The dream had scared him. He did not want to die.

"Damn bulb," he said to the light bulb above him that he couldn't see. He reached up to where the light fixture pull-string usually hung, found it, and pulled it. It gave a distinct "click," but no light appeared.

I'll just have to get me another bulb somewhere tonight.

Rising, and steadying himself by feel, he worked his way to the janitor's sink, knowing he always felt better with some water splashed on his face.

This evening the tap only provided a trickle of water, just enough for him to clear the sleep out of his eyes.

Nature called, and he made his way by memory and feel through the old boiler room in the darkness to the staircase, and began walking up the stairs.

Must have slept too late; it's already dark.

At the top of the stairs he found the door shut and let out a mild curse.

Pushing the door open, he could see late-evening daylight.

Good, the park's restroom will not be locked.

His thought is broken by a pain in his chest as a broken piece of board falls in and strikes him. It does not hurt much, but when he looks at it he can see a bent nail in the end of it has punctured him and drawn blood.

"Hell and damnation!"

He tosses the board aside and looks around for the prankster who set up the board to lean against the door. Oddly the alley appears to be strewn with a hodge-podge of debris and there is the smell of smoke in the air.

His head hurts as he crosses Prichard Avenue to Kelly Park and its public restrooms. After answering nature's call in the semi-dark restroom, he pauses to look in the mirror above the sink. His eyes see a gaunt-faced drunk, aged beyond his years, but in his mind he sees what those on the street call him. "Good evening, Pops," he says, and tries a brief toothless smile. He emerges from the public accommodation, feeling a bit better except for the hangover.

He sets out up Prichard Avenue and stops at 9th Street where he notices several fires burning in buildings in the area.

Where is the fire department?

Something does not feel right, and he walks almost to Prichard and 8th before he stops again.

The debris in the streets is getting worse and begins to register with him as he looks around. Something really big has happened but he can't quite place it.

What's this? Well I'll be.

Nick's vision clears enough to see all the telephone poles that line the street two blocks ahead have snapped off at their bases and are lying in the street.

"How can anyone drive with those wires lying in the street?" he says, and then notices the total lack of traffic. It is so quiet he can hear a baby crying. The cry is faint and is coming from inside a nearby apartment building.

Abandoning his intent to go to a dumpster behind a local pizza place, he stops, starting to feel really uneasy.

He carefully looks around and sees damaged buildings and roofs, trees shredded and fallen over, power lines down, multiple fires, the streets massively blocked by debris up ahead, as well as cars rolled over and even pushed into buildings.

"Yep, something's not right here," he says under his breath, and he shakes his head to clear it. He is immediately sorry, for the shaking hurts like hell.

Where is everyone?

This thought morphs out of the fog in his mind but it doesn't remain very long.

His eyes focus on a bag someone has left in the street near him. There is something odd about it. It looks as if someone has made a shirt into a bag. Then his eyes focus. It is not a bag; it is a shirt, and there is one arm sticking out. It is a headless, legless body, with one arm, lying in the street.

"Holy crap! Oh my god, jeezes!" he says, stepping back in horror.

Fear floods in, gradually at first, and then stronger. He knows somewhere in the back of his mind that he should do something, but what? He decides that walking away quickly is the best thing to do at this time. He will tell the first policeman he sees about the body, but on second thought, he never does get along well with the cops.

They'll think I cut up that poor man back there.

He looks back, and it is still there.

I need a drink.

He retreats up Prichard to 9th Street, which looks better toward the east, so he sets out that way. This is a really good choice, he decides, because not more than three blocks down the street he knows he will find, at the corner of 9th and John Briggs Road, the Taconic Spirits, a fine liquor store, where the dumpster there gave him a half bottle of good Russian vodka last week. So he picks up his pace, intending for a little refreshment to clear his mind.

Puzzled that he still hasn't seen anyone, the area reminds him of a ghost town, and this bothers him.

There is no one to touch. Now how is a man to make a living if nobody is out and about?

The entire front window of the liquor store is shattered, the door is standing open, and excitement wells up in him. Scanning the mess of broken glass all over the floor, he can smell the place reeks of booze. Amazingly many bottles of wonderfully colored liquids are still sitting on their shelves in pristine condition.

Nick looks around and calls out "Hello, anyone home?" He pauses and then tries again. "This here is Pops. Martin, you in there?"

Martin is a good man. Where the hell is he?

Then it strikes him; bonanza! It is obvious there is no one in the store and no one on the streets.

Can you believe this, Pops ol' boy? Ain't nobody guarding the chicken house!

Giddy with his find, he enters, and like a kid in a candy store, goes from shelf to shelf, looking at the treats.

"Hello, baby!" he says, placing a dirty hand on one of his favorites. He caresses several of the bottles and finally chooses two, slipping them into his pockets. He takes another of his favorites, opens it, and takes a long pull on it.

"Ah! Damn that is good." The warmth spreads through him.

The fear he felt earlier is gone. All he wants to do now is go back to his warm hidey-hole and drink his dinner, so he starts back down 9th Street.

But something is nagging at him. It's in the back of his mind and he just can't quite place it. He knows he should be ecstatic about the evening ahead of him with his new-found liquid friends, in fact several evenings of pleasure considering how much booze he picked up for free. He pushes the uneasy feeling out of his mind.

At Prichard Street the unease comes back and now he knows why. It is hanging over him like a vulture circling a corpse. There, above him, on the side of a warehouse is an old ad, painted on the red brick and faded by years in the weather. The faded words say "Quality Perambulators." He can barely read the long word and doesn't have a clue what it means, but the picture shows a mother with a smiling baby in a carriage, and he remembers the crying baby he heard earlier. Looking toward 8th Street, he wonders if the youngster is still crying. There is still no one in sight.

"That poor little tyke has nobody. Damn his mother anyway; ain't she got no responsibility?"

Reaching his boiler-room entrance, and wrestling with the baby's cry and the siren call of the booze, he knows if the booze gets him downstairs he won't come up until tomorrow.

Finally his conscience gets the best of him, and after taking another long pull and stashing all his bottles except the best behind a dumpster in the alley, he sets out up the street to see if the baby is still crying. He knows helping the baby is a good thing, and he feels good about himself for deciding to help.

Out in front of the apartment building he can still hear its cry, intermittent and fainter now. He becomes even angrier at the mother.

Where is that woman? Why doesn't she care for that baby?

When he enters the lobby of the apartment, his anger is washed away. There is a lady lying on the floor at the base of some stairs. She is lying with her head in a pool of blood and has one arm outstretched with her hand on a wheel of the overturned stroller. Nick tears up at the sight of this evidence of a mother's love.

"Poor, poor, lady. Poor baby."

What's this world coming to?

He walks over and looks into the baby stroller. The baby cries harder when it sees him. Nick feels at a loss as to what to do.

I can't keep you, little feller. I ain't no good as a babysitter.

His head is starting to hurt again and he doesn't feel good. He really just wants to go lie down and drink a little, but this little bawling baby has somehow gotten under his skin.

"I guess I gotta be your rescuer, little child."

The sooner I get help for the baby the sooner I can go home. Gotta do it.

So he fortifies himself with a swig; then he rights the carriage and pushes it out of the apartment building, starting out on a long walk to the only place he can think of taking the child; the church at 9th and Main Street where they feed him on Friday nights.

I'll just leave the carriage there; knock on the door, and leave.

"They will take care of you; you'll see," he said to the infant.

At the church Nick finds Rabbit sitting on the church steps with his head in his hands.

"Hay, Rabbit. Whatcha know, man?" Nick says.

Rabbit looks up.

"Oh, it's you, Pops. I'm glad to see the bomb didn't get you. Whataya got there?"

"Would you believe, a baby? The mom's dead. Gonna leave this little guy here. The good church folks will take care of him."

"No man, you can't do that," Rabbit said, agitated. "There ain't no one here. The police told everyone to get out."

"Get out?" questions Nick, looking around. "Where did they all go?"

"Most folks that got wheels have done left Yorksberg. You gotta go too."

"The hell I do," Nick responded with anger, and thinking of his once-in-a-lifetime stash of liquid back at the warehouse. "Why are you here?"

Rabbit seemed slow to answer. "Well, I hid out when they come by. Things are open now, if you get my drift. I figured, why pass up the opportunity?"

Nick thought he knew what Rabbit was hinting at. If the liquor store was wide open, then why not other places?

"Well, I don't know about that," Nick lied, not willing to admit he had been dipping into the open treasures himself. "I need to find someone to give this kid to. He'll die with no one to help him."

"You a good man, Pops," Rabbit said, and stood up to point toward the hospital several blocks farther west. "The docs at good ol' Saint Mary's, they will take care of that kid. Take him there."

Nick looked toward the hospital.

"Yah, Rabbit. That's a good idea. But listen, I have something I gotta do back up 9th there. Would you mind pushing the little guy over there?" He pointed toward the hospital with a boney, suntanned finger that was shaking a little.

"Sheeeeet," Rabbit said while shaking his head. "I ain't no baby buggy pusher. You picked 'em up; you take him."

He was not feeling too well and he desperately wanted to get back home. "Look, Rabbit, I know I'm asking a lot, but I live way back down the other way," he pointed the shaking finger again, "and that, my friend, is a long walk. I know you live down at the end of the rail yard. Hell, that 8th Street overpass is right past the hospital. You're going that way. Just drop the tyke off."

The baby had been silent, but now broke out in a cry that touched both men's hearts. Rabbit looked at the overpass he slept under, then at the hospital, and back to Pops. Pops could tell Rabbit knew he was right, but to his dismay he saw him shake his head.

"There ain't nothin' in it for me, Pops," he said with finality. "Ah ain't gonna do it."

"Wait man," Pops pleaded in desperation. He reached into his soiled coat and pulled out the one beverage container he had not stashed. It was a small bottle of beautiful gold-select rum. They both knew it was smooth, and expensive.

"If you'll take the tyke to the docs, you can have one long swig on this."

"Hooeee!" Rabbit responded with enthusiasm, his eyes lighting up. "Is dat select? I ain't seen dat in years. Dat's a man's drink! Make it two, and you got a deal."

Nick thought about it for a moment, unsure how much rum Rabbit could swallow in two long pulls on this small bottle.

"Deal, here ya go." Nick handed Rabbit the bottle and Rabbit handed it back half empty.

"Man, you took half my hooch!" he said to Rabbit, a bit in awe.

Rabbit smiled. "Hooeee! Feel dat heat. Damn, man, dat is fine stuff."

Nick took a swig, capped the bottle, and stuffed it back into his coat.

"We got a deal?" he said, pointing at the now-silent baby.

"I got you covered, Pops. See you around." Rabbit got up and began pushing the carriage toward St. Mary's. Nick could hear him talking to the baby as he moved away.

Nick watched him go, not sure if he could fully trust Rabbit, but finally turned and walked back east on 9th Street, feeling good about the good deed he had just done and eyeing the fires burning in the downtown district.

By the time he reached his place of refuge, he was experiencing diarrhea and felt very weak, so he staggered over to the public restroom. Too ill to return to his boiler room mattress, Nick slipped down onto the restroom floor in a corner and sipped his friend one last time.

Analysis of Chapter 13

Nick's survival is not in question at first. He lives far enough away from ground zero and below ground. So he misses the heat, light, and blast. The alcoholic fog keeps much of the situation from his thinking mind. When his friend Rabbit says the word "bomb," for example, he does not pick up on it.

His focus is on drink, and that focus insulates him from reality.

Many of us have a focus that is not drug induced, but nonetheless keeps us from seeing and dealing with reality. This is particularly evident in the lack of leadership and preparation in our large-city communities to assure the maximum number of people survive a terrorist's nuclear attack. Given this lack of preparedness, you and your loved ones have little chance of surviving, unless you change something.

Will you and your loved ones live <u>after</u> surviving the explosion?

Do you, for example, have your "GO pack" ready and standing by? If not, why not? A GO pack, sometimes referred to as a "Get Out Of Dodge pack" (G.O.O.D. pack), is a backpack or suitcase prepared ahead of time for a quick escape from your home. It should contain all that is important (food, clothing, credit cards, medicines, shoes, water purifier, and even a weapon), especially things you will wish you had if you have to leave and never return. Take copies of your will, driver's license, passport, mortgage papers, birth certificates, marriage certificates, etc.

Think of the man who hurriedly escaped ahead of a hurricane, which subsequently removed his neighborhood from the face of the earth. When he tried to return, the police would not let him back into the neighborhood because he could not prove he really lived there. When he tried to file an insurance claim on the house, he did not have the policy number and could not describe the lot or section numbers of his subdivision.

Prepare a GO pack that will keep you going after the disaster, whether it be a tornado, hurricane, tsunami, meteorite fall, sinkhole, pestilence, or nuclear bomb.

So why isn't your GO pack ready? The answer is you are like most people, distracted by work, family life, some "important" sporting event (there is always one more), or the latest television show; or you have convinced yourself you will never need it.

Just remember this: to be ready you must take the time to get ready. You want to be ready to leave at a moment's notice with everything you will need to live away from home for a while, maybe years. Make it so. Search the internet for "go pack" or "survival lists" and you will find some well-thought-out lists.

Do you own pets? What are you going to do with them if your city is attacked? This should be part of your planning also. If you are not home when the bomb explodes, do you think you can go home to pick up the pets? This could cost you your life.

Shelters in distant cities you might have to run to may not accept pets, as they struggle to make room for the tens-of-thousands of humans displaced by the attack. Do you think local shelters will allow everyone's pets inside? Where will the food and water come from for the animals? Who will clean up the animal waste in those confined spaces, and how will you keep your animals from transporting dangerous radioactive materials into the shelter? Each pet owner should think this through before they have to run to a shelter.

Preparation is needed for emergency services folks also. Have you prepared for a nuclear strike nearby? If not, why not? Chances are your focus has been on training to respond to a hurricane, fire, tornado, riot, or the local financial situation that squeezes your team constantly. You will never be prepared until you begin preparing. Reading a book like this one, intended to spur your thinking, is a good start, but then you must take action.

For some of you, finding financial resources will be the first big step. Radiation instruments are not cheap. How many will you need and how will your department pay for them? Building shelters is expensive, and changing the thinking of the powers that be to encourage them to always build new facilities with dual use in mind, will not be easy. There is always the tendency for people to cut the cost now for a need that may never occur.

Planning is not so expensive. There is much citizens and their leaders need to talk about.

How will you coordinate with other counties and hospitals?

How will you use available resources such as school buses to extricate people from the high radiation zones? Buses that are used to move people may become unusable due to contamination and may have to be cleaned or buried.

What are the political and financial implications of the loss of the county's entire school bus fleet?

How will you control and direct traffic after the radiation is falling?

Get some smart heads together, brainstorm, and come up with some ideas. Most importantly, obtain the buy-in of those in control of the resources to implement whatever plans you make.

You should realize Nick is a dead man. He has accumulated too much radiation damage from the radioactive materials that fell in the downtown region of Yorksberg. He is a hero for attempting to save the life of the infant, but will be sick and too weak to stand by the next morning. He will die within a few days and will not be found for months, if that soon. Rabbit will not survive either.

Does the child live? No. The baby was exposed to several hours of harmful radiation coming from the fallout outside the apartment building before Nick came on the scene. When he took the infant outside, its radiation exposure increased during their walk to the church. The accumulated dose is the key factor.

Fallout patterns after a nuclear explosion are capricious. Testing in the American desert and in the South Pacific revealed higher dose rates were commonly found some distance from where the explosion occurred. These little pockets of higher radioactivity were deposited just because of the weather and the way the air was circulating in the atmosphere. In one case, radioactivity was concentrated on the far side of a mountain, and this was believed to have been caused by precipitation due to the movement of air over the mountain range.[13] Example fallout pattern contours can be seen in the Part 1 Chapter 7 analysis of the Sonny Summers story, "Caring for Others."

Just as there can be concentrations, there can be areas that receive less fallout, and the pattern of these distributions is largely unpredictable.[14] The huge updraft into the mushroom cloud carries much of the radioactivity high into the air above the explosion site. If there is a significant wind blowing at high altitude, then by the time the uplift slows and the radioactive load the updraft was lifting begins to fall out, the cloud will be downwind of the explosion point. This is why we see the dose rate contours are usually higher just downwind of the blast site.[15]

Interestingly, it is possible to find dangerous total doses at sites far from the blast site. For this reason, many communities far downwind will have to be evacuated or moved to shelters.[16] Examples of the effects of fallout at places distant from Yorksberg are covered in the Chapter 21 story of Amiee Moller ("Gentle as a Lamb") and in the Chapter 22 story of Luther Rheems ("Through a Glass Darkly"), both of whom live far from Yorksberg.

Looting

Some people may be tempted to loot the relatively undamaged stores, as Nick did, in a city hit by a terrorist's weapon. Remaining in the city for two or three hours to loot

---

[13] *The Effects of Nuclear Weapons*, Samuel Glasstone and Philip J. Dolan, United States Department of Defense, 1977, section 9.77. This concentration was seven times stronger than its immediate surroundings.

[14] Observations and theoretical speculation lead to the idea that of all the radioactivity lifted up in the rising mushroom cloud, the mushroom head contains as much as 90% of the radioactivity and the "stem" of the cloud holds the remainder. *The Effects of Nuclear Weapons*, Samuel Glasstone and Philip J. Dolan, United States Department of Defense, 1977, section 9.61.

[15] See *The Effects of Nuclear Weapons*, Samuel Glasstone and Philip J. Dolan, United States Department of Defense, 1977, Figure 9.77a, the Boltzmann shot in Nevada, and Figure 9.77b, the Turk shot in Nevada. Also, note the asymmetry of the fallout as exhibited in Figure 9.105, the Bravo test at Bikini Atoll.

[16] Unfortunately there are few shelters, and those that exist are mostly not maintained or stocked to support people. Evacuation will be the order of the day, and hopefully this can be completed before the fallout arrives.

could give you a case of radiation poisoning that will cripple or kill you, and all the loot will be highly contaminated and therefore easy to detect by authorities. No pawn shop will touch it.

Quiz on Chapter 13   (Answers are in Appendix A2)

1. Will people really abandon their stores in areas of an attacked city that are not destroyed by the blast?
2. Will the street really be empty of folks after the explosion?
3. Nick's hidey-hole was more than a mile from the blast. Why was he in danger?
4. Could Nick have survived somehow?
5. What is a "GO pack?" What is its purpose? What should be in it?

In our next short story we will look in on St. Mary's Hospital. Inside we will again find people surprised by the nuclear attack. Some will do well, and some... let's just say they could respond better. St. Mary's will prove to be a very busy place. The hospital is almost a mile and a half from ground zero. It is safe there? Read "Medical Mayhem" and see.

Author's Note: The following story does not come close to capturing the confusion, even bedlam, of a huge patient influx, emergency triage, contamination, lack of medical personnel and supplies, and the struggle to move patients without jeopardizing treatment, a large hospital in an attacked city would experience.

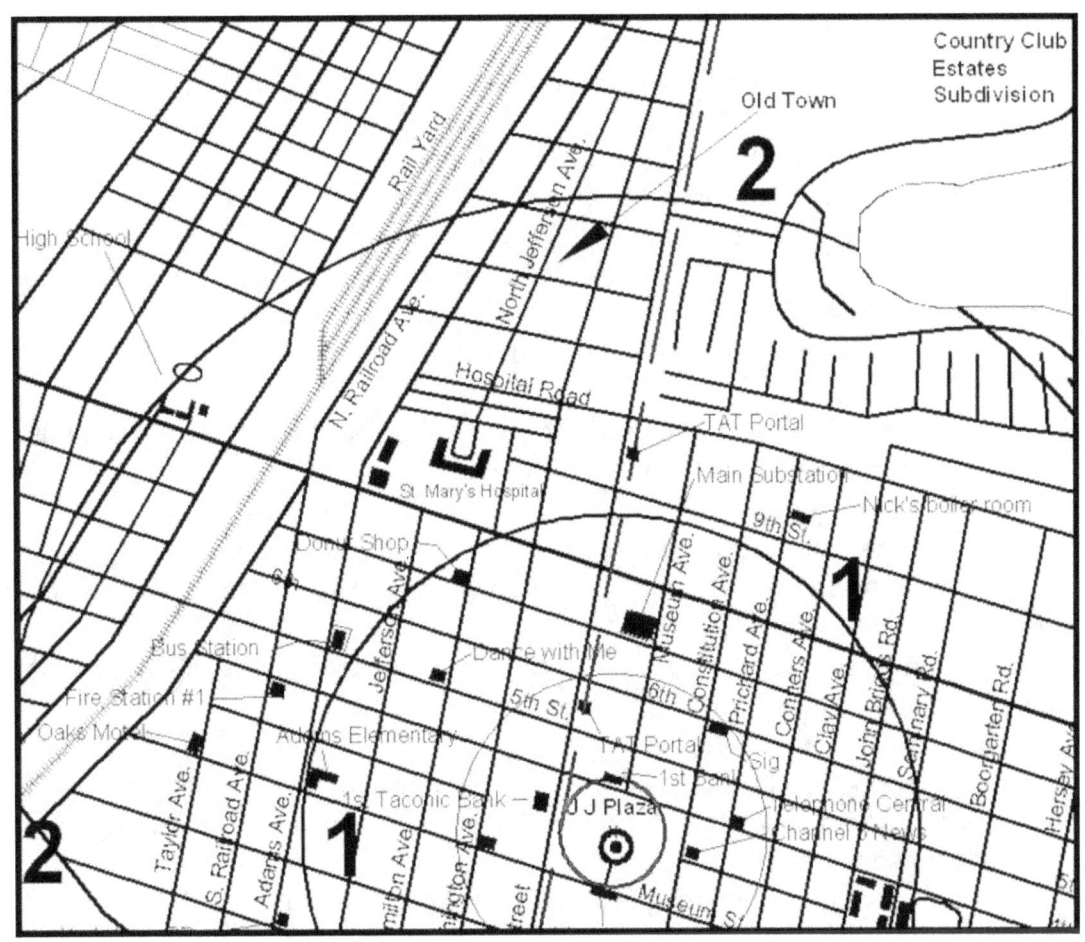

The Hospital's Position Relative to the Explosion

14 - Marcus Gingman – Medical Mayhem (1.4 miles)

Unpleasant events seem to come in threes, Frank Edwardson mused while recalling the coffee spilled on his slacks that morning. *Spilled hot coffee was the first event.*

As he stepped into the elevator he recalled the second event he had seen in the morning paper. It had shaken him. *Why does anyone ride motorcycles in the winter?* He punched the button for the first floor. The paper said ice was to blame. *Dr. Collins laid his bike down and skidded into a parked taxi. At least he wasn't killed.*

The elevator dinged as it passed the second floor.

Hate to lose a good doctor. What is event number three going to be? It couldn't be much worse than a shattered leg, could it?

The elevator stopped with a lurch on the first floor and as the door opened his eyes met those of his administrative assistant. She had several large, black binders under one arm and a cup of coffee from the cafeteria in her free hand.

Nice perfume.

"Good timing, Frank; thanks," Bonnie said. "I was just trying to figure out how to push the button with my hands full."

"You're welcome." He smiled at her predicament. "I'm off to see Ramos. I've got to get him to work second shift tonight to cover for Dr. Collins."

"I read about that. Good luck with Ramos," she said.

He reached in and pressed the forth-floor button for her and then stepped back out. "I'll be back up to the office in a few."

"Gotcha covered," she said, and the door shut.

Continuing toward the ER he spotted Nurse Bella Johnson sitting at a computer terminal work station in one of the hallway cubbies.

"Hey, Frank," she said, without looking up. "What's the rush?"

"Things are really popping today, Bella."

"Don't bring any of that popping stuff down to the ER," she said. "We like the quiet times."

She had a game of hearts going on the computer, so obviously this was a quiet time in the ER. He looked at his watch for the third time since noon.

It's 2:29 p.m.

"Now, Frank, don't you go and start nothing down in the ER," she said, wagging a finger at him. Without looking up she added, "A watched bed pan never boils. You got a hot date tonight or something?"

He looked at her, wondering how she saw him glance at his watch without looking in his direction.

The woman has phenomenal peripheral eyesight.

He laughed at her suggestion of an impending date.

"Bella, you are amazing. My wife Susan is the hot date, and she will be making roast beef tonight. I am already hungry."

"Ohooo roast beast!" Bella stopped fiddling with the game and looked at him. "Best with ketchup I say. You're going to bring me a slice tomorrow?"

"Perhaps. That depends—."

At that instant the hospital lights went off.

He looked up at the ceiling fluorescents and felt the building shake one time followed by the sensation of the floor rolling slightly for a second or two.

He saw Bella's eyebrows go up and her mouth drop open with surprise. "Earthquake? In this state?" she said.

She barely finished speaking when the building shook again, sharply, with a very loud boom as if some hotshot fighter pilot had loosed a sonic boom on the city. Mixed with this he could hear the faint sound of breaking glass and a very deep rumble that made the hair on the back of his neck stand up.

"Holy cow!" he said, and began to run toward the ER entrance. *Sounded like a large aircraft crashed nearby.*

As he ran down the hallway, he noticed that only every fourth ceiling light fixture had come back on.

The hospital emergency power generator is on. We've lost commercial power.

Passing through the double doors at the end of the hallway, he entered the ER lobby to find one of the entryway plate-glass windows missing and the floor strewn with broken glass. Several people were in the lobby, staring out the entrance.

"What happened?" he said to a man standing near the entry.

"There was this bright light outside and the window just crashed in," the man said, still staring outside. "Glass damn near hit me. There is something odd going on outside."

Frank turned his attention to the outside world as Dr. Ramos joined him from the ER examination area.

Looking down from hospital hill he could see across the entire Old Town subdivision. It appeared to be enveloped in a strange dust. Several trees were down or leaning, one completely across a road. One power pole leaned over at a precarious angle, and the cross bar on top of another had failed, leaving the wires dangling in a droop over the street. The roofs of a few of the houses had large patches of shingles missing. These were strewn all over the yards and street. Strangely, one of the cars parked along Hospital Road appeared to be burning on the inside.

The hospital PA system came to life.

"Maintenance contact second floor west nurse's station, extension 250. Maintenance, please contact second floor west nurse's station, extension 250."

Frank turned to the receptionist behind the counter. "Karen, give maintenance a call about this window, and call housekeeping to clean up this glass," he said.

"Okay, Dr. Edwardson," she said, picking up the phone.

The PA sounded again. "Maintenance, contact third floor east nurse's station, extension 350."

He picked up a phone and dialed one of the third-floor nursing stations.

"This is Frank Edwardson. Maintenance is being requested from multiple floors. What happened?" he said.

"Broken windows here," said the nurse. "We have five on this wing. Lots of cold air pouring in. We may have to move patients out of those rooms. The other floors probably have the same problem. Something blew up outside. One of our nurses is on the way down with some lacerations."

"Thanks," he said, and hung up. "Lacerations coming down from the third floor," he relayed to Dr. Ramos.

"Karen, get on the radio and see if you can find out what happened. It sounds like we might have some casualties. I'll be out front for a bit."

Halfway down the walk to the parking lot he met a man coming toward the ER.

"Any idea what happened?" he said.

"Downtown blew up," the man said while pointing up.

Frank looked up and felt a dark awe at what he saw. An elongated, wicked-looking, mushroom-shaped cloud of gray and black hung out high over north Yorksberg like a looming vulture. It had risen so high that a white, ice-crystal cap had formed on top. He had seen pictures of atomic explosions, but was shocked at the immense size of the cloud he now saw.

"Oh my God!" he said.

He turned and ran back into the ER where several injured people had arrived from other floors. These injuries looked to him like superficial face, arm, and torso cuts, probably caused by broken glass.

He corralled Dr. Ramos and the ER nurses. His voice shaking, he spoke to the group.

"This is a big one. It might even be a nuclear explosion downtown. Better call in all the staff you can and set up a triage area.[17]

As they moved off, he mumbled, "By God, they do come in threes."

Within fifteen minutes his world had changed. Standing at the ER entrance, Frank surveyed the scene. Cars were pouring into the parking lot with injured folks, and people were even walking from the old town subdivision to the ER. The four doctors who had come down to the ER from other floors were working on a group of injured people, some fairly seriously cut by flying glass. He noted a second group of people with less-severe injuries sitting in chairs in the ER waiting area, which having been filled with frigid winter air, caused him to shiver in his dress shirt. He asked one of the nurses' aides to start seating a third group of walk-ins around the room on the floor.

Outside, Frank could see a constant stream of people coming up the walk, with a line of cars extending from the ER entrance down the hill to the parking lot and even onto Hospital Road, apparently attempting to drop off injured people.

Nurse Stella Monson walked up as he surveyed the scene.

"Phones are out and there is no traffic on the radio." Stella said. We are receiving calls from ambulances, but only when they are near the hospital."

He pulled out his cell phone and confirmed his phone had no signal-strength bars.

Then, out of the blue, another thought came. "Radiation," he muttered. He turned to Stella and said, "We need all the radiation instruments down in ER immediately. Would you please send someone to find them?"

"You think there is radiation out there?" she said.

"We'll know as soon as those instruments are found."

Other hospitals have worked on drills for this sort of thing. I just never thought it would happen here.

"It's awfully cold in here with that busted window," he said to Stella. "Let's have the patients wait in the hallway down that wing." He pointed to the doorway. "It's still warm in there."

---

[17] Triage is the process of prioritizing sick or injured people for treatment according to the seriousness of each person's condition or injury. It is used when the number of injured people is so large that the medical staff cannot treat them all quickly. Each patient is evaluated quickly, and less-serious injuries are set aside to be attended to later.

A few minutes later he surveyed the scene with satisfaction. Many of the waiting patients were now in a warmer area, but the ER lobby remained full of newcomers.

A nurse walked up with three yellow boxes. "Stella told me to give these radiation detectors to you."

He could see a meter, a small black switch, and a handle on each. One at a time he turned them on. None of the three radiation instruments worked. He gave one to Stella to open, and handing another to an interested bystander, said, "See if they have a battery."

A minute later he knew. Stella was the first to comment.

"The batteries leaked in mine. There is that battery stuff all over the contacts inside," she said with disgust.

The batteries in the other two detectors had not leaked, but the devices were dead.

"Would you mind finding some batteries for these? And give that messy one to someone to clean up. Maxwell perhaps?" he said to Stella.

"I've got some nursing to do," she replied, "But I will find someone to help."

Jordan Maxwell, dressed in his maintenance coveralls, carried a piece of plywood into the lobby at that moment and set it by the broken window.

Frank tossed him a friendly salute and then picked up the telephone from the admissions desk and keyed in the PA code.

"Attention please, this is Frank Edwardson in the ER. It looks like this might have been a nuclear explosion downtown. There may be radiation outside. Please do not leave the hospital until our situation can be confirmed. We still need help in the ER if you can spare anyone. I'd like a report from each wing's nursing station on the condition of the building and any cleanup or other needs you have. Send that to me in the ER."

Not knowing what to say next, he looked around. One of the nurses nearby waved to catch his attention and pointed at an injured man who had bandages over his eyes.

"We need an ophthalmologist in the ER, Stat," he said over the PA system.

Five minutes later one of the maintenance staff walked up with two of the radiation instruments.

"We had a few batteries in the Maintenance Department, and now two of these detectors appear to be working. That's the good news. The bad news is on the bottom." He offered the device bottom side up.

Frank looked at the calibration sticker on the bottom. "Calibrated three years ago!" he said. "This instrument has not been calibrated in three years! That can't be good."[18]

"Well," the maintenance man offered, "that does not mean it won't work. Maybe it will be accurate enough."

---

[18] Calibration of the radiation instrument just means checking to see if what its radiation meter says is accurate. Frank has just discovered that over the last three years no one has checked to see if the detector would work as it should. Calibration checks should be done annually.

One of the ER assistants tapped Frank's shoulder. "Dr. Edwardson, someone wants to talk to you." She pointed at the east hall doorway. He glanced over and could see an old man in a hospital gown, standing there with a nurse. He looked rather frail.

"I don't have time right now. Tell him I will see him later."

He turned one of the radiation instruments on and the meter's needle immediately went off the top end of the scale.[19] "Is that good or bad? God help us!" Frank said.

"I'm not sure. Where is a nuclear physicist when you need one?"

Bonnie was standing across the lobby, sans coffee and binders. He waved her over.

"Thanks for coming down. I need all the help I can get."

The ER assistant persisted. "Mr. Gingman says you have to talk to him, or many people will die. He insists."

"What next?" Frank said under his breath, and walked over to talk to the frail old man.

"Hello, Doc. I am Marcus Horatio Gingman ." Frank noted his fingertips were bluish. *Circulation problems.*

"Pleased to meet you, Mr. Gingman... Mark. What do you need?"

Bonnie hovered nearby, listening.

"I worked as a civil defense director for Philadelphia for seven years in the late 1950s. I can tell you exactly what you need to do... that is, if you need my help. I have been well trained in the art of recovering from nuclear explosions."

"An angel just when I need one," Frank said. "I do need help. Tell me how to work this." He held out the radiation instrument to the old man.

"I can show you how to work that, but first you have to get control over who comes into the hospital and how they come in. Put guards on the outside doors. Do whatever it takes. A policeman works well but you probably can't find one."

"Why? What do you mean? We can't refuse people."

"That was a nuke downtown. Nothing else could have set those fires I saw from my window. A big chemical bang might break a few windows a mile away, but it does not set fires this far away," Gingman said. "Only a nuke could do that, and that means there is radioactive material falling outside. This stuff will be very hot, meaning intensely radioactive." He paused a moment as if expecting a reaction from Frank and Bonnie. "It will get carried into the hospital on patients' shoes, clothing, and hair."

"We have to find a way to admit them," Frank said. "We can't leave them outside."

"You can let them inside, but first get a broom and sweep the stuff off their clothes. Get them to shake it out of their hair. If it won't come off their shoes or clothing, then they should leave those articles outside. The less of this fine sand-like fallout you let in, the lower the exposure will be for all who shelter here."

"Bonnie, would you delegate this for me? Tap the staff and bystanders, and set up barriers and some sort of process to sweep and strip?"

"Sure," she said, and started to go off into the crowd of folks already in the ER waiting area.

"And discriminate!" Mr. Gingman shouted after her.

---

[19] "Off the scale" just means the indicating needle when its off the top end of the radiation detector's meter.

She stopped and turned back to listen.

"Look, if they can walk up here then chances are they can last for a 30-minute drive to another city. Tell them to go out of the city to another hospital. You admit only the badly hurt—you decide who that is. If they refuse, scare them with a little radiation talk. You will be telling them the truth. They really are better off far away from here."

"Okay, got it. Control the contamination from coming in. Discriminate," she said.

Frank was starting to appreciate this old man.

"May I sit down?" Mr. Gingman motioned toward Stella's ER Admissions area. They took him over to her desk where he sat down and pointed at her full cup of cold coffee. "May I?"

"You aren't contagious, are you?" Stella said.

"Not unless heart problems are catching, sweetheart," Mr. Gingman said, taking a big gulp of the cold black liquid.

"Hey, caffeine is not on the list for heart patients," Gingman's nurse said disapprovingly.

"Screw the list," the grizzly old man retorted.

When Gingman's hand carried the cup to his lips, Frank could see a tattoo of a sword on one arm with the letters USMC just peeping out from under the sleeve of his gown.

Gingman took another big gulp and half the cup was gone.

"Boy that is good, even if cold," he said.

"Okay, Mr. Gingman, what else would you suggest we do?" Frank wanted him to focus. He had an uncomfortable feeling that he did not have much time.

"Your hospital is amazingly well built for a radiation shelter. The walls of all your bottom-floor rooms on the south side have earth on the other side of them, and the ground on the north side slopes away. That's shielding. All a person has to do is stay in the southern rooms of this bottom floor. You have four floors above to keep the radiation from the dust on the roof from reaching you."

Gingman took the radiation survey instrument. "Let's see what we have here." He turned it on, and clicked the knob on the front.

"You had it set too far downscale. Now it shows us the radiation strength right here at this desk."

Frank leaned in with Stella and Mr. Gingman's nurse and looked. The needle sat on the number 5. "What does 5 mean?" Stella said.

"We call this the dose rate. First, this really was a nuclear explosion. There is a huge amount of nuclear radiation here. Second, we are getting 5 rem per hour right now."

No one said anything for a moment. Finally Frank said, "Okay, so what does that mean?"

"At that dose rate, if it continued, we would all accumulate a lethal dose of radiation in three or four days. The good news is that is probably as high as the radiation dose rate will get, unless you let people bring a lot of that radioactive fallout in here. Otherwise you will see this gradually decrease. Keep in mind this is inside the building. Outside the dose rate is undoubtedly higher."

Gingman took another swig of Stella's coffee and continued. "Grab a volunteer for me," he said. When they hesitated, he said, "Anybody that can run upstairs and walk quickly, and write some numbers down for me. This is an emergency."

Frank commandeered an uninjured teenage boy who looked to be about 17 years old and brought him over to Gingman.

Gingman switched on one of the instruments and showed it to the boy. "See how this needle goes full upscale? You click this range knob up one click." He did it as he spoke it, "and now you see the needle is near the middle. I want you do a quick survey. Go to all the wings at all the floors and take a reading. Try to click the range switch to keep the needle near the center. Write down what it reads at each location." Gingman handed the volunteer a yellow pad that he appropriated from Stella's desk.

"Also, go into the southernmost rooms on this floor and get those readings too. And step out front under the entry way overhang and take a reading outside. Then bring the readings back here. I will be better able to advise the hospital administrator if you will do that for me, quickly."

"I got it. I'll be right back," the boy said, and headed toward the stairwell at a run.

A commotion broke out at the ER entrance. A large man wearing jeans, sandals, and a wife-beater tee shirt pushed his way in, shouting.

"Who's in charge here? You can't send us to a far-off hospital. You are going to treat my wife right here or you'll have hell to pay." Red-faced, he held a petite woman's arm in his left hand and a black pistol in the other, pointed at the ceiling.

"In charge would be you," Gingman said to Frank. "He's got a gun; here, use this." He switched the other radiation instrument to a mode to produce a tone.

"The pitch of the tone will increase with the strength of the radiation. Scare him with it if you need to," Mr. Gingman said.

Frank walked over to the man holding the gun. "I am in charge," he said.

The fellow pushed the woman up close and continued loudly. "We pay taxes and my Chola is hurt. You have no right to send her someplace else. I want you to help her now!"

Frank noted the man's red face was not just from anger. The smell of booze wafted across him.

God help us! A drunk with a gun.

Frank sized up the situation. The man's concern for the woman made him think this could be easily defused. The woman had cuts on her face and forehead. Blood had run down her face and she looked a mess. But the wounds he could see looked superficial and free of glass.

"Nurse," he called, waving at one of the many who were watching the man with the gun. One brave soul came forward.

"We will fix her up right now," he said to the drunk, "but first I need you two to step back outside the entry way and let those folks sweep you."

"Sweep us?" the man said, looking back at the entry. "Say, this better not be a trick."

"No trick," Frank said. "Did you know that big explosion that hurt your Chola was an atomic bomb? It made radioactive dust fall outside. We sweep it off everyone so it won't kill them. You have some of it on you right now." He pointed to the man's shoulder.

"Man, you're full of it. I ain't going anywhere until she gets help."

The doctor raised the yellow box in his hand. "See this? It makes the sound you hear when it senses radiation." He moved it closer to the man's head and shoulders and the instrument's tone rose to a high pitch. When he pulled it away the pitch dropped. The man's eyes went wide.

"It's killing you and your Chola. Please let us sweep it off outside. I'll go with you." At that he turned the man and started him toward the ER's entrance. Once outside, the man stopped.

"Do it here. I am not going no further."

After thoroughly sweeping the man and woman with a broom and coaxing them to brush out their hair, Frank led them back into the ER and the nurse began treating the woman right in front of the drunk. She cleaned the blood off with wipes and saw the cuts were largely superficial. After she finished cleaning her up, the man calmed down considerably. Frank watched as the nurse applied antibiotics and patches to cover the wounds. The drunk now held the gun pointed at the floor.

"Now you and Chola need to leave the area. Leave Yorksberg. Get far away from here," Frank said calmly.

"We can't," the man said rubbing his head. "The car doesn't work anymore. I don't want her out in that radiation."

"The only way you can stay here is to give me that gun. We don't allow guns in the hospital unless you have a concealed carry permit and you keep it concealed per state law." Having no permit, and wanting to stay, the man surrendered the firearm and sat down in a corner with his sweetheart.

The volunteer taking Gingman's radiation survey came back in less than fifteen minutes, a little out of breath.

"Okay, let's see what we have," Mr. Gingman said to them. "On the top floor, closest to the radioactive material on the roof you wrote down 110 rem. You had to change scale to read that, didn't you?"

The volunteer nodded.

"Good job. Well, that is too much radiation. Doctor, you should move all patients and staff off the fourth floor. Put them down here." He pointed to the number written for the southernmost rooms of the ER level. "The radiation levels in those rooms are less than 1 rem per hour."

"Third floor is too hot also, 63 rem per hour. And the second floor is no good either at 37 rem per hour. Move them all down here. Start with the babies and children; they are more sensitive to radiation damage."

"Stella, I need you in the ER, but I want you to coordinate this via the PA. Make a general announcement that we are going to move everyone we can, pediatrics and maternity first."

"We only have one elevator working. This will take a while. What about intensive care?" Stella said.

"Talk to the doctor on duty there. We might have to leave them if moving them will kill them." He looked at Mr. Gingman.

Gingman had the cup to his lips and said softly over the last of the cold, black liquid, "Welcome to the world of the hard choices of nuclear war."

"War?" Frank said. "This might just be an isolated event, like a terror attack."

"Son, it's just a different kind of war. Wait until you see the casualty list and then you tell me if this is just a little terrorist event."

Gingman motioned Frank over and whispered, "These radiation levels are too high. You are going to have to evacuate the hospital."

"I thought you wanted the people moved down here," said Frank.

"Moving them down is the right thing to do. They will get a lot less exposure down here while waiting to move out. Not only is the radiation level too high, but you have food, water, and sanitation issues also."

A few minutes later a man in a Fire Department uniform walked up to the admissions desk. Frank had seen the man's shoes being swept when he first approached the ER entrance. The Fire Department officer carried a radiation survey instrument that he looked at as he walked. A uniformed policewoman was right behind him.

"Are you in charge here?" he said to Frank.

"Yes, I am the hospital administrator, Dr. Frank Edwardson." He started to shake hands with the Fire Department officer, but the man did not lift his hand.

"I am Walt Compbins, Fire Inspector. My hands are contaminated, so forgive the no handshake. This is Officer Melbourne. We've been sent here to make contact and get your status. Do you need fire or police?"

"Well, the staff got the fires put out. Just curtains in two of the rooms, but an officer for crowd control would be nice."

"The assistant chief thought so. Officer Melbourne will stay here. What else?"

Frank could feel fatigue. He looked at Gingman.

Gingman nodded.

"I would recommend evacuating the hospital as soon as possible. The bottom floor radiation levels are okay for a short sheltering, but there are a lot of people here, with more coming."

"All right, I'll see what I can do," the Fire Inspector said. "Melbourne has a portable radio with her. She will be your com center. All the central control centers are gone, but she will be able to hear and talk to police and fire vehicles. Command Com is now set up on Copper Ridge. I'll get back to you on the evacuation as soon as I know something. Meanwhile, we recommend you send folks away and tell them to get out of the area. Folks in neighboring cities will tell them where they can stay. Emergency shelters are being set up across the state."

"I'll get you some numbers and info on special needs," Frank said.

Hours later Frank received word that all but two critical-care patients had been moved to the bottom floor. He did a quick walk down of the area and found it to be cramped and stuffy with patients everywhere.

Staff members continued to send away all who were not critically injured and took breaks when they could, catnapping here and there. They had been told not to expect second-shift personnel to come to work, and had been asked to stay on. The wave of fresh patients had dwindled down to a much slower flow; apparently the police were getting the word out for people to leave the area. Surprisingly, there were very few broken limbs and fractures.[20]

About 9 p.m. they got word the National Guard would arrive at daybreak to transport those who could walk. Critical and non-walking patients would be removed throughout the night via ambulances, with drivers rotating to reduce their exposure.

Frank set up a rotation among the staff members so that no one person would spend too much time ferrying gurneys from the ER to the ambulances, which could be pulled up quite close to the building. By 10 p.m. the first ambulance evacuation had started, with a round trip taking about 20 minutes. Patients were taken only far enough to get them outside the contaminated zone and then transferred to "clean" ambulances or buses for the ride to distant hospitals.

He knew there were several hundred wounded who had walked in to St. Mary's and just stayed. This included several infants, one of whom was even brought in to the hospital by a vagrant. These wounded lined the lower floor halls and generally just tried to sleep. Vending machines on the bottom level of the hospital were soon empty, and lack of water and sanitation were a growing problem as Gingman had predicted.

Around daybreak, cell phones began ringing, and for fifteen minutes it seemed as if everyone lining the halls and crowded into the safer first-floor rooms were taking calls. Some were elated at having discovered their loved ones were safe, while others received bad news, or worse, no news.

"Haven't heard from Susan?" Stella said during a quieter moment.

Frank thought again about his wife, as he had off and on all night. Susan had never called, and his many attempts to reach her by cell phone resulted in nothing.

"No, nothing yet," he said with an ache in the pit of his stomach. "All I know is she mentioned shopping downtown with Listy, a friend, and Listy's daughter." Tears of fatigue and worry came to his eyes.

I have to stay focused.

---

[20] The records of hospitals in the Japanese cities bombed in World War II show the incidence of serious mechanical injuries was surprisingly low. In one hospital where 675 patients were seen, for example, there were no cases of skull or back fractures and only one case of a fractured femur. This is attributed to the fact that those with more severe injuries probably did not survive long enough to get to a hospital. *The Effects of Nuclear Weapons*, Samuel Glasstone and Philip J. Dolan, United States Department of Defense, 1977, 12.20.

Analysis of Chapter 14

Running a hospital 1.2 miles from a Yorksberg-sized nuclear explosion will be a problem because of the thousands of injured who will show up at the emergency room, and because of the deadly rain of radioactive fallout. For the sake of having a story to tell, we will assume the radioactive fallout around Yorksberg's hospital is not enough to require immediate evacuation of everyone. It would be a good exercise to consider what would need to happen if the radiation levels were high enough to cause death within ten hours for those who stayed.

The staff of Yorksberg's St. Mary's Regional Hospital has trained with the Yorksberg Emergency Operations Center (EOC) for hurricane preparedness and is able to handle multiple casualties. The problem is that a hurricane, for all its power and ferocity, is a slow beast. It takes hours or even days to throw its punches and all its nuances are well understood and expected. More than 50 feet above sea level and constructed to withstand hurricane-force winds, St. Mary's will weather the worst the Atlantic Ocean can send. Contrary to this, the monster that St. Mary's met this day is a very fast beast. It will do most of its killing and maiming within five minutes of its explosive appearance, and the number of dead and injured will far exceed those of a hurricane.

St. Mary's is located on a large, grassy quadrangle north and east of downtown Yorksberg. It is a relatively new facility with several features that provide protection for the people inside following the nuclear attack. This was not planned.

Look back at the map at the start of this chapter. North on this map is up. You can see that St. Mary's sits about 1.4 miles from ground zero, and that the blast wave will come from the southeast and strike the hospital at the point of its southeast corner. At that distance the overpressure is less than 2 psi. A blast wave will affect a structure the most if it hits perpendicular to a wall. The oblique angle of impact at St. Mary's Hospital softened the blow. This reduced window damage.

The bottom floor of this hospital is actually a half basement carved out of a hill. The natural slope of the ground is downhill toward the north. This means that standing south of the hospital one can only see three floors, but on the north side four floors are evident. The emergency room is located on this bottom floor (see sketch below).

Radiation emanating from radioactive fallout on the roof has a long distance to travel to reach the first floor, and must travel through the roof and three floors. The hospital is constructed out of cinderblock and poured concrete walls with pre-stressed concrete and steel panels making up the floors and roof. Built to withstand a hurricane, it is made of heavy, solid material, which will help shield those inside from some of the radiation resulting from the attack.

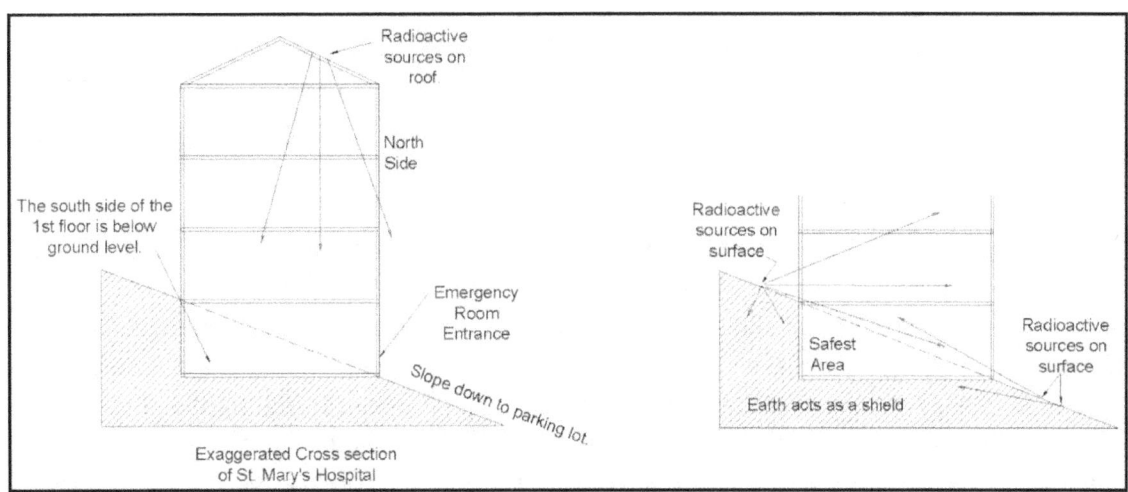

Where is the Lowest Radiation Exposure Rate?

Note the slope of the land provides natural radiation shielding from radioactive sources lying on the ground. Radiation emanating from particles on the ground outside the hospital building must travel through several feet of earth to reach the zone marked "safest area." Three feet of earth can reduce gamma radiation by as much as 0.007.[21]

If the radiation dose rate is 200 R/hr outside the shelter, for example, then behind 3 feet of earth the dose rate would be 1.4 R/hr. Keep in mind it is the density of the material that improves its shielding ability.

There are three factors that help reduce your radiation exposure: time (how long you are exposed), distance (how far you are from the radioactive material), and shielding (how dense and thick the material is between you and the radioactive sources).

Your hospital may have no such shielding safety factor. In that case, if fallout from the terrorist's bomb falls on and around it, your only course of action will be to immediately evacuate everyone.

Civil defense planners must determine how this will be done for each and every hospital in the area because no one can predict which way the radioactive mushroom cloud will move.

This hospital has its own electric generator, which automatically starts when power goes off and is wired to supply power to some lights and other critical portions of the hospital. These include one surgical suite, one elevator, the ER, X-ray and labs, and a few offices. The generator at St. Mary's is powered by natural gas from underground gas lines.

City planners would do well to consider natural gas-powered emergency electric power generation equipment. Historically underground gas lines seem to survive hurricanes and tornados well, and for an isolated event, like a nuclear attack, the gas lines may provide

---

[21] *The Effects of Nuclear Weapons*, Samuel Glasstone and Philip J. Dolan, United States Department of Defense, 1977, Table 8.72.

basically unlimited fuel… if not ruptured. Disadvantages of petroleum-type fuels stored in tanks include the possibility of fires following an attack and the finite amount of fuel that can be stored in a tank.

Could the gas lines be broken in a nuclear attack? Certainly, but such main line breaks will be limited to areas near ground zero. There is a chance that gas pressure outside that zone may remain sufficient until utility personnel have time to isolate the damaged lines.

The explosion in downtown Yorksberg slapped the ground so hard it sent out "P" and "S" earthquake-like waves. Waves in the earth tend to travel faster than the speed of sound in the air, so the first physical effect of the blast is the arrival of a seismic P wave through the earth. The P wave is actually a compression wave. It is quickly followed by S waves, or shake waves, which gives the sensation of the floor rolling slightly. This phenomenon is seen during earthquakes where the first sensation is often a loud "bang" as the P wave passes, and then a rolling sensation for many seconds as the S waves pass. This sequence is what Dr. Edmonson and Nurse Johnson experienced in the hallway. The lights went out first (loss of power travels at nearly the speed of light), a sharp shake (the P wave passing through the ground under the hospital), and then the sensation of the floor rolling or moving under foot.[22]

The blast wave at the hospital, a mile and a quarter from the explosion, was approximately 2 psi overpressure[23] and a wind gust of some 70 mph arriving about six seconds after the explosion. The overpressure is enough to blast some windows inward, but it is not able to substantially damage St. Mary's structure. Most of the blown-in windows will be on the side of the hospital facing downtown, the south and east sides, but acoustic effects and the large size of the ER entrance plate-glass windows caused one of them to also break.

Large sheets of glass in commercial buildings are made strong and in many cases may flex and not break. Such windows may even be blown out of their frames in one piece. In contrast, most window glass used in homes is quite fragile and may fracture into hundreds of shards, which are then accelerated into the room. Persons standing at the window may be severely injured and those across the room may also receive cuts.[24]

---

[22] The reader may remember the shaking was not mentioned in the previous story of Chief Ruffe at the Donut Hole (Part 1, Chapter 9). This was not an oversight. Seismic waves in the ground are felt with various intensities depending on the underground geologic structure and location. There was actually little shaking at the donut shop even though it is closer to ground zero than the hospital.

[23] From Table 2.1 in the Part 1, Chapter 9 analysis.

[24] Some readers may recall a scene from a 1950s civil defense movie showing children in a school ducking under their desks to be protected from a nuclear attack. Folks laugh at this because they think such a simple action cannot possibly protect kids from a nuclear explosion. That is an ignorant viewpoint. At distances beyond the zone of complete destruction, most well-built structures will not be totally destroyed, and flying glass may be the primary cause of blast-related injuries. By ducking under their desks, the children put themselves below the windowsill so that flying glass passes over them. This is presented in more detail in Rachael Miskins' story called "Elementary Knowledge" (Part 1, Chapter 11).

The tendency for the light from the explosion to draw the curious to a window is itself a hazard. A good rule of thumb is to avoid the windows so that any blast-propelled glass does not injure you. Don't worry about thinking a nuclear bomb is only a photograph flash. The flash from a camera is like a very quick blink. The light from even a small nuke will last for seconds. For a larger bomb, perhaps a one-megaton device, the light may last for ten to thirty seconds.

In several of these short stories, people at various distances from the explosion are not immediately aware of what has happened. The huge mushroom cloud is a fairly good telltale sign of a nuclear explosion, but we need to remember that large chemical explosions will also produce a mushroom-shaped cloud. The mushroom shape occurs because of the buoyancy of the hot gasses rising up after the explosion and not because the explosion is nuclear. The difference between chemical and nuclear explosions lies in how much heat is released, how large the resulting cloud is, and how high it rises.

Some might argue that no one knew the actual explosive power released in downtown Yorksberg and that the blast might have been a big chemical explosion with no release of radioactive materials. Our fictional blast released the energy equal to 19,000 tons of TNT. Loaded onto trucks capable of carrying 40,000 lbs (20 tons) of cargo each, it would have required the terrorists to park 950 tractor-trailer rigs with 20 tons of TNT on each in the downtown area to equal the explosive energy of the terrorist's nuke. All of that would then have to be exploded at exactly the same instant. That is basically impossible.

A nuclear explosion produces so much heat that the mushroom cloud will rise into the stratosphere, perhaps producing an ice-crystal cloud cap on top. Think of that height as where the tops of very large thunderstorms go. Chemical explosions will not produce clouds that reach that high.

Most people connect nuclear explosions with radiation and they know it is dangerous, but they do not know how it is dangerous or whether it will affect them. Since it is silent and painless there may be a tendency to assume they are okay where they are. This could have serious consequences. Communicating to the public at large about where the dangerous areas are following a nuclear explosion should be a priority of local authorities so that people who need to move out can do so as quickly as possible. Typically the most dangerous areas will be the zone right below the rising mushroom cloud and areas on the ground over which the cloud drifts.

In this story the Fire Department contacts the hospital about an hour after the event. This delay happens because it takes time for people to regroup and organize after being hit hard. Leaders are gone, resources such as vehicles and pumper trucks may be damaged, and communications will be down. Training for such a disaster should include preparing for the possibility of missing people and equipment. Training scenarios should be run with the EOC Coordinator assumed dead or missing, for example. This will force the team to fall back on plan B, which then would define who steps into the EOC Coordinator's position. This sort of command hand-down will eventually occur, but with training and forethought it will happen faster. A common understanding among the various branches of the emergency service organizations is important.

Preparations at hospitals should include planning in advance about what off-shift personnel should do in the case of a nuclear attack. Do they immediately report to the hospital, wait at home until called, or report to a distant hospital in another county? Key personnel should have a playbook of options prepared, which should be understood by everyone. Communications may be nonexistent after a nuclear attack, and previously written and agreed-on plans will be worth their weight in gold.

Radiation survey instruments are powered by batteries. Since these instruments are seldom used, they may actually be stored so long that the batteries are no longer useful. Hospitals, EMT groups, Fire Departments, Police Departments, and families that have radiation survey instruments must put into work a plan for storing batteries and replacing them at some periodic interval. Depending on the type of batteries used, it may be best not to store them in the instrument because some batteries may leak.

Calibration of radiation survey instruments is an important issue. The instruments must be calibrated for the instrument's readings to have meaning. Recalibration must be done periodically. Contact your instrument's manufacturing company for recommendations. You do not want to be in a 50 rem/hr radiation field with an instrument that lies to you and says the radiation field is only 5 rem/hr.

There are different kinds of radiation survey instruments. In Dr. Ramos' situation he actually needs one type for gamma radiation measurement and another for detecting alpha and beta emitters in localized areas such as shoes, hands, skin, and wounds. The survey of small amounts of radioactive particles on the shoes, clothing, and hair of persons walking in to the hospital may be masked by the much larger amount of radiation coming from general widespread fallout around the building or tracked in by people.

This means that sites where people congregate or shelter following a nuclear attack should in fact have two kinds of detectors, both calibrated and ready, with personnel trained to know how to use them.[25] One detector should assess the overall radiation dose rate, and another should be able to find small, hot spots.

In this St. Mary's scenario, the areas outside the hospital are highly contaminated; the ER waiting room is contaminated to a lesser degree by radioactive material carried in by people; and techniques of stripping, cleaning, and sweeping are used before people can be admitted to the examination area of the ER, the hallways, and rooms of the basement level

---

[25] Seems like a daunting task, doesn't it? Where will the city get the money to prepare and maintain shelters? Who will do the work of training people, setting up the shelters, checking them regularly, and maintaining the survey instrumentation? Well, the usual way today to accomplish this is to spend billions of dollars, perhaps with Uncle Sam's help. You will end up with a further bloated payroll, higher taxes, and Sam's nose in your tent. Another way is to remember that the people have a vested interest in this. Educate them about their own survival. You need only organize and delegate authority, use city or county authority to designate shelters in existing buildings, and offer the people the chance to raise their own taxes to provide shelter necessities and a minimal number of paid employees (off-duty police officers would be great – they already carry the authority to make a shelter work). Get creative!

of the hospital. This effort is to keep the radiation dose rate in the "safe" shelter areas as low as possible.

Hospital workers should consider how contamination control could be done at their facility and which supplies (such as brooms, disposable gloves, booties, and tacky mats) need to be stocked. We have a robust nuclear power industry that has figured out radiation control in detail, and there are many commercial products available designed specifically to help you with contamination control. You do not need to reinvent the wheel.

Some general guidelines on contamination control of persons in need of medical treatment are available on the internet. Key ideas for decontamination summarized from one of these are as follows:

1. Triage and stabilization of patients take priority before initiating decontamination procedures.
2. Removing the clothing typically removes approximately 80-90% of the contamination.
3. Open wounds should be covered during skin decontamination.
4. Contaminated clothing should be placed in plastic bags and stored for proper disposal. These radioactive items should be stored away from casual human access.
5. After clothing removal,[26] the skin should be washed with soap and water, using gentle brushing. Do not scrub hard enough to abrade the skin.
6. Hair may be decontaminated using any commercial shampoo or by clipping.

Most hospitals do not have underground levels. In those cases where the hospital and its grounds receive significant fallout, the only course of action will be immediate evacuation to an uncontaminated zone. This brings up a whole new logistics problem, the one Frank faced the next day when authorities ordered that St. Mary's be evacuated. Preplanning will make this less painful.

In this story, one person with knowledge in your hospital or shelter makes a big difference. Just having read this handbook will put you ahead of the typical citizen. Where are all the civil defense directors from the 1950s and early 1960s who know something about recovering from a nuclear explosion? Most are either gone or retired. It would be instructive if you took two minutes and thought through what probably would have happened at St. Mary's if Mr. Gingman had not been there.

Funding for training for emergencies will always be an issue. If you live in the Midwest you probably train to respond to tornados. If you live in a large city on the Gulf Coast, you probably train to respond to tornados and hurricanes. If you live on the West Coast or in Alaska you train for mass casualties from earthquakes; large mass-transit

---

[26] The mass casualty situation at St. Mary's is not the place for complete decontamination, including whole-body washing, because the entire area, including inside the hospital, will probably be contaminated to some extent. Complete decontamination will have to be done at hospitals far from the nuclear attack; this is another reason for moving the injured out of the contaminated zone.

accidents; and terrorist attacks on schools, malls and transportation. But how many large cities have training programs for a nuclear attack of the magnitude described here? This is not a new threat and it is past time for such training to be organized and delivered.

Hospitals and emergency services near nuclear plants probably already have some radiation control training. This will be to their advantage if their city is struck.

The man with the gun was written into this story to start the reader thinking about the possibility of some societal chaos in a large-scale event such as a nuclear attack. Aberrations in human social behavior can be triggered by an individual's inability to cope with the stress of the event, particularly if the person senses a loved one in danger or his or her security threatened. Just the presence of a uniformed officer of the law can greatly reduce the possibility of such flare-ups. The breakdown of society due to a nuclear attack is further discussed in the story of Amiee Moller, called "Gentle as a Lamb" (Chapter 21 of Part 2).

Mr. Gingman made the comment that, "A policeman works well, but you probably can't find one." This is a telling comment. Hospital administrators would do well to have a uniformed officer pre-planned to show up at the hospital to help control the crowds that will come.

The plan to turn away those with non-life-threatening injuries and send them to out-of-the-area hospitals is a key idea. It greatly reduces the flow of contamination into the hospital and reduces the work load on everyone. Injured people from a nuclear attack will be far too numerous to be handled by local hospitals even if there was no radiation problem.

Surrounding communities across the state will have to be involved. That is why hospitals in cities a hundred miles from the target city should have training in radiation survey instruments and contamination control even if they figure no one will ever bomb their little town.

The only real answer to St. Mary's predicament is wholesale evacuation.

Some may wonder why the ER radio on police and ambulance frequencies was not used early on in this scenario. The answer is that although there was electric power for the radios at the hospital and in the vehicles, the blast destroyed all the antennas on the roof.

Quiz on Chapter 14
(Answers are in Appendix A2)

1. Name three problems hospitals within 100 miles of a bombed city should prepare for.
2. For hospitals in the bombed city that cannot provide radiation shielding for patients, what must be done?
3. What special instruments should hospitals have to respond to atomic terror attack injuries, and what three periodic events should occur with these instruments?

4. After the bombing, how will the next shift of hospital staff workers know whether to come in or stay away?
5. True or False. The injuries the hospital staff will see following a nuclear explosion will be unlike the injuries from a non-nuclear mass-casualty accident.

Next we will consider the effect of the bomb on the Yorksberg subway system, which is named the Taconic Area Transit System, or just the "TAT" to Yorksbergians. You will find interesting complications in that the subway passes under the Taconic River to south Yorksberg. Join Tammie Janos in Chapter 15, which we call "Trouble can be Good."

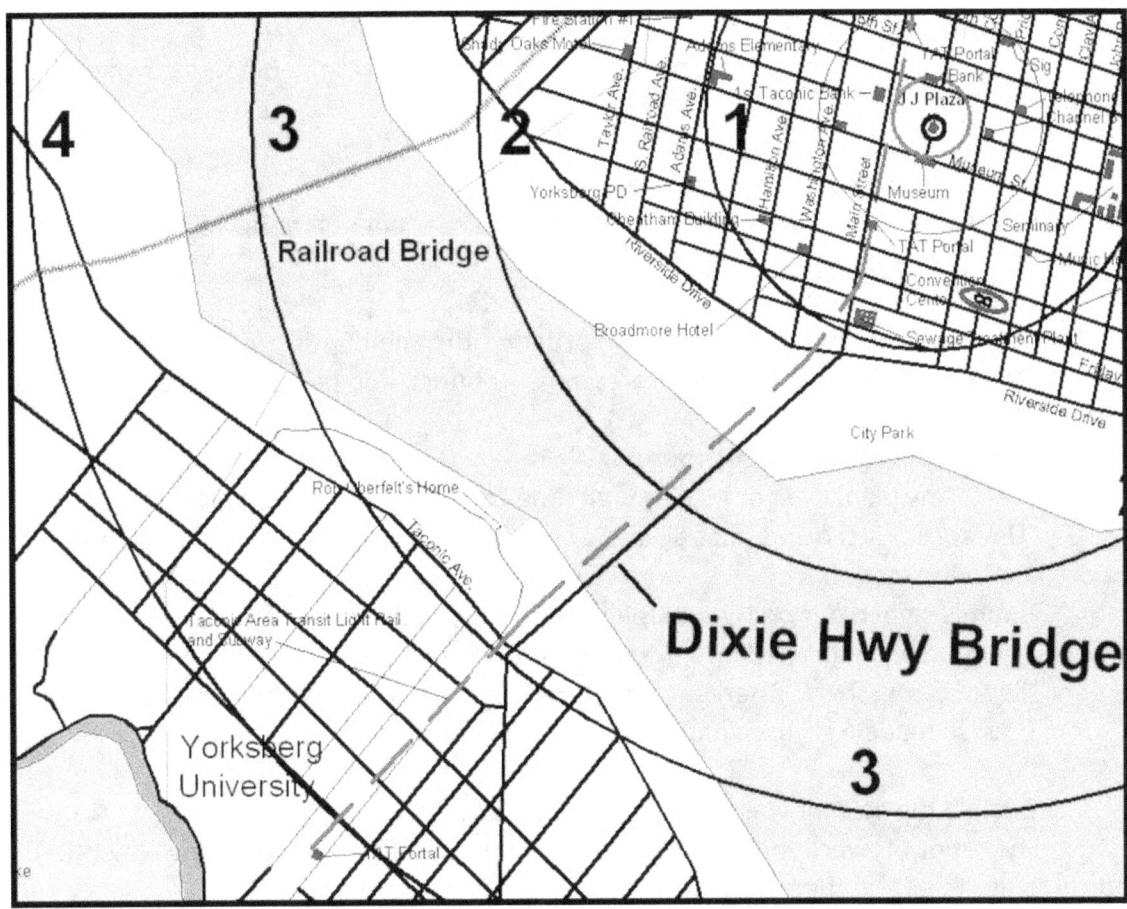

Toothache in the Subway

15 - Tammie Janos – Trouble can be Good (2 miles)

This day has been nothing but trouble. The toothache that kept me up all night, not getting up on time, breaking my favorite string of beads, and now this.

She walked across the bank lobby with her arms full of binders, embarrassingly aware that her watch alarm was sounding.

"Beep, beep, beep."

It would pick now, when I can't possibly shut it off.

She could see several of the bank's customers looking at her, some smiling, as she juggled the binders and beeped.

Just my luck it beeps when my hands are full. My luck is so bad I probably dropped a pen or something when I was 21, and Mr. Right walked by while I picked it up.

"You're beeping," a grinning Peggy Britton said as Tammie passed by her teller cage. Tammie waggled a little finger in acknowledgment and smiled back.

"Reminder of my dental appointment," she said.

"Here, let me help," Peggy said, rising and walking ahead of her to the printer room, where she held the door open.

"Toothache?" Peggy said.

"Yes, and it kept me up last night. Thanks." Tammie set the binders down with a thump.

"Who are you going to see?"

Tammie silenced the beeping watch.

"I go to the university's School of Medicine. The students there will practice and I will get relief on the cheap."

"Really? I've never done that. Are they good?"

Tammie carefully set the binders in order on the shelf.

"Never had a problem. Their professor is a dentist, and he keeps a pretty close eye on them."

"Good luck; see you in the morning?"

"That's my plan. I've got just enough time to TAT[27] over to the university."

"Under the river? God, that always gives me the creeps," Peggy said, and walked back to her teller station.

Tammie signed out on the board in the employee's break room, put on her coat, grabbed her purse, and leaned into her boss's open office door.

"See you tomorrow, Theresa. I'm off to the college of drills and Novocain."

Theresa made a grimace and said, "Ouch. See you tomorrow."

Outside the cold air was like a slap on the face.

She set out toward the corner of Main and 4th Street, trying to decide which TAT portal to use to get on the subway.

On a nicer day I'd go for the museum portal, but this wind is hell.

Her decision made, she turned and walked up Main Street to the 5th Street TAT portal, keenly aware of the biting cold on her ankles.

At the portal, she briefly looked at the schematic of the subway routes laid out in colors with all the stations numbered. The diagram showed that TAT ran under the city up north out to the airport, ran south under the river, and then ran above ground as a light rail system approaching the university TAT station.

She walked down the concrete stairway into the underground, bought her pass for two bucks from a vending machine, and then passed through the turnstile to the waiting area along the tracks. She could see about twenty people were already standing there. The air felt cold there too, but without the wind she felt warm in her winter coat.

The racket of the oncoming 2:15 university-bound train announced its arrival. It pulled up right on time and squealed to a stop. Stepping into a car through the automatic doors, she saw a young man enter just before the doors closed. He grabbed the strap next to her.

---

[27] Yorksberg's light rail subway system is the Taconic Area Transit, or the "TAT" to Yorksberg's citizens.

Tammie immediately felt a little uncomfortable. *Is he looking me over?* She could not bring herself to look at him. Men on the subway gave her the creeps. Then he spoke in a friendly tone.

"University-bound history major, right?"

They all leaned back as the car accelerated through the tunnel. The darkness outside brightened each time a light whizzed by.

You're in a well-lit car with about fifteen other people. You can talk to him.

He looked to be a little taller than she and in good shape. She noticed a book under his arm.

"I'm university bound, but not for a class," she said. "How did you know I'm taking a history class?" The paranoid idea that he had followed her for weeks crossed her mind and she shoved it aside as being stupid.

He pointed at the DVD case sticking out of her purse and read the title.

"*The American Heritage Series, with Historian David Barton.*"

"Good guess, Sherlock," she said, and tried a slight smile. "I watched the DVD and am returning it to a friend. I guess you're a beer salesman?" she said.

"A beer salesman?" he said surprised.

She felt the lean on the overhead straps increase again, signifying the train decelerating into the museum TAT portal between 2nd Street and 1st Street, the last portal before the track dove down 65 feet below the Taconic River into ancient bedrock. That thought made her uneasy.

The young man looked down at his clothes and shoes, trying to see what had pegged him as a beer purveyor.

Tammie laughed at the expression on his face and his personal exploration.

"It's not your clothes," she said; "it's the book you have."

He looked at the cover of the book and then he broke out laughing.

An automated voice in the background said, "Please stand clear of the doors. The doors are closing. Please take a seat or hang on tightly. This train will be starting momentarily."

Tammie liked his laugh. It was a happy laugh of someone really amused, but she wasn't sure what amused him.

He held the book up for her. The title said, *Corona Discharges and Lightning Mitigation*.

Now she laughed. "Sorry, all I could see was the word *corona*."

The train accelerated from the station and the voice said, "The next stop is Yorksberg University Station."

She looked at her watch and saw that she still had plenty of time. It was 2:29.

They never take patients in at their appointed times anyway.

"What is a corona discharge?" she ventured to keep the conversation going. Her tooth hurt and she rubbed it with her tongue.

"First, my name is Alan Craig," Alan said as he shifted the book to his hand on the strap and offered his other hand.

Tammie juggled the purse and shook his hand. "I'm Tammie," she offered, and then on second thought gave her last name, "Tammie Janos."

The train rolled on and shortly began a steep decline down to the under-river section of the tunnel.

Oh my God. I hate this part. She closed her eyes.

"This part gets to me too," Alan said. "Imagine being under the river. I always wonder what would happen if the ceiling caved in."

"I don't want to think about it," she said hurriedly. "Tell me what a corona discharge is." She still had her eyes closed and wanted some distraction from the thought of going under the river.

"You know if the tunnel caves in, having your eyes closed probably won't help you," Alan said.

She opened her eyes to his smile.

Is he teasing me?

"A corona is an electrical discharge that happens near conductive sharp objects when a high voltage is applied."

"You must be a physics major," she said.

"Close, electrical engineering, with a physics minor."

The train reached the under-river section and leveled out. The tunnel lights whizzed by in the darkness outside as the train moved under the river at its top speed. Tammie tried not to think of the millions of gallons of cold, brackish water in the riverbed above them.

Their conversation waned for a moment, so she started to ask him how he liked the university. Her first word was cut off when the lights went off and the train began decelerating. A fraction of a second later the entire train lurched as if it had hit something.

An emergency light was on at each end of the car, giving just enough light for her to see everyone thrown violently forward and to the side as the train came to a sudden stop. There was a strange deep rumbling sound and a rough shaking of the car that faded after a few seconds. Then a few seconds after the lights first went out, Tammie felt her ears pop. It was not the ear popping of a slow change of altitude; this was sudden and so strong it hurt.

The final lurch ripped her hand from the strap and she landed on the floor, aware that several other people had also fallen. As Tammie picked herself up, she heard a woman cry out in pain. There was considerable commotion as people helped each other up. A small group collected around the hurting woman and Tammie heard someone say the lady might have broken her wrist when she fell.

"Are you all right?" Alan said with concern. He had managed to hang on.

It's nice to have someone who cares.

"Yes. That was a hard fall, but I think I'm in one piece. What happened?"

"Maybe we derailed," he said.

The emergency lights comforted her. There appeared to be no other lights in the car or outside.

As people got up and began finding their seats, or straps to hold onto, it was very quiet, so quiet that she jumped a few minutes later when the train operator spoke over a car-to-car intercom.

"Ladies and gentlemen," he said, "the train has derailed and apparently all power is off. Please take a seat until we can get you out of the tunnel. If there are any doctors or nurses on board, please identify yourselves to me. We have several injuries that need to be looked at. If anyone was injured in your car, please send someone forward and let me know."

One of the men in Tammie's car volunteered. He had a small pocket flashlight and after he and another man pried one of the doors open, he stepped out into the tunnel. Tammie could see by his small light that there was a walkway along the track apparently designed for this sort of event.

Tammie sat down and Alan sat next to her. "This is scary," she said.

"Not comfortable," he responded. "That pressure is what scared me."

"You felt it too? That hurt my ears."

"I thought maybe the tunnel collapsed and caused the pressure, but I guess not; otherwise we would all be under water."

"What are we going to do?" she said with concern. "How are we going to get out?"

"Just wait on the man to tell us what to do. I am sure the TAT folks are trained for this sort of thing."

About fifteen minutes later, which seemed like an eternity, the operator's voice with its faint Brooklyn accent came again. He didn't sound too optimistic.

"Well folks, I've got good news and bad news. First, the bad news is the train is off the track. The good news is we are about half way through the under-river tunnel and there is a walkway along the tracks. I am unable to raise anyone on the train's radio, so we must begin walking out of the tunnel. If you have a light with you, please use it to help others onto the walkway and as we walk out. I estimate it is about a mile and a half to the university station. You can guide yourself with the railing along the walkway. Just stay together and move slowly and we'll be out of here before you know it. Now, everyone please exit the cars and line up along the walkway."

"I wonder why we don't just wait for them to send another train to pick us up. Surely by now our arrival has been missed at the university's station," Tammie said.

A man standing nearby answered.

"It might be the derailed cars are shorting the tracks. The power is below us on a power rail."

Alan agreed. "That would stop another train from coming."

They exited the car, being careful to step over the gap between their car and the walkway. It was necessary to step onto the edge of the walkway and then climb through the rail. This was hard to do in the dark and several of the men helped the injured woman, who was still suffering with the pain in her wrist. Tammie felt for her and was pleased to see her arm in a makeshift sling.

Once on the walkway, everyone hushed. It seemed to Tammie that everyone wanted to be able to hear the operator. She was comforted by the fact that there was enough light coming out from the line of train cars to allow everyone to see something of each other, but it was very dark. When she looked at either end of the train there was nothing but total blackness beyond.

"Listen!" Alan said. "Is that water?"

"Oh my God!" Tammie said when she heard its roar in the distance. It sounded like a waterfall coming from up ahead of the train.

Alan had a keychain LED light in his hand and shone it down under the cars. "Crap," he said. "Look."

She could see water under the car and it was just about deep enough to cover the rails. Worse than that, it was flowing rapidly back down the tunnel toward the Yorksberg side of the river.

Tammie felt the first wave of panic and grabbed Alan's arm. "Oh my God, oh my God! We are going to die down here."

"No, lady," the man behind her said. "We are going to walk out. Now be quiet so we can hear the man up front."

This brought her up short. The firmness in his voice steadied her.

This is the story of my life. I finally meet a nice guy on the train and then we both drown under the river. She smiled at the dark humor of that thought.

The train operator passed by them, walking back down to the rear of the line, counting heads. When he got to the end he started shouting so everyone could hear him. He had a very bright light in his hand.

"Everyone, I have placed a volunteer at the front to lead you out. Wave your light, Bill."

All heads turned and could see someone up front shining a bright light at them.

"You will follow Bill. I'll take the rear to keep from losing any stragglers. I have a flashlight like the one I gave Bill, and will use it to help you see." He waved his light, playing its strong beam along the walkway. "Walk as quickly as you can, but do not run. We don't want anyone else getting hurt."

The plan was a good one. Tammie could see Bill's light at the front, shining up the tunnel, and could see the line of people walking behind him. The light from the operator at the rear of the line of people constantly played along the walkway, making it fairly easy to see. She relaxed a little.

As they walked, the sound of cascading water grew louder. Eventually Tammie could see Bill's spot light stopped on what looked like a large stream of water gushing into the tunnel from overhead. It was a heavy roaring stream that appeared to be under great pressure. As they approached this cascade, the air was filled with mist and smelled like river water, a kind of fishy, seaweed smell.

As they passed the cascade, most of the people in the line ran through the spray. It was loud, and everyone got a little wet.

"Is that my imagination or is that water spray growing?" Tammie said after they were some distance past the leak in the tunnel's wall.

"Leaks only get bigger," Alan said. "They teach that in engineering. Look," he said, training his small light at the tracks, "we must be going uphill. The tracks are dry here."

Sure enough there was no water on the tracks. All the water spraying into the tunnel appeared to be flowing back downhill to the wrecked train. Tammie felt encouraged at this fact.

After walking another thirty minutes she noticed the walkway and tracks had ceased their steep climb and had leveled off.

"We are not under the river anymore," Alan offered.

"Thank God," Tammie answered back, smiling a big smile.

It took about twenty more minutes of steady walking before they heard shouting from up front. They could see why. There was light at the end of the tunnel, and nothing had ever looked so good.

As Tammie walked, the subway finally reached the point where it came up out of the ground and proceeded as an above-ground rail line leading up to the university portal.

The cold intensified when they became exposed to the wind. Her legs had gotten wet when she ran through the spray from the cascade inside the tunnel, and the cold was almost painful.

Thank God my coat is warm.

She could see the rail line was fenced in on either side to keep people away. This fencing forced them to walk along the tracks the rest of the way to the university station. Tammie noted the excitement their emergence caused in the people at the station.

"Were you folks in the tunnel when the bomb hit?" a man asked them as they came up to the station. "We thought you guys were goners!"

"What bomb?" Alan said. "Our train derailed under the river."

"Yorksberg got nuked!" The man practically yelled as he pointed north.

They turned and looked back the way they had come. The city was peppered with raging fires and enveloped in a huge cloud of smoke and dust. Sirens could be heard wailing in the distance.

"Oh my God! Oh my God!" was all Tammie could say as she thought of her office and the people she worked with, the people she had seen less than two hours ago. Then a sobering thought came to her. *Saved by a toothache. Wait until I tell Mom.*

Analysis of Chapter 15

The fireball from the nuclear explosion in John Jay Plaza grew to about 900 feet in diameter within the first second after the bomb exploded. This diameter encompasses part of the 1st Taconic Bank of Yorksberg and thus the unusual weather in the bank lobby that day – high temperature of 6,000 degrees with a supersonic wind. Nothing much will be left of the bank except for some reinforced concrete with bent and melted rebar sticking out. All the people Tammie worked with are dead.

Sometimes things happen to us that we perceive as "bad," when in fact they really act in favor of us. A car dawdles down the road and we are in a hurry, so we become upset, never realizing that had we not been hindered, we may have been T-boned at the next intersection and killed. This is what happened to Tammie. She has a toothache and because of that she survives an un-survivable situation (i.e., she survives even though she works 900 feet from where a nuclear explosion occurs).

Many large cities have subways as part of the transit system and it is interesting to speculate what effect a nuclear bomb might have on them. Our fictional city of Yorksberg has a small system consisting of one rail line, part subway and part above ground. It runs above ground from the airport (north of the city) and then goes underground as it nears the hospital TAT portal. It continues as a subway all the way through the downtown district and then under the river. On the south side of the Taconic River it remains a subway for a while and then emerges to run once again as an above-ground rail line up to the University TAT portal.

The subway downtown actually passes within a city block of the bomb's detonation point (see map). Under these circumstances, it is likely the seismic energy at the tunnel will be huge and this may result in a part of the tunnel collapsing at some point. Fortunately there were no trains in the downtown area of the subway at the time of the explosion. The north-bound train was just leaving the hospital TAT portal heading toward the airport, and like Tammie's train it stopped when the power went off. No injuries were suffered there by the blast since that portal is some two miles from ground zero and the geologic strata there did not focus the seismic wave.

It is likely that any people who walked from their stalled train and exited the subway system at the hospital portal would be exposed to the intense radioactivity present in the air by the time they came up out of the subway. With little information available to them and transportation unavailable, it is likely that many of these people would be severely exposed.

This makes the point that one of the biggest logistics problems for city emergency planners will be the urgent necessity of moving people out of the radioactive zones. There will be hundreds of thousands of survivors clueless about the danger of the radioactivity. If they are not removed from the area soon, they will suffer enormous radiation damage to their bodies, leading to sickness and even death.

Much of the preparation for such an event lies in educating the general public and placing intelligent resources prior to the explosion. This means shelters for the people to lie low in until transportation can be brought in to extract them. Well-equipped shelters will have supplies of drinking water, an air filtration system, food, sanitary facilities, medical supplies, and cots or blankets for people to sleep on. This is an enormous undertaking that many cities and counties will balk at due to the required expenditures and the perceived waste if no nuclear attack occurs.

Cities and counties can save money by doing nothing and blaming the evil men, after the huge, unnecessarily large death toll is revealed. Eventually, in hindsight, the media and others will point out how cheap it would have been to save the countless thousands of lives lost, if better planning and wisdom were applied to the expenditure of construction funds.

The solution lies in creating facilities that are used every day, but are designed so that they can quickly become functional shelters when a radiological emergency arises. Think of structures that are already scattered around a city for the convenience of the citizens: libraries, schools, and other public buildings that if designed with the additional function of a shelter in mind, could be used if the need arises.

These structures are already doubling as polling places and tornado or hurricane shelters, so why not also use them for nuclear attack survival? If your city has to construct such multi-use places from the ground up, yes, it will cost more than building a single-purpose facility to be used solely as a shelter, but the multi-use structures will be more efficient because they can be used for more than one purpose.

The first effect on the train under the river is the loss of power. This happens almost instantly because the explosion destroyed the main power substation downtown, which feeds that portion of the rail system. The lights go out in the train and it begins slowing down; battery-operated lights immediately come on in each car.

The second effect is the arrival of the explosion's powerful ground wave, like an earthquake, which jolts the tunnel hard enough to derail the train. Once the wheels come off the track the train slows down violently causing everyone and everything inside to be thrown forward.

Would the seismic wave from the blast really be able to derail a train a mile and a half from the blast point? Remember that the strength of seismic waves in a particular location depends on more than the energy release at the blast site. Seismic waves reflect and refract through the various materials and layers underground. Thus they are diminished at some places and amplified at other places. For our scenario we have assumed the blast did derail the train and was strong enough at one point of the under-river tunnel to cause a fracture in the rock. This resulted in river water incursion into the subway tunnel ahead of Tammie's train. Had the electric-power-driven train not derailed, the passengers would still have had to walk out.

For those interested in what eventually happened, you should know the entire tunnel under the river was eventually flooded, but no one drowned in the tunnel. Years later the tunnel would be dewatered by powerful pumps, the fracture repaired, and train service restored.

We assume in our scenario that the pressure wave from the explosion is somehow ducted into the underground system and that this results in an ear-popping pressure wave reaching the train about seven seconds after the blast. This corresponds to sound traveling about a mile and a half in that time.

Will such a pressure wave traverse the subway system in real life under this situation? The answer is that it could, and it could even be much more powerful if the bomb is detonated in or near a subway portal.

Hopefully your city's emergency planners and the folks who operate and maintain the transit system have considered how to handle a train derailing in a tunnel. Yorksberg had the wisdom, and it is common practice, to provide a walkway along the underground rail for emergencies and for rail and tunnel maintenance.

Aware that their trains run through tunnels that would be completely dark if power is lost, the TAT authorities made sure that each train carried powerful hand lanterns and that their batteries were kept fresh. They also maintained the train car's emergency lighting system. You should consider what would have happened to Tammie and the other folks on the train had it derailed under the river and had the emergency lighting system not been planned ahead of time.

Many folks carry keychain lights and a few might have a flashlight with them. In the case of Tammie's train, we surmise the folks could have walked out holding the walkway rail and using only a few keychain lights; however, it is likely their progress would have been much slower, and as the cascade of water leaking into the tunnel increased in volume as time passed, this could become a concern.

Being underground in an enclosed area is claustrophobic for some people, especially in the dark and under a river. Tammie's panic at the thought she was going to die will be a real occurrence in many people in this situation. Good emergency lighting will help such folks cope. It might be wise to train transit personnel about their options in dealing with a claustrophobic person.

Could a nuclear blast break an under-river tunnel and cause leaks? Very possibly. In fact most such tunnels have groundwater leaking into them all the time, with the water being constantly pumped out. If a direct leak path from the river into such a tunnel does happen, the rate of water intrusion will be very high due to the depth of the river above and the height of the water above the tunnel. High flows are known to enlarge the leak-flow path as time passes.

Could a nuclear explosion happen a mile and a half from an underground train and the folks on board not know it? The answer is yes. They will suspect an earthquake at first. Since normal AM and FM radios do not work well underground and the subway communication system may not work when the power is out, how will they find out about the attack? They will likely find out the same way Tammie did, when they exit and meet other people.

City planners should seriously think about designing the entrances to subway tunnels with the ability to be closed off and sealed. Most subway entrances in big cities today are wide open, negating the potential for people to go underground to escape wind-borne radioactive dust. Certainly the underground will provide some shelter, but contaminated dust will easily enter and be deposited on all the surfaces within the underground near any of the subway entrances.

Civil defense planners should also carefully consider the effects a nuclear attack will have on the subway ventilation system. Will the flow of air draw radioactive materials into the subway near the blast; perhaps even transport it to non-contaminated parts of town? It might be wise to shut down such systems after a nuclear attack until the effects on the transport of contamination can be understood.

Finally, for the romantic readers, yes Tammie and Alan continued to see one another. Mr. Right did not get away this time. For the sake of our story, we will tell you that these two survivors of the Yorksberg nuclear attack eventually married and have three healthy children. They are presently living in Austin, Texas, where he works for a local power distribution company and she teaches history at one of the city's high schools.

Quiz on Chapter 15
(Answers are in Appendix A2)

1. To make sheltering in the subways realistic, what preparations will the citizens have to make?
2. Sometimes it is good when bad things happen in our lives. True or false?
3. Is it possible for a nuclear bomb to damage a subway deep underground?
4. Can subways transport radiation to distant locations?
5. Moving tens of thousands of people out of a nuclear-bomb-damaged city quickly will be very difficult due to clogged roads, lack of transportation, fires, stalled or abandoned vehicles, and radiation. Suggest an alternative to this need for a quick exodus.

Hopefully this short story and the analysis gave you some things to think about. We have seen several city dwellers who survived; now it is time to watch what happens to a suburbanite three miles from downtown. Could the bomb significantly affect people that far away? Well, it can, both in ways you might anticipate and in ways you might not think of. Read on, and see what happens to Laticia Washington in a story we call "Shooting from the Hip."

And please don't do what she does.

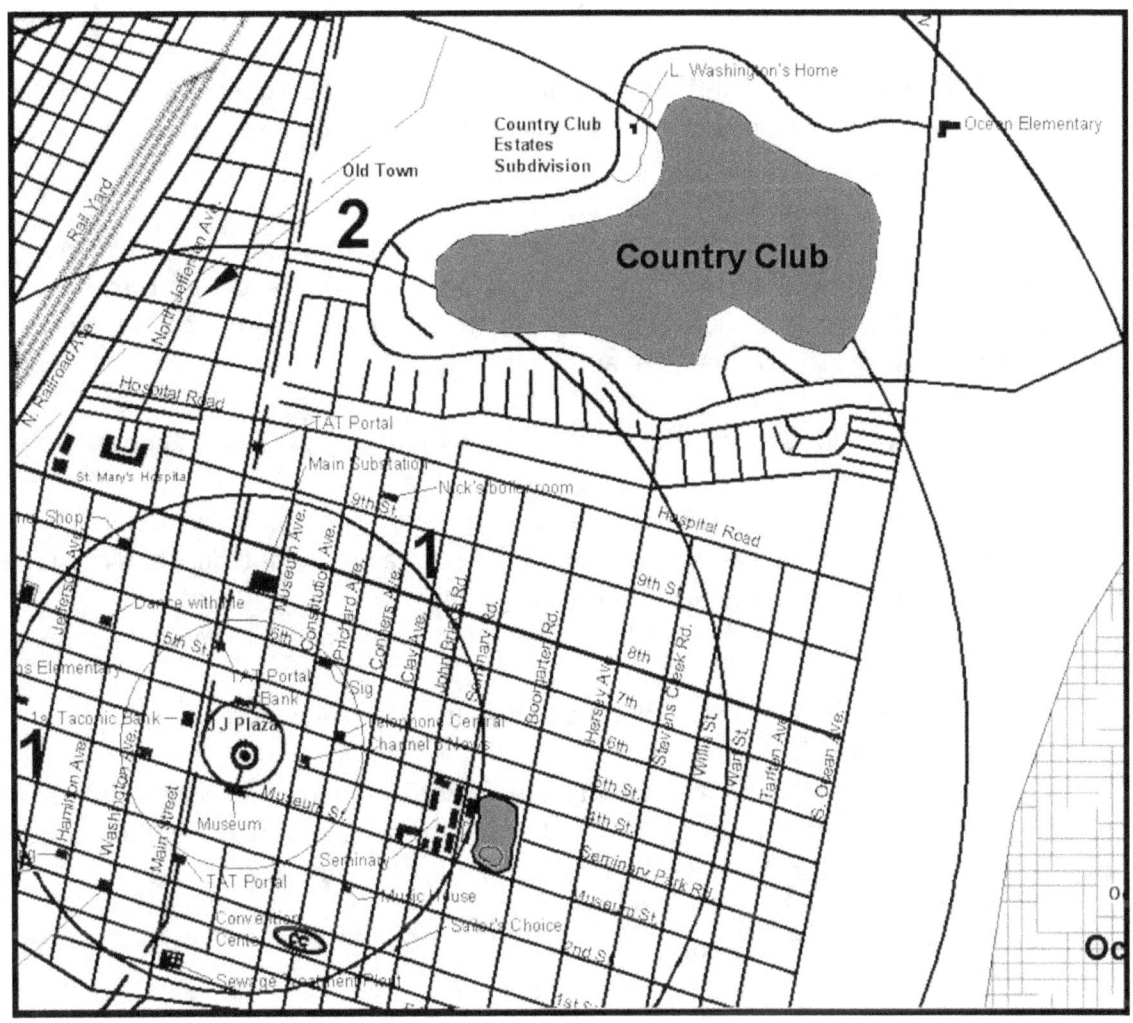

Don't do what Laticia did

16 - Laticia Washington – Shooting from the Hip (3 miles)

Jeremy had placed the can of rat poison, a rope, duct tape, and a very sharp knife in the bag the day before, and then taken that bag to find Carla, a dark purpose implied.

Laticia placed the wet laundry into her dryer, cleaned its lint filter, and set it in motion. She then began folding the towels and sorting various items all the while watching a small TV she had tuned to today's episode of "Days of Stars and Trailer Trash." This soap opera had all of her neighbors talking, and she was glad the story line was finally getting back to the confrontation between Jeremy and Carla.

"How did you find me?" Carla said, while eying the bag in Jeremy's quivering hand.

"Does it matter now?" he said. "You must pay, you know."

"Pay? Pay what? It is you who should pay. I know about you and Shelia. I intend to tell my father everything…. Jeremy, what are you doing?"

Laticia's towel-folding hands froze in midair, as Jeremy reached into the bag.

"This is your fate, you lying cheat!" he said, slowly withdrawing his hand from the mysterious bag.

The television went off and the basement was plunged into darkness.

"Noooo!" Laticia moaned at the now-silent television. She heard the washer stop and the dryer spin down to a quick stop.

"Oh shoot-a-bug!" she said loudly.

She threw the towel down and began to walk toward the light from the open basement door at the top of the stairs. When she placed one foot on the bottom step, she felt the whole house shudder once and heard a distinctive, deep "crump" sound, and then the sound of breaking glass somewhere above.

In the hallway upstairs she found one of the two frosted-wineglass keepsakes from her honeymoon, broken in pieces on the floor.

"Damn," she said upon seeing the damage, forgetting her normal kid-friendly "shoot-a-bug" expression of exasperation. She pulled out a broom and dust pan from the kitchen pantry and began sweeping up the glass.

"What happened, Mom?" said Brad, peeking out of his partially opened bedroom door.

"Don't come out here. There is broken glass. It went everywhere."

"Was that an earthquake?"

"I don't know, honey. I think that was too short to be an earthquake. Your father went through one in California and said it made a boom sound and then the floor rolled for about 10 seconds. This felt like someone dropped something really big and heavy."

"Oh," Brad said, and coughed and sniffed.

"How's the Hardy Boys book?"

"It's really good. "Thanks for suggesting I read it. They have found a haunted house."

"Well, get back in bed and cover up. The house is chilly."

He didn't answer, but Laticia could hear him cough his way back to his room and then the rustle of sheets.

She started to get the vacuum out of the hall closet, but then remembered the power was off, and instead cleaned up the glass with a broom and dustpan. Then, taking a flashlight from a kitchen drawer, she went back downstairs to retrieve her coffee and the latest *World* magazine.[28]

Sitting in her breakfast nook with the magazine in her lap, she looked out the window and across the nearby golf greens, which were mostly winter brown, and sipped her still-warm coffee. After a few moments, she decided to call her mother and pulled out her cell phone. It did not work. *I should have known. Duh.*

Holstering the cell, she picked up her magazine and opened it to an article about some lawyer suing because American soldiers were praying at the Air Force Academy, but

---

[28] www.worldmag.com/index.cfm

couldn't get into it. The house was so quiet she could not read. Something about the quiet bothered her, so she took stock of the situation.

The central heat is off, so no there's no heat available. The fridge isn't running, and the freezer in the garage isn't making any noise, she thought of the small chest-type freezer, which always sat in the garage entry way, making its normal repertoire of whirrs, bubbling, and intestinal-gas-like squeaks.

But she sensed something else softly audible in the quiet. It was voices, distant voices that sounded as if they were coming from in front of her house. *Typical,* she thought, *neighbors out talking about the power going out.*

She got up, walked to the living room, and peeked out the Venetian blinds. She could see Meg, Rachael, and some blond lady she didn't know in front of Meg's house, talking and looking down the street to the south. Meg's two-year-old ran circles around them all, so cute, all bundled up like an Eskimo, in a puffy blue outfit with a white, fur-lined hood.

"Brad, the furnace is off. Stay under covers or get your pants and jacket on until the power comes back on," she said with a motherly command voice.

"Okay, Mom," came his muted voice. "They're going in the haunted house," he said.

Slipping on her coat, she called back to Brad. "I'm going across the street to talk with Meg. I'll be back shortly."

"Okay, Mom," his distracted voice came back.

She closed the door behind her and walked across the street to talk to the women.

"I wondered when that shaking would get you out," Meg said as she walked up. "You have to help us figure out what happened. She pointed toward Yorksberg's downtown.

Laticia looked that way, and then up, high above Yorksberg.

"Oh my gosh! What is it?" she said. She could see a monstrous, very high, black-and-gray cloud arching high over them, moving northeast at a slow pace. She couldn't see the skyline of the city because of the smoke.

"Looks like smoke to me," the blond lady said.

"I think the power system must have exploded downtown," Rachael added. "That's probably why the lights went out."

"Just when Carla got the bad news," Laticia said.

Meg laughed. "So, you were watching that too."

"I think we all were," Rachael said.

"Well aren't we the group?" Laticia observed. "It's a good thing our husbands don't know how we fritter our time away." They all laughed.

"I thought I saw Brad peeking out the front window about an hour ago," Rachael said.

"Yah. He's home with the sniffles. Kathy hasn't got it yet." Laticia paused and then added her favorite expletive, "Damn."

"What are you damning about?" Meg said.

There was a knot of anxiety forming in her stomach. "Kathy's class went to the museum today." She looked at her watch and back toward the city.

"Aw, honey, those teachers will take care of the kids. Don't worry. I'll stay with Brad while you drive over to Ocean Elementary to wait for her if you want."

"Oh Jesus! Look!" said the blond lady. "The bank building is gone."

They all turned and looked. Laticia could see the base of the smoke column had mostly drifted clear of the downtown area. As the smoke between them and downtown became more transparent they could just make out the city skyline. It had changed. Entire buildings were gone, including 1st Taconic Bank, the tallest one.

Instantly, Laticia felt a wave of sickness flow over her like an electric shock. It settled in the pit of her stomach as raw fear for her daughter. Propelled by a shot of adrenaline, her heart began to race. She let out a little "Oh, God! Kathy!" and without another word to the ladies she began running back to her house, all the while pulling out her cell phone to call her husband. She had the "husband" button pressed halfway through the case before she remembered the phone did not work. She burst into the house and yelled for Brad.

"Brad! Get up, now! Bring your book and a blanket! Hurry!" He had never heard his mother in a blind panic before.

"Okay, Mom," he said in return, still distracted by the story. "Just let me finish this chapter. The Hardy Boys have just found a secret passage."

"No, Brad!" She knew she was screaming, but didn't care. "I want you in the car right now! You can finish it there!" Laticia felt both fear and frustration. She had gathered up her purse and had the car keys in her hand.

A minute later Brad, in his house slippers and dragging the blanket and book, walked quickly into the garage. "What did I do wrong?"

"Nothing, sweetheart," she said, "just get in the back."

The three ladies were still out front, staring at the broken city when they saw Laticia manually raise her garage door, back out rapidly, and take off down the street with a little tire squeal, the car's cold engine leaving lots of white vapor disappearing behind it in the chilly air.

She drove around Country Club Circle to where it dead-ended on North Ocean Avenue directly in front of the elementary school; there she could see buses piled up in front of the school and what looked like a group of parents trying to get their kids off the buses and into their cars.

Not wanting to get caught in the crush of autos and people, Laticia parked some distance away and then, leaving Brad buried in his book, ran back down to the school to where she could see the principal standing amid a group of adults.

"Principal Fogal, have they come back from the museum field trip?" she said breathlessly as she ran up.

"Not yet," the principal said. "They should be on their way."

"Can you call them on the radio?" someone said frantically. Several other mothers had gathered around. She guessed they all had kids on the field trip.

"Don't the buses have radios?" someone else said.

"They do," he said, "and we have tried to contact them. But the bus radio repeater is not working. We can call other buses that are nearby, but the ones over in the city are down among the buildings and our radios just can't reach them there."

Laticia looked at the ragged skyline and bit her lip. It looked even worse now. She blinked back tears in fear for her daughter. Looking toward the city she could see the massive dust cloud, now gray with tinges of orange, had come noticeably closer.

A distraught man spoke up. Laticia knew him as the roving science teacher, Charlie Nelson, a favorite of the children. It seemed to Laticia that he must have been trying to convince the principal of something because he spoke as if the conversation had not been finished.

"Fogal, I'm telling you, you have to order these buses out of the county and do it now."

"Charlie, we don't know what kind of explosion that was," Principal Fogal said in a mildly aggravated tone of voice. "If it wasn't nuclear, I'll never hear the end of it. The parents and board will have my hide and my job."

"Nuclear?" Laticia heard several ladies say, and the idea shocked her. She looked again at Yorksberg.

"And if you are wrong," Mr. Nelson said, "then neither you nor any of these kids will probably survive. Look at that cloud." He pointed. "We will be in the bottom of it in just a few minutes. Look, man, get logical... a flash so bright that several of our kids are still seeing spots, a white-hot ball of fire as big as the whole downtown... Carmen said she could feel the heat from the fireball at the playground," here his voice became almost a shout, "and we are three miles from the city! And the mushroom cloud! "That should be enough to convince you!"

"I think you might be right," Principal Fogal said angrily. "But I can't authorize such a major change in plans without direction from the district office. They will have to tell me where to send them so that parents can pick the kids up later."

"Oh my God," Charlie said. "You don't have time to wait on the school board. You should send them west... but you better have them run north to State Road 42. They can go fifty miles due west and be out of the way of this cloud." When the principal did not respond, Charlie said, "Do you want me to do it?" and grabbed for the bullhorn the principal held.

The principal tried to keep the bullhorn and a scuffle began for the device.

Parents were shouting and several were crying. Laticia did not know what to do, so she ran back to her car. She had panicked again at the first suggestion that this might be a nuclear bomb, so as soon as traffic allowed she pulled out and poured on the power heading for the city. A crushing, twisting knot of fear for her little Kathy drove her south down Ocean Avenue and into the eastern edge of the downtown district.

She passed an ever-increasing stream of cars coming out of the city. Many of these were driven by people who were obviously panicked, aggressively passing as many cars as they could, honking at anybody who held them up. This forced her to slow down and blow her horn several times as the idiots came at her.

She could see a lot of dust and smoke hanging in the air, so she closed the car's vent, shut off the heater, and made sure the windows were all up and tight. She knew the quickest way to the museum, and by the time she reached S. Ocean Avenue and Museum Street, she began to doubt Mr. Nelson's warning about this being a nuclear explosion.

She noticed a few fires but found little substantial damage to the buildings along S. Ocean Avenue. Shingles were all over the road and tree limbs down everywhere, as if a strong wind had blown through. At one point she passed a dead pine tree with its top branches smoking like a smoldering torch in a vacant lot.[29] She thought it must have been hit by lightning, but she dismissed that thought as silly in December.

Laticia shook her head to clear it. There were so many thoughts racing through her mind, but the primary and primeval one told her to hold Kathy safe and warm in her arms.

Turning the corner onto Museum Street she could see the debris increased farther down. Near Museum and Seminary there were three cars burning and beyond Seminary lay absolute, total chaos. Telephone poles were down across streets, parts of buildings were lying in the road at places, there were fires in many of the buildings, many of the trees lining the road were either uprooted and tossed helter-skelter or broken off at the trunk, and smoke was everywhere. The cold, hard knot of fear in her belly tightened into the beginnings of a protective, numb resignation and disbelief.

She pulled over and stopped at a burning car near Museum and Seminary, her heart racing and her palms sweaty. She ran the wipers to clean the dust off her windshield to better see something yellow a couple of blocks up Museum Street in the jumbled mess.

Is that a school bus?

"Mom, what are you doing?" Brad's voice came from behind her with a note of fear. She realized he had come up out of his book when she stopped and had seen the devastation ahead of them.

"Mom, that building is on fire. It's a really big fire," Brad said. She ignored his comment.

"I am going to go look for your sister. There has been a big explosion. Stay in the car and keep the doors locked. Don't open the windows. I'll be back quickly; I promise."

With Brad protesting in fear, she got out, shut and locked the doors, and started walking, half running, west on Museum Street.

After a block or so, she realized the yellow object she thought might be a school bus was a bit farther away than she had guessed, but she pressed on.

She passed a body lying on the sidewalk in the next block. She did not look at it. Her focus remained on the crumpled yellow thing amid what looked like a building or a wall fallen in the street. The way got more difficult, and she found she had to climb over a horizontal power pole, never once thinking the wires might be dangerous.

Her Kathy was probably on that bus. She figured she would be able to get her out and rush her to the hospital, so she pressed on.

As she approached the jumble of debris, which included the yellow object, she came across a dead child. He looked like a ten-year-old, badly burned, and folded over in an awkward position. She ran forward not daring to look at him further, seeing several live people in each block as she passed. They were either prone on the ground, sitting with

---

[29] See *The Effects of Nuclear Weapons*, Samuel Glasstone and Philip J. Dolan, United States Department of Defense, 1977, note to Figure 7.63, documenting a fire started on the top of a wood pole 1.25 miles from the explosion at Hiroshima.

blank looks on their faces, or walking like zombies, their clothing tattered or completely missing. Many had terrible burns.

For Laticia there were few sounds on this strangely silent journey. The fear for her Kathy kept out the voices calling for help from the broken buildings, along with the sounds of the crackle of fire, sobs, distant sirens, and somewhere in the distance a small airplane or helicopter.

She avoided looking at the people she passed and noticed the damage to the buildings grew worse the farther into the city she ventured. At first it had been just blown-out windows, but soon it became shattered structures, missing roofs, rooftop air-conditioning units smashed in the street, sections of walls collapsed, smoke from fires—so many fires—and dust everywhere.

The debris field finally became impassible when she reached the twisted and bent street sign that read Clay Avenue. She could see the paint on the sign was completely gone from one side, as if someone had applied a blowtorch to it, while the other side remained readable, barely, but it was blistered and scorched.

The yellow object could be seen clearly now, and her heart sank as she identified it as a school bus, or what remained of one, twisted and compressed like an accordion, sitting high up on a ragged, smoldering pile of metal and concrete rubble with broken electric poles and wires lying everywhere. No one responded to her repeated calls. She wanted to look within, but realized she could not climb up the massive debris to where the bus had come to rest. She made out the insignia on the side of the bus and felt relief that it came from a neighboring county. The thought of the many mothers who would be grieving that day brought tears to her eyes, and once they came, she began weeping uncontrollably.

She wanted to search further, her mind filled with the horrible image of her Kathy lying in a street, hurt or burned, crying for her mother to come and rescue her. But she could see it would be physically impossible. A few feet from where she stood the jumble of debris became too thick.

Her emotions surged again and she began sobbing. She now knew that, except for a miracle, her Kathy would not be coming back, that the buses would have come down Museum Street and taken Ocean Avenue back to the school. She knew this for sure. She remembered such museum field trips she had chaperoned with other classes, so she knelt in the rubble and cried, her mouth dry, her eyes burning from the smoke of the fires, and her adrenaline-driven strength now gone.

Rising, she turned and walked back toward her SUV and Brad, defeated and shaken. In her grief she did not see the man until he walked up to her with a stumbling gait and stopped, staring past her. He stood before her with gaunt eyes, awful gashes on his face and neck, no clothes on except boxer shorts and one sock, and blood covering his entire body.

"Help me," he said. "My wife—" his weak voice trailed off.

Laticia, overwhelmed, did not respond to his plea, but broke into a run back to the SUV. She could only think of getting away from this horrible place.

She found Brad had forgotten his book and still sat in the car, but now had a terrified look on his face. He had seen the body lying nearby. She realized he had seen the injured man staring after her and reaching out to her for help.

She got into the driver's seat and closed and locked the doors.

"Mom, what happened? Who is that man? Why are you crying?"

She could not answer for a moment, and when Brad tried to hug her over the back seat, she held him off. "No, honey, later. This dust on me might not be good for you. Wait until I wash it off." She used the rearview mirror and noted her coat, hands, face, hair, and eyelashes were dusted with a white-gray powder. It floated everywhere in the air like soot following a forest fire. She could even see it on the dashboard inside the car.

Only then did it occur to her that she might be in danger.

Didn't the Japanese people die of radiation after the nuclear bomb fell in World War II?

A new cold fear caused her throat to tighten. She turned the SUV around and, dodging debris, sped back to Ocean Avenue and then north to the elementary school, where she pulled up to the empty parking lot. One empty school bus remained.

She sat for a moment and thought of her husband. Cordell had been far enough away that he had probably escaped the explosion. This thought comforted her, but she desperately wanted to go to him. She thought about going back and working her way over to Copper Ridge Mall, but remembered what Mr. Nelson had said about the mushroom cloud, so she decided to do what he had told the principal to do. Go north and west.

Traffic continued to flow out of the city and suburbs, with cars moving north on N. Ocean Avenue, bumper to bumper but moving steadily. She pulled out and moved with the crowd to Shell Road where the caravan of cars had to slow as they passed around orange traffic cones someone had set up to block the road leading into the city. Traveling as fast as she could, she finally reached SR-42 about fifteen miles north of Yorksberg and turned west, intending to get on the interstate and go north, but as she approached the intersection of the interstate and SR-42 she changed her mind.

Remembering her sister lived about two hours northwest of Yorksberg, and figuring the county roads, the little blue roads on the map, would have light traffic, she drove under the interstate highway and onto familiar roads, which would take her to her sister's home, roads the family had often driven because of their pastoral beauty and lack of traffic. She looked at the dashboard. *I have enough gas.*

She drove for about twenty minutes when suddenly her cell phone began beeping the "you have a message" tones. She put it to her ear, one hand on the wheel, as Brad looked up expectantly. Cordell's voice sounded concerned, but calm.

"Honey, I hope you and the kids are okay. I am fine. I tried to get home, but the police were keeping people from going into the city. They sent me down to Bakersville where I am getting a motel room. Call me as soon as you can. I am really worried. I'll call your mother and sister and if I don't hear from you I will head to your mom's. She has enough room for us all. The police have the roads blocked off and there is no way I can get back to Yorksberg, so if you are still in that area, try to get to your mom's. Call me. I love you."

She could hear the stress in his voice. She called him back and he answered immediately.

She could not prevent the release of grief she hit him with. "Oh, baby, Kathy's gone," she wailed. She began sobbing again. "I found a wrecked bus; it wasn't Kathy's. The whole downtown is a wreck—" she tried to continue, but could not.

She slowed down and pulled over. She shook with grief, forgetting that Brad was listening from the rear seat.

Cordell cut her off. "Baby, baby, calm down. I'm so sorry, honey. Is Brad with you?"

"Yes, Brad is fine. I'm fine too. But Kathy went with that damn field trip to the museum."

Cordell paused, and then said, "Okay, honey, okay. I am so sorry. Maybe she made it out and will show up later. Where are you now?"

"On the way to Emily's. About an hour to go," she said.

"Okay, okay. Here is our plan. You stay the night with Emily and then bring Brad to your mother's tomorrow. I'll drive to your mom's place tomorrow morning. You got it, babe? That's our plan." His voice hinted he felt sorrow, and that made her sob more.

The cell connection faded a bit.

"Let me talk to Dad," Brad urged, and she handed him the phone and wiped the tears from her cheeks. Laticia drove on down the road while Brad talked to his dad until the connection was lost.

She continued on in light traffic, along a route that moved her away from Yorksberg. Brad tried to ask about Kathy. Through her tears she could not answer his questions.

"Later, honey. Let me drive right now."

Twenty minutes later they came to an intersection with a northbound state road where a DuckBurger fast-food business stood on the corner, and when Brad saw it he spoke up.

"Mom, I'm hungry. Can we get something?"

Laticia wanted to stop too because both hunger and nature were calling for her to stop. Besides that, the skin on her hands, arms, and the back of her neck prickled with the sensation of heat rash, and this alarmed her. She thought it too cool for heat rash and she felt an urgency to wash. So she parked under the DuckBurger sign, a smiling, giant duck holding a hamburger in its right wing.

After a restroom stop, she took her pajama-clad, blanket-wrapped son to the counter, and they each ordered a double-duck sloppy, an order of duckweeds (fries), and a drink.

They ate in silence, and Laticia found the normalcy of eating somehow comforting. It took her mind off Kathy, if only for a moment.

On the road again and relieved to know Cordell was safe, she turned on the radio. She couldn't find music on any of the stations. Instead the airwaves were full of news commentaries on the events at Yorksberg. She learned it had been a nuclear explosion and the city had been declared a national disaster area. The governor was on the way for a firsthand look, and FEMA had been activated. The National Guard had been mobilized to provide the manpower necessary to control all the roads leading into the contaminated area.

Contaminated?

Laticia suspected this word might apply to her, although she had little idea of what it meant or what the consequences of it were. She just knew that somehow it could be detrimental to her and Brad. The word made her want to shower more than anything else at that point, so she drove faster.

At last she could see her sister's home, situated on several acres, and turned down the long, familiar driveway. She pulled up to the country farmhouse and beeped her horn. She could see lights on inside and shining out into the early dusk of the winter evening.

Thank God they have electricity here.

Emily came bounding out the door and down the porch steps. She ran to Laticia and gave her a big hug before she had stretched the fatigue out of her joints. There were tears in Emily's eyes.

"Oh my God, oh my God," she said. "I thought you were dead. They showed it on the news. They're saying it's worse than 9-11."

"Maybe you shouldn't hug me or Brad. We kinda got dusted looking for Kathy."

"Don't be silly," Emily said. "I always have a hug for family." She gave Brad a big squeeze. "Did you find Kathy?" she added, apparently realizing what Laticia had said.

"No," Laticia said and broke out in sobs. She cried in Emily's arms a few minutes before Emily could get her into the house, seated at the kitchen table, and calm enough to talk. Through tears, she told Emily the story about her fears that Kathy had been near the bomb blast and about finding the bus. She could not bring herself to mention the dead child or the desperate man she had seen.

"Can I fix you two something to eat?" Emily said.

"No thanks, I'm not hungry. What I really want is a long shower."

"Well you know where it is. There are robes in the hall closet, and I will wash your clothes while you shower. Brad, are you hungry?"

"Not really. I'd like a shower too."

"Okay, showers it is. You can use the second bath. Just leave your clothes outside the door for me.

After cleaning up, they all watched television. News monopolized all the channels. When Laticia saw the explosion, apparently filmed from a helicopter, she said, "I knew Mr. Nelson was right." She had seen films of this sort of thing sometime in her past.

Laticia went to bed early after calling and talking with Cordell again. She could hear the concern in his voice when she told him about going near the site of the explosion. Laticia did not feel well and this alarmed Cordell.

"It's just the fast food and stress," she said.

She had mild diarrhea and dizzy spells, but felt better when she lay down. Emily promised to wake her if Cordell called again.

Laticia woke to the sound of Emily's persistent knocking.

"Come in," she said, still in the fog of sleep.

"Cordell called; he said he's on the road coming here, and he said we have to take you and Brad to the county hospital right away."

"Right away? He didn't mention it earlier."

"He insisted. Apparently he watched some news show and they talked about radiation in downtown Yorksberg. He is very concerned, Laticia, and he told me not to let you say no."

"Can't we wait until morning? I'm so tired."

"Cordell said I'm to call 911 for an ambulance if you refuse. Please get up. I'm afraid for you and Brad."

Analysis of Chapter 16

"Shooting from the hip" is an expression that means taking quick action without a lot of thought. Shooting from the hip is not a good response to a nuclear terrorist attack. Shooting from the hip is what Laticia does in response to the events involving her and the Yorksberg attack. We will look at Laticia's mistakes in this analysis so that you do not repeat them if a real attack comes.

Laticia lives 2.5 miles from the big bang. Her soap opera was interrupted because the main power substation downtown was destroyed in the blast. Electrical power moves much faster than either the bomb's air blast wave or the ground seismic wave. This is why Laticia does not connect the shaking with the power loss. The blast wave did not reach her house until about fifteen seconds after the power went off.

Extended power loss over a wide, populated area, particularly in very cold weather, can be lethal. Our public servants, as well as our city and county officials, cannot be expected to keep everyone warm. Individuals need to take charge of their own needs and work with their neighbors as much as possible to survive. In Laticia's case, the temperature inside her home continued to fall for days after she left, and the goldfish in Brad's bedroom soon succumbed.

Folks who find it necessary to shelter in place might find the lack of heat to be serious, especially if there are elderly, very young, or sick persons in the shelter.[30]

---

[30] You don't have to live close to the bombed city to be affected. If you live where the winters are cold, consider what you would do if power was off for a month or more with temperatures well below zero. Beyond your personal discomfort, consider that water pipes in the home may freeze, as well as any emergency water you may have stored. With no liquid water, sanitation (the bathrooms) will be an issue. You might have to use a large bucket, like a five-gallon paint bucket, along with one of your toilet seats. Just line the bucket with a sturdy kitchen trash bag. You can tie the bag closed and at the end of the day place it outside where nature will keep it refrigerated for you. For those who can make it work, a wood stove is a wonderful source of heat. Wood is inexpensive in most parts of the country, and a small stove will keep your

The neighbors are like Laticia, raised during the late '70s and '80s, upper middle class, and untrained in any aspect of civil defense. They are written into this story as clueless because that is what many of our citizens are today: clueless. They do not see the importance of learning to be prepared, and would choose their soap opera rather than a three-hour lecture on what to do when terrorists strike. The good news is that since you are reading this book, you are no longer among the clueless.

Shortly after Laticia and Brad departed for the school, the primary fallout began in her neighborhood. The nuclear fireball vaporizes everything it touches. Concrete, steel, wood, everything is heated until it is a white-hot glowing ball of plasma. Think of it as a vapor as it rises and radiates its heat away. As it cools, the vaporized materials in the plasma condense back onto tiny pieces of material the bomb threw into the air; sort of like moisture in rising air condenses into water on tiny motes of dust or salt crystals.

These tiny particles are thus coated with nuclear fission products that are highly radioactive. The larger particles, the most radioactively dangerous, fall close to the site of the explosion. This is the "primary" fallout. The lighter particles are carried a longer distance and fall farther away. This is the "secondary" fallout. The very smallest particles are carried on the winds around the world and settle out everywhere. By the time they settle, their radioactivity has decreased to the point where they cause little harm.[31]

The base of the bomb's dust cloud is about half a mile (0.8 km) in diameter. The 15-mph wind will carry this dust about one-fourth of a mile in a minute. Thus the dusty base of this huge cloud began to pass just west of Laticia's neighborhood about ten to fifteen minutes after the blast. Twenty minutes after the blast the base of the cloud was north of the neighborhood and moving away. This cloud is highly radioactive and best to be avoided. If you are outside, you will receive significant radiation from it even if it passes some distance from you. This radiation from the cloud is called "shine." If you stay in the area as the cloud passes over, you will also receive radiation exposure from the radioactive materials it leaves on the ground along its track of passage.

The rapid transport and dissipation of the cloud does not account for ground turbulence, especially in downtown Yorksberg. There, vestiges of smoke and dust will remain for some time, caught in eddies and wind currents among the taller buildings. Fires will loft this radioactive dust and present a hazard to emergency and news aircraft in the area. Authorities should close the air space above the city to prevent aircraft exposure.

---

home toasty warm. There are even stoves today that have catalytic converters that make them smoke free, something that might be required by city codes in high-population density areas.

[31] The long-term effects of small amounts of widely distributed radioactive materials are not in the scope of this handbook. Suffice to say the vast majority of living humans on the earth will never be adversely affected by this worldwide fallout. Some may develop cancer due to the fallout, but the cancers caused by the fallout will be mixed with the general background of cancers caused by cosmic rays, chemicals, bacteria and viruses, and human lifestyles (smoking), so noticing a difference in cancer rates will be difficult.

Meg and Rachel are two of the crash test dummies of this story. Without warning from the authorities, they will stay in their homes, not in their basements where some sheltering is possible, until they have received a lethal dose of radiation. They may not hear the helicopters circling overhead broadcasting "get out of the area" until the accumulated dose of radiation damage in these nice ladies assures their illness or death. Had they jumped up and run when they had first seen the mushroom cloud, they would have survived unscathed.

Laticia's home is placed approximately three miles from the blast to demonstrate that even in a really big nuclear blast, if you are several miles away and inside, you may not be aware of what has happened. Note the lesson here: if the house suddenly "bumps," it might be a good idea to go out and see what caused the bump. Most likely it is your friendly garbage man setting the dumpster down too hard, but you never know.

Again we see the hand of chance played out in the fact that Brad is at home and his sister is in the wrong place. You can do nothing about this sort of circumstance. If you prohibit your kids from downtown field trips, a 747 may crash on the school or a deadly swine flu may infect your child at the mall. What you can do is educate yourself and your family so that mistakes such as what Laticia does in response to the event do not cause further, unnecessarily harm.

Schools are mentioned in several of the vignettes in this handbook for a reason. They are complicated places full of our most precious possessions.[32] As depicted here, we have an uneducated staff who has trained for fire drills but not for a nearby nuclear explosion. When Laticia arrives, she finds what you will almost always find in untrained populations: different opinions; a leader with political complications attached to every decision he or she makes; a press for time; and lots of interested, and in this case scared, people (parents). This combination will only grow chaos and unnecessary deaths. Education, training, and accurate, uniform knowledge are the only cures.

> Do your children know what you expect them to do if they survive the terrorist's nuclear explosion in order to continue to survive? What you say to them ahead of time may save their lives.

Often there are people who know what needs to be done, in this case Mr. Nelson, the science teacher. But will the person holding the power of decision listen to the one who knows? This is an age-old problem that can be helped by educating the authorities, the leaders, and governmental representatives, so that when a nuclear terror attack happens,

---

[32] We must comment that our schools are one of the sites most vulnerable to terrorism in our society, and we as a people have not adequately prepared to defend our children. We do not teach our school's staff civil defense and, using some form of idiotic logic, have in most states declared our schools "gun free zones," thus guaranteeing that the bad guys will be able to kill hundreds of our children, any time they want to, before they can be stopped. Simple observation reveals that where weapons are readily available to good people, crime decreases every time. If 20% of the staff at each school were trained and given access to weapons at school, the bad guys would not have a free hand at killing and would probably pick some other gun free zone.

people do not stand around in the falling rain of radioactive material, arguing about what to do.

Indeed, our Mr. Nelson is a hero. He saved a whole school of children who were about to be sent on regular bus routes to their homes, and to their deaths.

For those who want to know, in our story the buses quickly transported the children and most of the teachers to a county forty miles away where they were sheltered until the children's parents caught up with them. Many of the clueless parents were actually saved by being forced to follow their kids. The few parents who insisted on picking up their kids and heading home—well, you can guess what happened to most of them.

Laticia panicked and drove downtown. The police are overwhelmed and have not had time to organize and respond by sealing off the city. There are policemen out in cars all across the city, but every one of them has ten emergencies to handle, so control of traffic trying to get into the blast area is nonexistent.

County officials outside the city are fairly quick to recognize what needs to be done, and thus when Laticia finally drives off trying to follow the plan Mr. Nelson suggested, she encounters the first of many road blocks (orange cones and police tape blocking the incoming lane) that must be set up to control access into the contaminated zone.

The fire department has lost its downtown station where the chief has his office and where the dispatcher's console is located. The units outside the city center respond and are fighting many fires, but soon leadership recognizes that many of the larger fires are way out of control and that whole city blocks will have to be abandoned. In addition to this, wiser heads prevail with some fear of radiation (they have a few instruments capable of measuring radiation), so the fire folks retreat to the west and south of the city, many of their engines taking the interstate across the river to be washed off and staged near the university, to be deployed as wisdom dictates.

Lack of communication is as big a problem for the fire department as it is for the police department. Without high antennas and repeaters, in some places one can talk for no more than a mile and a half with terrain and buildings blocking signals. There is a tendency for governments to locate the police/fire radio dispatchers and antennas downtown, which is both a blessing and a curse since the tall buildings allow for antennas to reach out a greater distance, but the downtown is more likely to be the target of the bad guys.

We can see that having a pre-arranged plan would make communication after the disaster simpler. Sending a patrol car to the top of Copper Ridge to act as a relay station, for example, would bring patrol units south of the river in contact with anyone north and west. As the Yorksberg police and fire departments get organized they will eventually implement this.

Gasoline for emergency vehicles may become a problem because of the lack of electricity to pump fuel out of storage tanks. It would be wise to have hand pumps or generator-powered pumps capable of doing the pumping. It would also be wise to move at least some governmental fuel storage out of the downtown districts.

It is appropriate to comment here on what can be described as the zone of survivable destruction. Near the site of the explosion, survival is next to impossible. As we examine the damage caused by exposure to heat, blast, and radiation farther and farther out from ground zero, we find the destruction diminishes and the chances of survival increase. A certain distance away from the point of the explosion we will begin to see a few survivors. These are likely those who were deep inside a building or other major structure that protected them. Farther out we find survivors in damaged structures but still no survivors who were out in the open. Farther still from ground zero we finally reach the point where a few people who were outside on the street survive. Eventually we will reach a distance from the explosion where almost everyone survives the initial blast, heat, and radiation.

Thus there exists a ring centered on the explosion point beyond which survivable injuries will occur when a nuclear weapon is exploded in a city. The size of the inner edge of this ring where a few people survive, and the outer edge of the ring where everybody survives, depends upon the energy released by the weapon used. For the Yorksberg weapon, estimated at 19 kt, the inner ring is presented as approximately 0.5 miles from John Jay Plaza. The outer ring is just beyond 1.5 miles. Most of Yorksberg's immediate injuries will be found in this zone, the Yorksberg zone of survivable destruction. We see this as Laticia moves toward the ground-zero point. She finds little damage and no injured people along Ocean Avenue. As she drives down Museum Street, however, there is more and more damage.

For a weapon that yields more energy, such as a 5,000-kt weapon (five megatons), the zone-of-survivable-destruction ring will be much farther from ground zero. Consider the following example of data taken from nuclear testing.[33] The table below shows the distance from ground zero for a wood-frame building to sustain severe damage (low probability of survival) and to sustain moderate damage (higher probability of survival).

Surface Explosion (Yorksberg Example)

Weapon Yield	Distance for Severe Damage	Distance for Moderate Damage
19 kt	5250 ft, 1.0 miles, 1.6 km	6750 ft, 1.2 miles, 2.1 km
5 MT	41,250 ft, 7.8 miles, 12.6 km	43,500 ft, 8.2 miles, 13.3 km

Notice that for the 19-kt weapon, the zone of moderate damage is a ring two-tenths of a mile wide (1.2 – 1.0 = 0.2 miles), centered on the explosion point. When the weapon yield increases to five megatons of TNT-equivalent explosive power, the moderate damage ring is 0.4 miles wide (8.2 – 7.8 = 0.4 miles). Significantly, the moderate damage ring for the 5 MT explosion starts at 7.8 miles while the moderate damage ring for the 19-kt explosion starts at about 1.0 miles. You can see the zone of probable survival would be much farther away from ground zero for the larger explosion but only slightly wider. Keep in mind the wider the ring, and the larger its circumference, the more people it contains.

---

[33] *The Effects of Nuclear Weapons,* by Samuel Glasstone and Philip J. Dolan, Third Edition, 1977, p. 218-219.

The numbers we just covered in the above table apply to damage of structures sitting in direct line of the blast wave with no intervening buildings or hills. The distances used in our Yorksberg examples have been modified (reduced) somewhat to compensate for the large number of intervening buildings.

You might be interested in the effects of an air burst for comparison. These are in the following table.

Air Explosion at Optimum Height

Weapon Yield	Distance for Severe Damage	Distance for Moderate Damage
19 kt	7000 ft, 1.3 miles, 2.1 km	9000 ft, 1.7 miles, 2.7 km
5 MT	55,000 ft, 10 miles, 16.7 km	58,000 ft, 11 miles, 17.7 km

Laticia's fear for her daughter drives her to where none should go, downtown, and she unthinkingly takes her son with her. No one can describe what she would see downtown after such an event. The author has only scratched the surface of this gruesome situation. You know the fate of the 28 elementary school kids from the neighboring county. They died almost instantly, being too close to the blast. They were on the first bus to leave and had they departed three minutes earlier and not been stopped by the light at Museum and Conners, they would still be alive. The overpressure at their bus when the blast wave hit was strong enough (50 psi) to kill them outright, and the blast dynamic pressure (wind) exceeded 300 mph; thus the bus was squashed and tossed on top of rubble, to say nothing of the intense radiation they received. They were just too close.

The description in this book of the wounded and dying is actually a small part of the actual effects of such a bomb in a city the size of Yorksberg. For more details and pictures we suggest you do some reading at the public library on the after effects of Hiroshima and Nagasaki. Little can be done for most of these people except to comfort them. Those this close and not sheltered by a building or earth will receive on the order of 300 to 1000 rem of radiation just from the initial explosion. That, coupled with the high radiation from dust and fallout, will place most of these people in a condition that is beyond modern medical science to help.

Laticia could not save anyone who was close to the bomb and exposed to deadly levels of radiation, and she could have further injured herself or Brad by staying in the area longer. The hurt man calling for help for himself and his wife is a good example. Unknown to both he and Laticia, his wife is already dead and there is nothing the best medical folks can do for him except comfort him as he dies from massive radiation exposure. Laticia may have seemed unfeeling to leave him, but unknowingly she took the correct action.

Laticia's run to her sister's home is fraught with errors of which she is totally oblivious, except for a vague sense that the radiation may be a problem. That last phrase is an understatement! First of all, her SUV is highly contaminated. Everywhere she drives she leaves a trail of alpha, beta, and gamma emitters that will take many months to find and clean up. Whole chunks of pavement will have to be transported to radioactive waste dump sites.

The itchy feeling on her skin is the beginning of beta burns.[34] Laticia has collected enough radioactive beta ray emitters on her skin that it is being burned, much like sunburn, even while she drives. This itching and burning sensation may appear during the first 24 to 48 hours. Within a day or two these symptoms typically disappear. Two to three weeks later skin damage shows up as increased pigmentation in the form of dark-colored patches and raised areas. Within a year normal skin pigmentation and appearance typically return.

The DuckBurger, fast-food restaurant will be shut down by authorities, raised, and hauled off to a waste site by men in protective white suits. An attempt will be made to contact every person who ate there after Laticia and Brad contaminated the men's and women's restrooms, the eating area, their table and chairs, and the countertop they touched. Several folks who stopped at "The Duck" after Laticia and Brad were later found to have internal radioactivity because Laticia and Brad unknowingly brought in radioactive particles and deposited them on the table. When the diners who came in afterward touched the table, they picked up these radioactive emitters and then transferred them to their food just before they ate it. Contamination was also found in the vehicles and homes of people who had stopped at "The Duck" after Laticia and Brad.

As Cordell Washington arrived at Emily's driveway well after 4 a.m., he found a lone, county patrol car parked there with its running lights on and its blue lights flashing. He could see police barrier tape blocking the entrance to the driveway.

"Are you Mr. Cordell Washington?" the officer said as Cordell got out of his Chevy.

"Yes I am," he answered.

"I am Officer Yates with the Claymore County Sheriff's Department. Your wife has been taken to the county hospital in Rainey."

"I came through there," Cordell said.

"You will find your son and wife's family in quarantine there. They have established an area for contaminated folks to spend the night. You will be able to talk to them, but not go near them. They are all highly contaminated from the Yorksberg bomb."

"My God!" he said, starting to realize the magnitude of what had happened. "Are my wife and son okay?'

"I can't say, sir. I arrived after they were transported. I suggest you take that question to the medical people, good people, at Rainey General."

"Okay, thanks officer. By the way, why the police-barrier tape? I thought all the contaminated people went to the hospital."

"General orders from my watch commander. I'm here to keep people out until relieved. FEMA experts are supposed to be here tomorrow to check it out."

"Check it out?" Cordell emphasized the word "it."

"Yes, sir, the property. It is undoubtedly contaminated now. It will have to be cleaned or buried."

---

[34] *The Effects of Nuclear Weapons*, Third edition, U.S. Department of Defense, 1977, sections 12.155 through 12.162, with photographs of beta burns on the neck and feet. Using an internet browser, search for "beta burns on the neck" and you can view an actual photograph of this skin damage.

Cordell was speechless for a moment. Finally he said, "Thank you, officer. Sorry you got stuck here tonight."

"My job, sir, but thanks. Now you head for that hospital. And watch your speed. They will be there whether you drive 55 or 90."

"Right," Cordell responded, and got back in his car. He did not drive 90 miles per hour, but it was close to that on the straight sections of the road.

Emily and her husband are loving people and they welcomed Laticia with open arms and without question. This was not wise. Days after they were all evacuated to the hospital, a team was deployed to their property in protective suits to scan the driveway and grounds. They sprayed little puffs of bright orange paint on any spot registering as a radioactive source. They did the same for the house. When Emily and her husband were allowed to return several months later, they found the driveway and front yard pockmarked with holes. The front steps, porch, door, and entry way had been ripped out. Much of the oak hardwood floor had been removed, especially in the kitchen and hallway. The refrigerator, sink, cabinet fronts, dinette set, and living room furniture and rugs were gone. The television remained, but the remote, which Brad had handled, had been sent to a radioactive waste dump. The bathroom where they showered was a gaping hole at one end of the house. The beds Laticia and Brad had slept in, bedroom rugs, and some of the furniture in the bedrooms had also been hauled off. All the sewer and drain pipes were removed from the house clear out to the street because this is where the bulk of the radioactive material washed off Laticia and Brad came to rest after their showers.[35] All the removed material was shipped to a radioactive waste disposal site opened specifically for the Yorksberg incident. Officials told Laticia's sister and her husband they were lucky to have anything left.

Please do not think we have presented Laticia as foolish or stupid for what she did. She is neither. Laticia is the quintessential mother who forgoes life and limb when she sees one of her children in danger and takes innovative and decisive action to try to help save her young one. Were her decisions the best she could have made? No, we can see that by the consequences that fell on her health, the DuckBurger joint and her relatives. Would she do the same thing had she read this book? You decide.

It would be extraordinarily difficult in situations like these to refrain from chasing after your child to rescue them, and to instead remember to think about the future of their families, which will be a lot brighter if the parents are still alive after the catastrophe is over.

---

[35] At the Hanford Project in Washington State in the years after World War II, a worker took a contaminated wrench home with him. Such tools were tracked to assure that none got out of the contaminated area, so when it was found to be missing, teams of men in protective clothing and armed with radiation detectors literally followed the man to his house. They found contamination on the bus everywhere he touched it. They could even tell which seat he sat in. They arrived unannounced at his home and quickly located the wrench. They then proceeded to clip radioactive contamination from his carpet and the coverings from the family's chairs where he had left radioactive emitters (particles). Contaminated objects they could not clean or clip they removed. They did not leave until every emitting particle was removed. Other people on his bus were traced and visited; their homes were scanned and radioactive particles removed.

The take-home message is… try not to let your emotions rule over sound judgment, which is a dilemma every parent may face.

Did Laticia and her son Brad die? Of course they did, but not because of their radiation exposure. Laticia was sickened for several months by her exposure and it was more than a year before her body recovered and she returned to normal health. Twenty years later both she and Brad developed nodules on their thyroid glands that doctors said were probably the result of exposure to radioactive iodine from the Yorksberg explosion, but there were no further health consequences. Laticia died at age 55 from breast cancer (it runs in her family), and Brad perished in the crash of flight 1901R just outside Cincinnati many years later. The FAA found wing icing to be the cause of the crash.

Quiz on Chapter 16
(Answers are in Appendix A2)

1. Is it possible that neighbors would actually stand out in the yard after a nuclear attack and watch the mushroom cloud drift toward them?
2. Why are schools a particular problem following a nuclear terror attack? Explain.
3. What are the two major mistakes Laticia made?
4. What is the difference between primary and secondary fallout?
5. What is the "zone of survivable destruction" and why is it important?

What really happened to Laticia's daughter Kathy? You will read her story in the next chapter called "Kind, Intelligent Eyes." You can skip it if you do not want to know, but if you skip it, you will miss some pretty interesting technical comments about exactly what happens near an exploding nuclear bomb.

Fifteen feet from the bomb.[36]

17 - Kathy Washington – Kind, Intelligent Eyes (15 feet)

There is a place so far away, so swirled in cloaking light and impossible possibilities, that one might never find it in a thousand lifetimes, even traveling the distance of the width of the universe in the blink of an eye for a hundred billion years. It is a very close, hidden place, where jewels dance and thoughts can be set to singing, a place where desires are made real and matter is superbly insubstantial. It is where little girls go when their earth suits are destroyed. It is Kathy Washington's new home.

We will go there now to visit her because she wants you to hear her story. But don't worry; we won't stay long, and the trip to get there will only take as long as it did for Kathy.

Are you ready? One, two, and there she is, standing in a grassy field with a soccer ball in her hands. If you blinked, you missed the trip.

"Hi, Kathy, are you happy here?"

"I am. Did you bring all those people?"

"I did. They are reading your story right now. Tell them how are you doing here in this amazing place."

"Great. I miss Mom and Dad, and Brad too, but He said they will be here soon, so I just play with my friends and learn all kinds of new things."

"Learn new things? What do you mean?"

---

[36] The small circle is a fountain; the double-line circle is a driveway that surrounds the fountain. The "X" is where the terrorists explode their bomb. Kathy is sitting in a school bus 15 feet from the bomb as it explodes. The big circle is the size of the white-hot fireball the bomb creates in a tenth of a second. This is Kathy's story, and, we hope, some interesting physics.

Setting the ball down, she said, "Listen to this," and then began singing a complicated English madrigal in four-part harmony. When she finished, she said, "That was John Farmer's 'Fair Phyllis.'[37] Did you like it?"

"Wow! I am astounded! How did you sing all four parts at once?"

"It's easy here, but I can't show you how until you finally come. You may know in part, but not in whole. That's what He told me to tell you if you asked."

"All right, thank you for sharing your song. Are you ready then to tell us about yourself and your last day?"

Kathy smiled and nodded. "I have been thinking about what to say."

"Please go ahead."

"I always wanted to be a ballerina when I grew up, until Mom read me the story of Florence Nightingale and I decided I could help more people get well if I became a nurse, probably in a tent in a jungle somewhere, or in one of those fancy operating rooms with people in blue-green smocks. Then I entered the horse phase. I saw the movie *Black Beauty* and wanted a horse so bad. I would name her Sugar, and she would be a golden palomino, and she would be able to do fancy steps and come when I whistled.

When I came out of the museum that day with my class, I had been thinking about history and about what it would be like to be a curator like Mrs. Thompson, and about Thomas Jefferson's pen. I got to touch it! I wanted to go home and tell my mother what Mrs. Thompson told us. She said we cannot know who we really are as a people unless we know our history, why our nation was formed, what its guiding principles are, and where they came from. Without that knowledge we are lost as a people and may stumble into many dark and dangerous places."

"You mean like those men blowing up your city?"

"No, that is not what I meant. The men blowing up the city was a nexus point, but I am not allowed to talk to you about those. You may know in part, but..."

"Not in full. I know, but you make me curious. Please continue."

"Okay. I'll skip the part about walking to the buses. When we got to our bus, our teacher Miss Prichard told us, 'Stay in line, children.' She is our teacher and is very nice. Did you know she is only twenty-five and had just gotten engaged to be married the next month? 'Everyone check to make sure you know where your partner is,' she said."

"I am amazed that when you say her words you sound just like Miss Prichard. How do you do her voice so perfectly?"

Kathy waved her index finger at me and said, "Can't tell you." Then she continued her story.

"She told us to know where our partners were because she made us pair up to help her keep track of everyone. My partner was Elizabeth. Miss Prichard also gave each of us a number.

'Raise your hand if you can't find your partner,' Miss Prichard said.

When she said that, Bobby raised his hand.

---

[37] http://www.youtube.com/watch?v=8eeVMEMxlkc (for those who want to hear it). Or – for a very different King's Singers version try http://www.youtube.com/watch?v=OYbN_2hqFoI

'Okay, Bobby, I see your hand. Class, Bobby can't find George. Does anybody know where George is?'

Of course almost everyone raised their hands when she asked that, and many of us pointed to the end of the line.

'He's hiding behind that trash can,' several of the girls and boys said. George was like that, always doing something to get attention. When he heard he had been spotted, he stood up grinning.

Then Temka Lumpkin said, 'Move up with your partner, George.'"

"You spoke Temka's words with a new voice. That's an exact copy of Temka's voice, isn't it?" I said.

"Yep, that's her. She's the volunteer assistant with our class," Kathy said.

"'Temka, I got a count of thirty-two. What do you get?' Miss Prichard said.

'Thirty-two,' Temka said. 'We have all our little ducks in row.'

That made some of the kids look around," Kathy said and smiled.

"'Ducks? Where are the ducks?' several of the kids said and immediately began looking for the ducks. That is so silly. That's when Janet spoke up.

'There are no ducks. It's just an expression. I also counted thirty-two, Miss Prichard.'

She is one of the more grown-up girls and always likes to help.

'Thank you, Janet,' Miss Prichard said.

And then I heard her say to the bus driver... 'Okay, Homer, open her up.'

She made an opening gesture with her hands and Homer grabbed that big silver handle at the front of the bus and the door folded open.

'Everyone get on the bus and sit with your partner.'

Miss Prichard said that and we got on. I followed Elizabeth. Several of the boys asked Homer 'Where is Bart?' as they passed. It is an old joke, but he always smiles when he hears it. I always thought Homer looked like Santa Claus because Homer is slightly bald and has white hair. Even his beard is white. I think he used to work in the post office, and I heard him say once that he has eight grandchildren.

Once we were all seated, Miss Prichard told Homer to close the door and then she told us to count off. We started with the number one and each kid yelled out their number in order. When the numbers got to twenty-three, George's number, most of the kids looked at him because he usually does something to make it seem like he is missing. Julie, in the seat in front of him, stood up and pointed down at him and said, 'twenty-three' real loud.

Miss Prichard told Julie to sit down, and then called out George's name with a stern voice, and he finally yelled out his number. With everyone counted, Miss Prichard told Homer to go."

"How do you do all those voices so perfectly?" I said.

"Do you want to hear that 'now you can know in part' thing again?" Kathy laughed as if it was some kind of private joke. I laughed with her.

"No, I just forgot. So what happened next?"

"Well, I had the window seat and looked out. We were passing one of those rental trucks like my dad rented one time, only this one had that bomb in it. The last thing I remember on earth was looking down into the truck's cab and seeing this man with something in his hands. I thought he must be praying. I must have blinked, because here I am. I don't know how I got here. I learned later what had happened."

"You didn't see the explosion?"

"Nope. He let me see it later from across the river... oh! I wasn't supposed to tell you that."

"Know in part again?"

"Yah. I hope you don't mind."

"No really, it's okay. So you didn't feel any pain?"

"Nope. I am indestructible.... Oh my gosh, I did it again. I am going to have to stop talking with you. I think it is time for you to analyze what happened to me. Be sure to tell them about the intense soft X-rays and the disassociation of molecules."

"Wait a minute; you're a 5th grader. How do you know about those things?"

"I used to be a 5th grader; besides, they teach nuclear physics here if one is interested in such things. Dang, I did it again. He is wagging a finger at me. I must go."

"Wait; before you go, who is this 'He' you keep referring to?"

"He said you might ask, and told me to say that I answered this question in the first sentence I spoke to you."[38]

Analysis of Chapter 17

Not much can be said about survival fifteen feet from the bomb. The author just wanted you to know about Kathy and the people she knew. Such pathos-drenched tales could be told for each of the hundreds of millions of children all over the world throughout all the history of mankind who died because of the "stinking thinking" of some adults.

Unlike many of them, Kathy did not suffer. She was not injured by the nuclear explosion to die hours later. The explosive blast never reached her. Here is why.

Within 0.000006 seconds (six millionths of a second), the nuclear reaction was over. All the energy that would be released had been released. The core of the nuclear material had been heated to tens of millions of degrees. This core grew very rapidly due to the enormous pressure within. In .01 seconds the nuclear fireball reached the size of a football field and its growth started slowing down. By then the moving van is gone, the evil men are gone, the buses are gone, the fountain is gone, and the ducks are gone. Miss Prichard, George, Temka, Janet Smith-Barnes, and Kathy Washington are gone. And none of them felt a thing.

---

[38] To learn more about this "He" and what human life is really all about, read "*Why You are Alive on Earth*" by V. G. Blanchette, Jr., ISBN 9780692800447.

Why? Because while the nuclear fireball is still within the truck, the enormously high temperatures within it immediately begin to radiate energy in the form of soft X-rays. In fact, the primary thermal radiation leaving the fireball at this point in time is in the X-ray region of the spectrum of light.[39] This intense emission of soft X-rays is the method by which the extremely hot material inside the growing fireball radiates heat energy out of the fireball. This huge amount of X-rays actually heats the air and everything else for several meters around the point of explosion. This includes Kathy's bus.

The X-rays are so intense that Kathy, her friends, and the entire bus vaporize into incandescent, white-hot gas in a thousandth of a second. There is no time for nerve impulses that might signal pain to reach the brain before the brain is gone. The gasoline in the bus's tank does not even have time to burn before it too is heated so hot by the X-rays that all its gasoline molecules are disassociated (broken down) into its constituent atoms: carbon, hydrogen, and oxygen. The tires don't melt because the material in the tires, including the steel belts, instantly becomes broken down into a white-hot gas.

This happens so fast that by the time the blast reached the bus nothing remained except glowing plasma, which was expanding outward.

Photos have been taken with a special camera to try to catch the very first millionths of a second of the fireball's growth.

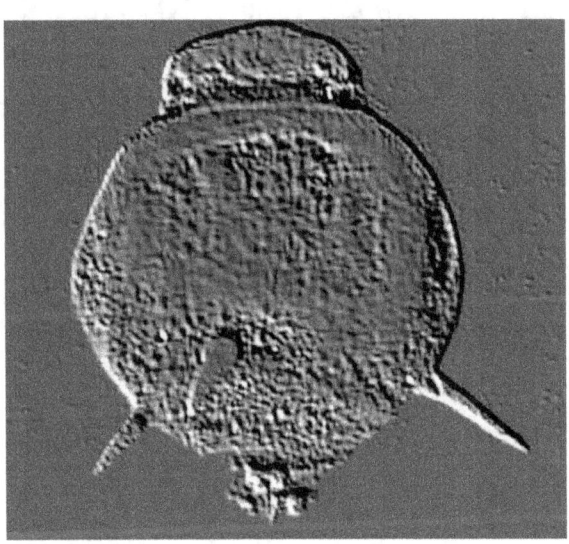

Rapatronic Photograph of a Nuclear Fireball[40]

---

[39] *The Effects of Nuclear Weapons*, Samuel Glasstone and Philip J. Dolan, United States Department of Defense, 1977, section 7.75. "Most of the (primary) thermal radiation is then in the wavelength range from about 0.1 to 100 A, i.e., 120 to 0.12 kilo-electron volts (keV) energy, corresponding roughly to the soft X-ray region--."

[40] The Rapatronic camera used was designed for taking a picture of the nuclear explosion. It had a special electronic shutter that was extremely fast. Search Google Images for the word "Rapatronic" to see many different examples of these fascinating pictures.

You can see the effect of X-rays vaporizing things outside the expanding fireball in pictures taken by a very fast camera, called a Rapatronic camera, which shows the nuclear bomb very early in the explosion. In this high-contrast image you can clearly see the steel guy wires (that support the tower containing the bomb) being vaporized by the intense X-ray emissions at the instant of the explosion. You cannot see the wires or the X-rays, but you can see three sharp points. Those are the wires being heated by X-rays and vaporizing ahead of the rapidly expanding fireball.

Some readers might be interested in a deeper, technical description of this X-ray emission. If so, read the next two paragraphs. Otherwise, skip them; you won't miss anything.

"Immediately after the explosion time, the temperature of the weapon material is several tens of millions of degrees and the pressures are estimated to be many millions of atmospheres. As a result of numerous inelastic collisions, part of the kinetic energy of the fission fragments is converted into internal heat and radiation energy. Some of the electrons are removed entirely from the atoms, thus causing ionization; others are raised to higher energy (or excited) states while still remaining attached to the nuclei. Within an extremely short time, perhaps a hundredth of a microsecond or so, the weapon residues consist essentially of completely and partially stripped (ionized) atoms, many of the latter being in excited states, together with the corresponding free electrons. The system then immediately emits electromagnetic (thermal) radiation, the nature of which is determined by the temperature. Since this is of the order of several times 10^7 degrees, most of the energy emitted within a microsecond or so is in the soft X-ray region--."[41]

"… If the burst occurs in the lower part of the atmosphere where the air density is appreciable, the X-rays are absorbed in the immediate vicinity of the burst, and they heat the air to high temperatures. This sphere of this white-hot air is sometimes referred to as the 'X-ray fireball.'"[42]

Rest assured, Kathy and her classmates never felt a thing.

Quiz on Chapter 17
(Answers are in Appendix A2)

1. When the bomb explodes, how long does it take for the nuclear reaction to be completed?
2. How long does it take for the nuclear fireball to grow to the size of a football field?
3. Why are these facts important to your survival?
4. Was Kathy's skin burned by the exploding bomb? Did she feel pain?

---

[41] Glasstone and Dolan, section 2.107.
[42] Ibid., section 2.110 in part.

5. At the instant of explosion, how is energy transferred out of the nuclear material (what form of energy vaporized Kathy and her class)?

We started this *Nuclear Terror Survival Handbook* with a piece of a story involving Rob and Tessie Oberfelt. Remember the busted window and cracked fish tank in the preface? The next chapter is their story of the attack on Yorksberg. Read on to find out what happened to them in *The Power of Knowledge*.

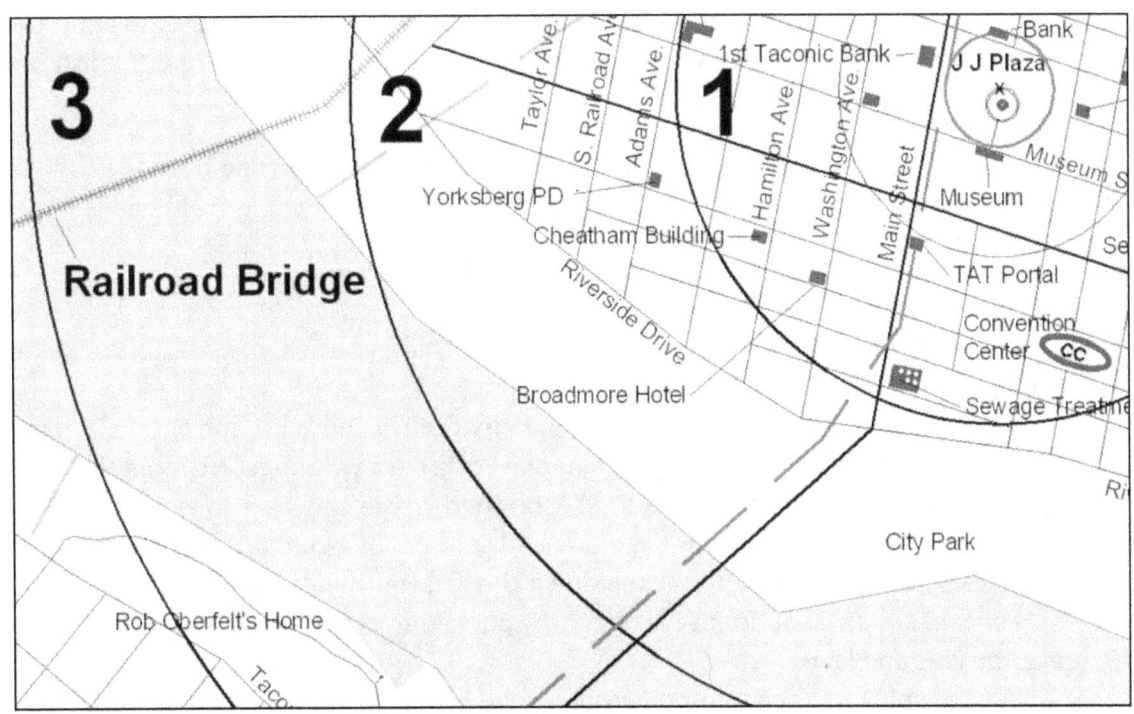

Rob's house, directly across the Taconic River from the city.

18 - Rob Oberfelt – The Power of Knowledge (2.6 miles)

A stark white light suddenly filled the room, and over Tessie's shoulder Rob could see through their picture window what appeared to be a white-hot star rising from Yorksberg's downtown district across the river. Its brilliance kept him from looking directly at it. For a second he hesitated, and then he saw it - a circle of disturbance spreading rapidly toward them across the river. Recognizing the spreading circle as evidence of a blast wave coming from the explosion, he grabbed Tessie's arm and pulled her out from in front of the window.

"Rob! You hurt my elbow!" she said just before the window shattered into the living room and the house shuddered under a singular, loud boom. A strong, cold wind briefly blew in along with a distant, deep, horrible rumble, like continuous thunder coming from across the Taconic River.

"What happened?" she said.

"That was close." Rob shook a piece of broken glass off his shoe. His heart raced and his hands trembled from their close call.

"My fish!" Tessie wailed at the sight of their broken fish tank.

"Ten gallons of water on the rug and dying fish are nothing compared to what the folks over there are going through," he said, pointing out the window. Forget the fish babe. Yorksberg has just been nuked."

"Nuked? You mean that was a nuclear explosion?" Tessie turned from the fish and looked at the mushroom-shaped cloud rising from the distant city. She grabbed his arm. "Rob, what do we do?"

"I have to go to work," he said.

"You're the Yorksberg Emergency Operations Chief; you tell me... this is the fallout scenario, isn't it? What do I do?"

"It is the fallout scenario. You go get the emergency check list and G.O.O.D. pack."[43]

The gray and black cloud rising high above Yorksberg was huge. He mentally checked through the EOC supplies he had in his truck, and then Tessie was back in a moment. She held the list they had prepared over the years and set her "bug-out kit," a large aluminum frame backpack, on the couch and looked down the list. Her hands were shaking.

"For the fallout scenario it says to get my purse and credit cards, turn off the power, and take the kids and leave."

"We are going to have to modify that on the fly. Look, Tessie, I am going to have to go to work right now, so listen closely and do what I say. You and the kids will be okay."

She nodded.

He put on his winter jacket, the hooded one with a parka-like fur ring around the face opening. "Exeter County EOC" was printed in black letters on the back.

"Take your pack and the kids' packs too, get in the car, and pick up the kids. Thank God their schools are on this side of the river. Then head for either your folks' place or mine."

"I'll go to Dad's. He's closer."

"Good. Stay there and I will be in contact with you as soon as I can. It will be awhile... more than a week is likely. Move quickly. You need to beat a half million people to the interstate or you will be stuck in a colossal traffic jam."

"Rob, I'm scared."

"So am I, babe." He embraced her. "Now get going. There's going to be a lot of traffic. Try to beat it and do not go toward the city." He kissed her.

"What about our neighbors? Shouldn't we warn them?"

"Just get the kids. Most of our neighbors are at work. It's okay to be kind, but you don't have time to save everyone. If you engage them you will end up being their after-the-fact emergency coordinator and instructor. You don't have time to teach them about radiation and what to pack. I guess a one-minute conversation would be okay with a couple of them, but for God's sake don't get into a long chit-chat. We don't know how much

---

[43] G.O.O.D. is an acronym for "Get Out Of Dodge." It is also called a "bug-out kit" and is usually a backpack prepared ahead of time for an emergency that requires you to leave home in a moment, when you don't have time to pack. What to put in your "bug-out" pack will be discussed in the analysis section of this chapter.

radioactive fallout will come here, and I want you to beat the traffic jam flowing out of town."

"Isn't that heartless?"

"Some would call it survival of the prepared. Now I have to go. Grab your cell charger and don't forget your credit card. And turn the furnace off. We don't want to heat the entire state."

As he went out the door he heard her say, "What do I do about the window?"

He yelled back, "Just leave the window."

Rob got into his pickup, started the engine, pulled out of the driveway, and drove down the street to the west, passing a group of people huddled on the front lawn, looking at the distant, distorted mushroom cloud with ashen faces and pointing fingers. He stopped, rolled the window down, and yelled, "That was an atomic explosion. You folks need to drive to a safe place out of town, south of here would be best, before the radioactive fallout comes. Don't delay; go now!

Starting toward the Dixie Highway Bridge he hesitated.

Survivors will be coming across the bridge, and that path takes me too close to downtown. So he pulled over and took out his two-way radio from his tool holster.

"Any EOC, this is EOC Chief." He repeated the call but no one came back. A moment later his radio crackled to life.

"EOC Chief, this is Patrol 6."

"Go ahead, Patrol 6."

"Rob, this is Officer Swanson. I am at Copper Ridge Mall. I can hear EOC Central at the airport. He has been calling you."

"I can't hear him. Ask him what the radiation levels are there."

"Will do. EOC control, EOC Chief wants the radiation levels there. Please report." There was a short pause.

"EOC Chief, EOC Central reports they have been watching the rad levels. Currently at 750 mR/hour and rising fast. He says the base of the mushroom cloud will be on them in about 8 minutes at current wind speeds."

Rob thought for a moment. He guessed the grounds around the EOC building would soon see several hundred rem per hour. Inside the building would not be much better. If they ran now they would receive a smaller total dose than if they stayed put and ran later.

"Patrol 6, tell EOC Central to evacuate to Copper Ridge Mall. Emphasize that they are to put on respirators and run for it. Tell them to leave everything and go. Tell them to bring EOC Mobile to the Copper Ridge Mall."

"Roger, EOC Chief. EOC Central, Chief says you are to don respirators and run for Copper Ridge Mall. Bring EOC Mobile with you. He emphasized the word 'run.'" There was a short pause.

"Chief, they are on the move. I don't think any of them wanted to stay."

He wondered what they would have done if he had been downtown and there was no EOC Chief.

"Thanks, Swanson. I am jumping on the interstate. Be there in five."

Turning right onto the interstate he headed north. He noted that traffic was sparse in the northbound lanes, but the other side of the interstate was heavy with traffic heading south out of the city. A glance to the right across the river he could see many parts of the city engaged in fire. Dust was everywhere, particularly north of the city's downtown district.

Up ahead he could see the mall situated on the outer extremities of Copper Ridge, the highest geographic feature in the area. The mall sat 150 feet above the city. *Not much elevation but it would be enough to provide decent radio coverage.*

As he pulled up to Officer Swanson's patrol car, he heard several EOC units, including the fire liaison, calling. He took time to apprise each contact of his situation and give all of them initial instructions. This was easy with the EOC Play Binder open on the seat next to him.

"EOC 4, proceed to the south side of the Dixie Bridge and set up a coordinating point. We will have wounded coming across the bridge. Work with the EMTs out of the University Hospital. See if you can set up a shuttle back and forth across the bridge. Give me a radiation reading when you get there. If it is too hot, we will have to move you. Get some civilian help as you need it."

EOC 4 acknowledged.

"EOC Chief, this is Fire Leader 2, Fire Assistant Chief Parker. The Chief was downtown. No one has heard from him or from Headquarters."

"Roger that. You have the ball, Phil. Please status your folks and let me know what you need."

"You got it, Rob; Fire Leader 2 out."

This went on for several minutes until the EOC RV pulled up. Rob signaled for the driver to stay inside and retrieved a radiation survey meter out from under his seat. When he switched it on it went full scale and an alarm sounded. The officer standing near him stepped back.

"Wrong scale," Rob said, trying to be reassuring. As he rotated the scale control he found they were getting about 200 mR an hour. As he approached the EOC RV the radiation detector's indicator went further up the scale. He changed scales and got a reading, about 800 mR per hour on the front and left side. He motioned for the driver to come out.

"Hello, Jerry. Thanks for getting this beast out from under the cloud."

He offered his hand and Jerry held back. "You never know," Jerry said, showing Rob the palm of his hand.

"Right," Rob agreed. There was no point of getting contaminated by a friend.

"Marty and Tyler are on console, trying to reach the Governor's office. Go on inside if you like."

"Officer, would you take me up the ridge." He pointed to the nearby Copper Ridge and could see smoke rising from up on the ridge. "I want to see if we can raise adjacent county EOCs. We are going to need lots of help."

"Can you reach other counties from up there?" the officer said.

"We tried this in the past and found that it depended on weather conditions. Sometimes we could communicate with other EOCs and some days not."

As they started to get into the patrol car, a van pulled up with a bumper-mounted antenna and the RACES logo on the side, identifying it as a mobile Radio Amateur Emergency Services vehicle. The front plate read "W2ZZR."

Rob was glad to see them. They must have been monitoring the EOC frequency. He had worked with the amateurs during hurricanes and found they could be invaluable for health and welfare traffic.

"Bad day, Roy," Rob said to the W2ZZR amateur rolling down his window.

"Damn bad. We are here for you. I'll keep the hams off your tail. You call us when and where you need us."

"Thanks. I will need you." Rob got into the patrol car and they headed up the ridge.

As they came up on the ridge crest, Rob could see that the smoke he had seen on the ridge seemed to be localized in what looked like the wreckage of an aircraft, and when they came to a stop near the cell phone tower, a man ran up to their car.

"News helicopter caught a guy wire. One survivor. Her name is Kasey Tellure[44], from Channel 5 News. Can you get some EMTs up here?"

He made a quick decision. "Nope. None to spare. But I can get a stretcher and," as he looked at Chad's truck, "by God I know where to find a pickup truck."

A few minutes later, Rob had tried the EOC channels of the three adjacent counties. To his delight, all three came up promptly. "God bless this cold, clear air," he prayed. He described the initial situation and received assurances of their support. He then called down to EOC Mobile. "Jerry, I have a fire pumper truck from Sharpsville on the way. He should be at the mall in twenty minutes. He is uncontaminated so let's keep him that way. Cordon off a section of the mall parking lot with good drainage and hose EOC Mobile down. Get the rads down as low as reasonable and then bring the beast up on the ridge. You can reach all the counties from up here today. Send the amateurs up here too."

"Okay, boss. Marty copied that and is on it. Several others of our EOC team have arrived."

Rob continued talking as he used binoculars to survey the city from the ridge.

"As the team assembles, let's begin preparations to start the first radiation survey per the play book."

"EOC Mobile copies. Boss, I have a few injured folks showing up in cars. Some are in pretty bad shape."

"Send them to out-of-county hospitals unless they are critical. Send them south and west. Criticals go to the University Hospital. Find someone to coordinate that… and find out what is happening at St. Mary's. They were really close in and we haven't heard from them."

He drove back down off the ridge to find media people raising a small dish antenna from their van.

"Officer, would you please back the news folks off? The other end of the parking lot would be nice. I do not have time for them now. Promise them a briefing at…" he looked at his watch… "make it 6 p.m."

---

[44] You will read Kasey's story, and the story of Chad the tower rat and his buddy Tom, in Part 2 Chapter 20 *Belief is not Enough*. In that story you will learn why Kasey was high above Copper Ridge when the bomb exploded.

"Will do. By the way, the sergeant has assigned me to you for the time being."

Rob got out of the patrol car and headed toward EOC Mobile. Someone called out the door, "The Governor is on the line for you, Rob."

Taking up the handset he thought, *Now we will get the big dogs launched*.

"This is Rob Oberfelt," there followed a slight delay that suggested their signal was traveling a long way. Rob wondered if these transmissions were encrypted. They were probably being monitored by media personnel somewhere.

"Rob, this is Governor Corbin Stewart. I have the President on the line. You will be speaking to him and the FEMA folks and many others. Please give us a two-minute status of your situation. Then I will ask you what you need. Go ahead."

"Okay, Governor... Mr. President. I can confirm a very large explosion has occurred in downtown Yorksberg. I saw the explosion myself and the mushroom cloud. We have large amounts of radiation downwind, which suggests this was a nuclear explosion. The city is presently in a huge pall of dust and smoke with many fires out of control. We lost our main fire station, water supply, and it appears electric power is out across the county. The airport is not blast damaged but was directly downwind of the explosion and I have moved my EOC team from there to our present location on Copper Ridge about eight miles east of the city. Radiation levels were climbing when they left the airport. Most of the folks who survived appear to be leaving the city... the roads are full. We are starting to see critical injuries showing up at our site... lacerations, burns, etc., and are sending the ones we judge as critical to a local hospital. The others are being directed out of the county. The fire department is overwhelmed but they are in the thick of it. We are going to need a lot of help."

Analysis of Chapter 18

The first clue the terrorists have struck is the stark white light flooding Rob Oberfelt's living room through a window that faces the city. Rob later recalled a sense of heat in the room flooded with this light.

Several factors determine the amount of heat from a nuclear explosion that falls on a surface: 1. The energy yield of the bomb, 2. The height of the explosion above ground, 3. The distance from the explosion, and 4. The prevailing atmospheric conditions.

The temperature the exposed material reaches depends on the angle of incidence of the incoming heat radiation, its duration, its intensity, and the ability of the material to absorb the radiation. This last factor can be correlated to the color of the material. It is well known that darker materials absorb more heat energy than light-colored materials. This effect can be seen in the photograph of burn patterns on the skin of a person

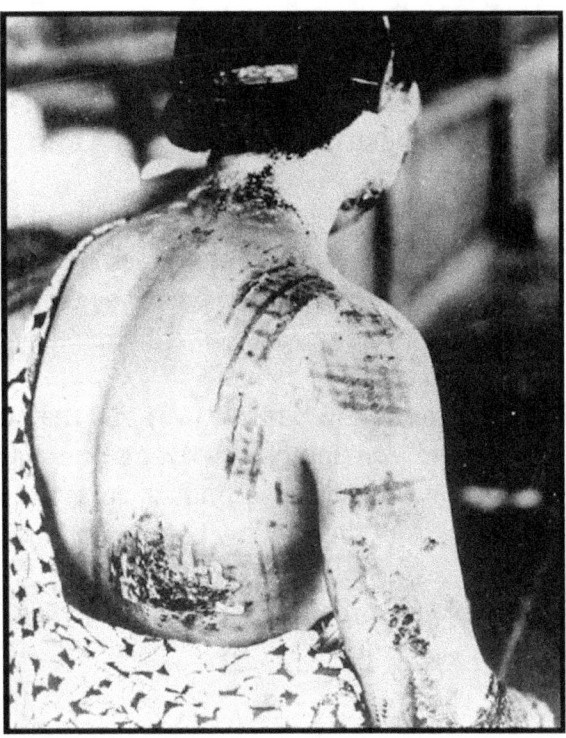

Evidence that dark-colored fabric heats up faster when
exposed to the flash and heat of an atomic explosion.[45]

exposed to the flash and fireball of one of the bombs dropped on Japan to end World War II. Dark parts of the fabric became hotter and caused more severe burns, effectively transferring the pattern of the fabric onto the skin underneath.

Because the amount of radiated heat from a nuclear explosion is very large, the surface temperature of materials within several miles of the blast will rise rapidly and extremely high temperatures can be reached. From the bombs dropped in World War II, for example, it is estimated that directly below the air burst surface, temperatures may have gone as high as 5,400 to 7,200 °F; 3,200 feet away (six tenths of a mile) temperatures may have reached 3,270 °F.[46]

Avoid Windows

Some people who have a "near death" experience report being in a tunnel and seeing a bright light at the end of that tunnel. They feel a need to walk toward the light. In the case of a nuclear terror attack, you do not want to go look at the light as Tessie did. She walked to the window to see what was causing this amazing, bright light in the middle of the

---

[45] *The Effects of Nuclear Weapons*, Samuel Glasstone and Philip J. Dolan, United States Department of Defense, 1977, Figure 12.72.
[46] Ibid., section 7.26.

afternoon. It was so bright she had to shield her eyes from it. She had seen films of nuclear explosions that Rob had brought home, but the actual sight is so unlike what she had seen in the films she did not connect the two. Rob had seen filmed nuclear blasts many times during training sessions he had attended or given, and yet he too "forgot" for a moment and looked out the window.

This "forgetting" lessons learned is something we all do. That is why retraining is important. Our leaders in emergency services should remember that telling once is not teaching. Good teaching uses the principle of three because most people need to hear instructions three times before they begin to stick, and if you really want them to remember something, ask them to teach it.

The fact that Rob and Tessie were 2 ½ miles away and that Rob saw the shockwave coming across the river saved them from injury. The river is one mile wide where the Oberfelts live. It took the shockwave a full five seconds to cross the river. That was enough time for Rob to pull his wife away from the window before the blast wave hit their house.

Failure of Overpressure-Sensitive Materials[47]

Approximate side-on peak overpressure (psi)	Structural Element	Failure seen during nuclear testing
3.0 – 10.0	Brick wall panels, 8 or 12 inches thick and not reinforced	Shearing and flexure failures
1.5 – 5.5	Concrete or cinder-block wall panels, 8 or 12 inches thick and not reinforced	Shattering of the wall
1.0 – 2.0	Wood siding panels, standard house construction	Main connections of structural panels fail, allowing whole panels to be blown in
1.0 – 2.0	Corrugated steel or aluminum paneling	Connection failure followed by buckling
1.0 – 2.0	Corrugated asbestos siding	Shattering
0.5 – 1.0	Glass windows, large and small	Shattering; occasional frame failure

The table above shows the blast wave overpressure effects on various structural elements of buildings. These are from testing in Nevada. These might mean more to you if you consider the following blast wave strengths roughly estimated for the Yorksberg fictional explosion.[48]

---

[47] Ibid., Table 5.145.

[48] These numbers are a combination of the sea level wind velocities of an "ideal shock front" (Glasstone and Dolan, Table 3.07) and Excel spreadsheet calculations using Glasstone and Dolan's, Table 3.73c values extrapolated with the scaling formula given on page 114 of that reference to convert overpressure values from a 1-kt yield to a 19-kt yield. Although by no means precise, this calculation formed a basis against which the

Distance (ft)	Miles	Overpressure	Wind (peak)
2668	.51	10 psi	294 mph
4003	.76	5 psi	163 mph
6671	1.26	2 psi	70 mph
10,000	1.9	1 psi	--

At one-half mile from the Yorksberg ground zero, for example, we could expect shearing and bending failures for unreinforced brick wall panels, 8 or 12 inches thick. This data also indicates that one might expect to see the shattering and occasional frame failure at distances almost two miles from ground zero.

Halfway across the river as the blast wave approached Rob's house, its overpressure likely dropped below 1 psi. By the time it reached the Oberfelts at 2.5 miles (13,728 feet), it probably could break few windows except for the whimsical nature of acoustics and variations in window construction. In this case the flat surface of the river and the slope from the Oberfelts' back yard down to the river's edge managed to concentrate the blast wave pressure enough to shatter their large picture window. Pieces of flying glass flew into the room and busted out the side of their aquarium. Had they not stepped away from the window they would have been cut by the flying glass.

If you see an unusual bright light outside, like some sort of giant flashbulb going off, do not go look out the window to see what is happening. It might be prudent to count to fifteen before looking.

The dynamic part of the blast wave (wind) at the Oberfelts' home was well below 70 mph by the time it reached the house. For a home built to modern hurricane standards, this was no problem. Not a single shingle was torn off. The Oberfelts experienced the dynamic part of the blast wave phenomenon as a brief cold wind blowing into their shattered window.

Rob tells his wife to "just leave the window" (i.e., do not attempt to repair it or cover the hole). Some would argue they had time to nail a piece of plywood over the hole, but did they? At that moment they had no idea whether or not harmful levels of radioactive fallout would start falling in their neighborhood. They are only 2.5 miles from the blast, and most of the radioactive material is high over them. Fifty thousand feet above them, the mushroom cloud may spread out to ten miles in diameter before being blown off to the north, depending on prevailing winds at those high altitudes. The heaviest, most radioactive material usually falls out first (i.e., close to the blast zone). So it is quite possible that if the Oberfelts had spent a half hour boarding up the house, they might have received damaging amounts of radiation before they left the area. The point is they do not know what radioactive materials will fall, and when you don't know, it is best to act cautiously.

Everyone should have a sturdy backpack at home filled with items that will help them survive if an emergency requires them to leave quickly, with no time to think or pack.

---

fiction in this book could be written with consistency and some degree of accuracy as to the effects of a 19-kt explosion over various distances.

This backpack is referred to as a "bug-out kit," a "go-pack," or a "Get Out Of Dodge" kit. This kit can be used for any emergency, not just a nuclear terror attack.

What should the "bug-out kit" have in it? The answer will depend on whose kit the backpack is, but the individual's kit should allow the person to survive for 48 to 72 hours with nothing else. Here are some things to think about when packing your go-pack. Not all these are for everyone, and keep in mind this is just one list:

- Enough food and water to last 72 hours. This includes:[49]
  - Water for washing, drinking, and cooking. U.S. recommends 1 gallon (3.78 liters) per person per day.
  - Non-perishable food.
  - Water purification supplies.
  - Cooking supplies.
- A first-aid kit.
- Fire-starting tool.
- Maps and travel information.
- Weather-appropriate clothing (e.g., poncho, headwear, gloves, etc.).
- Bedding items such as sleeping bags and blankets.
- Enough medicine to last an extended evacuation period.
- Medical records.
- Battery or crank-operated radio.
- Lighting (battery or crank-operated flashlight, glow sticks).
- Firearms and appropriate ammunition.[50]
- Cash and change, as electronic banking transactions may not be available during the initial period following an emergency or evacuation.
- Positive identification, such as a driver's license, state I.D. card, or social security card.
- Fixed-blade and folding knife.

Those unfamiliar with radio power supplies may wonder why Rob's radio works when the cell phones do not work. The answer is that Rob's radio is a hand-held walkie-talkie with batteries. He talks to an officer in a patrol car in direct line-of-sight, with no cell towers required. All cars and trucks have both a battery and a generator driven by the engine, so loss of commercial power will not affect them. Ambulances, fire department vehicles, police cars, and other emergency vehicles should have radio capability after a small nuclear bomb attack such as this one in Yorksberg.[51] The problem they may have is

---

[49] This is a partial list from Wikipedia.com. There are many go-pack lists on the web. See "survival lists".

[50] Following hurricane Katrina, and due to the lawlessness that occurred at that time, some states have passed laws that allow people without carry permits to carry their home protection firearms with them during an emergency evacuation. Check your local state laws before transporting a firearm in your go-pack.

[51] Very large high-altitude nuclear explosions can produce a powerful electromagnetic pulse (EMP) capable of destroying sensitive electronics in vehicles. In that case, radios that survive the EMP should continue to work on the vehicles' battery power.

that of communicating over large distances, from locations amid tall buildings, or over interposing hills. The radio "repeater" towers may be down or no longer powered.

Most large communities have an Emergency Operations Center. This is usually a fairly secure building capable of surviving the area's typical recurring disasters: hurricanes, tornados, earthquakes, forest fires, or floods. This building may be wholly inadequate, however, for coordinating a response to a nuclear terrorist attack.

Yorksberg's EOC facility is a concrete bunker-type building constructed on the grounds of the Yorksberg International Airport near the U.S. Weather Service Facility. It is high enough to avoid flooding from even the worst hurricane (Yorksberg's repeating disaster of preference) and is built strong. Unfortunately it is directly under the fallout zone from the explosion. The building was not built as a fallout shelter and its reinforced concrete block walls and roof are not thick enough to protect those inside from radioactive fallout. Rob wisely orders everyone out.

Emergency planners should reevaluate the facility they have selected as their EOC. In this age of potential nuclear terrorism a new facility may be needed. An alternate plan is to have the EOC go mobile so it can be moved out of the path of the upper wind-driven fallout. Our fictional Yorksberg has both a fixed facility and a large recreational vehicle (RV) converted for EOC team use.

Rob has a binder with him, which he calls his EOC Play Book. In it are outlines of critical steps to be taken for a number of different emergency scenarios. These have been contributed by many people, and rewritten and revised over several years. The idea is to have critical steps listed so that none are missed when stressful crises occur. These steps can always be modified on the fly if a crisis throws you a curve. The important concept here is to do your emergency planning ahead of the problem and during a peaceful time when people can think clearly.

Assemble a group of civic leaders and people of knowledge, and brainstorm different scenarios. Ask many questions and instruct someone to record and publish the outcome. For example:

1. "How can we best facilitate the mass evacuation of the city in the case of a nuclear attack?" Coastal cities that face hurricanes probably already have such plans, but cities inland probably do not.

2. "What is the chain of command for police, fire, the EOC, and utilities, down to the precinct sergeant and station captain?" When the leadership is decimated by the bad guys, everyone must have a copy of this list and the new command structure should immediately begin functioning.

3. "Who will carry radiation instruments and report back radiation levels so that a contamination map can be created? Where can fire and police go without overly endangering themselves? Where can you leave people in place?"

4. Many other questions, such as "What are the legal ramifications of ordering city workers into zones of high radiation? What if their exposure is kept short enough to prevent harm? How will you measure that exposure?" After the attack is not the time to decide these issues.

The early use of masks cannot be over emphasized. Respirators that seal against the face with HEPA filters are preferred. These are sold at many hardware stores and building supply stores and are not expensive. Emergency workers should have mask training and be able to correctly don a respirator shortly after a nuclear attack if they are anywhere in the dust and smoke. This could be at most lifesaving and, at least, able to limit the whole-body burden of short-lived radioactive isotopes and the specific isotopes (such as iodine) that are biologically concentrated. Those without masks should get out of the dust as soon as possible. Breathing through some filter, such as a wet tee shirt or towel, is better than nothing at all.

Keep in mind that filters on masks will concentrate radioactive dust and will become highly radioactive. Change cartridges and store the contaminated ones away from people.

Emergency organizations such as fire departments may already have masks. Others such as county EOC teams may have to purchase and store masks. The rubber seals on masks have a lifetime that can be shortened by improper storage and care, which in turn, means that training is necessary. Masks should be carried with the individuals they are assigned to at all times. Leaving your mask in the EOC near your chair is worthless if you are elsewhere when the terrorists strike.

Kasey Tellure (of Part 2 Chapter 20), the lady lying in the bed of a pickup and being driven down the highway in the cold winter air, may sound unrealistic, but what else would you do with a news reporter with two broken legs and no vans or ambulances available? This type of event, a terrorist explosion of a nuclear bomb in a city, requires rethinking of what is proper and improper. Many innovations will have to be done on the fly to help people and save lives. Keep your mind open and think outside the box. Even with traffic backed up and moving at 20 mph down the freeway, Kasey was at a hospital within three hours. Compare that to leaving her lying on a cot at the mall for several hours until an ambulance could be freed up, if ever, and you see the expediency of making do with what you have.

Aid will be available from other counties near your city; however, they will have to maintain some of their resources, such as fire engines, to deal with local problems. Trying to find additional equipment to fight fires after a nuclear explosion will require careful pre-planning similar to the planning and coordination electrical utility companies do in preparation for supporting each other during hurricane season.

Depending on how far the loaned fire trucks get into the city, many of them may be irreparably contaminated while on the job. Other counties may want to loan trucks and crews but may not want to lose the trucks to contamination or have their firefighters injured by radiation.

Water will be a big problem if the municipal water system is shut down (you should plan on it being down). At Yorksberg the Taconic River provides many places where that water can be tapped, but only fires along the river and a few hose lengths into the city can be fought. It should be realized before the event that most fires will not be fightable and will have to be left to burn themselves out. Keep in mind that as a radioactively contaminated structure burns, the fire will lift radioactive particles into the surrounding air, adding to the existing radiation from the contaminated ground. A good rule of thumb is that after a nuclear attack, where there is smoke from fires, there is radioactivity in the air.

Ambulances borrowed from other counties will probably never return to those counties. This is because they will have to traverse into radioactive areas and carry people who are both injured and contaminated. It may be possible to designate ambulances as either clean or contaminated. The clean ones transport only non-contaminated people. You can begin to see the need here for many good radiological instruments and the trained people to operate them. Tacky mats, disposable gloves, rolls of paper, dosimeters[52] and other such common radiation-control materials will go a long way toward helping the ambulance crews keep their vehicles and themselves as clean as possible. Training is important here.

Rob orders the EOC Mobile unit hosed down by a borrowed pumper truck. Why did he do that and will that work? Fallout had already started raining down on the airport while the EOC team was at the EOC fixed facility. The EOC Mobile unit roof, sides, protuberances, wheels, wheel wells (once they started driving the unit), and engine were all contaminated by radioactive dust. The EOC Mobile unit brought some of the airport contamination to Copper Ridge Mall, which was still relatively uncontaminated. Since the EOC team members would be required to occupy the EOC RV for weeks, their total exposure might be too large if the unit could not be cleaned. Their total exposure could be significantly reduced by simply washing the dust off.

Will they get it all off? No, but they can reduce the exposure and then reevaluate dose rates inside the mobile unit. They might have to abandon the mobile unit and move their equipment into another van or RV. For our story we assume they cleaned it up sufficient to continue to use it.

Where did the radioactive dust go that was washed off the EOC Mobile Unit? You need to be asking these questions. It is in the water runoff. Where does the water go? Rob's only reference to this is his telling Jerry to pick a place with "good runoff." That indicates a place where the runoff cannot be driven through by other vehicles, which would contaminate them. It indicates the runoff should go to a storm drain or ditch such that the radioactive materials are kept away from other humans. Have you thought out where you will decontaminate vehicles and people? How will you do it in winter and summer? Again, preplanning is worth its weight in gold.

The Fire Department needs radiation survey instruments, dosimeters, and a preplan so they can protect themselves.

---

[52] A dosimeter is a small device that measures an absorbed dose of ionizing radiation over time. These can be made of film that darkens as exposure increases, or they can be electrostatic. The electrostatic dosimeters are charged up and then worn on the lapel or front pocket of a worker. As the dosimeter increases in exposure, its electrostatic charge discharges and the exposure can be read by looking through the device.

In this scenario, the Copper Ridge Mall site is receiving injured who are self-transporting to the mall parking lot. Rob is working without a triage team. But in an event this big, survival of those who can be saved will be expedited by having many triage stations where those transporting the wounded can be directed to take their injured. The best Rob can do at this point is to send those who come to his location out of the county hospitals or to the University Hospital in South Yorksberg (and this could change depending on possible fallout 5 to 8 miles south of J. J. Plaza.)

Radiation will complicate any triage effort. The team will have to scan each injured person. Some with relatively minor injuries, such as lacerations or a simple broken leg, but who are highly radioactive from contamination, may have to be stripped and washed before they can be grouped with non-contaminated individuals who are waiting for treatment. There is danger both to the other patients and to the medical personnel.

At some time after the attack there will be a conversation between a local authority and state and national leaders. It is likely that the federal government and state government will virtually move in and take over directing the recovery and cleanup. You should expect this and just do what you can to help. This will take time to get rolling (remember Hurricane Katrina's slow FEMA response), so if you are a survivor in the city you should help yourself and others. Uncle Sam is not likely to come rescue you for many days.

Just to round out the story, we want you to know that the injured Channel 5 reporter, Kasey Tellure, spent three hours lying in the back of a pickup truck moving slowly down the interstate, heading toward a hospital in the next county south. Tom the tower rat was driving. His partner Chad sat in the truck bed, parka clad and freezing, keeping blankets and tarps around the injured lady in the cold wind blowing by the truck. Kasey received little radiation exposure, and is a Yorksberg survivor.

Quiz on Chapter 18
(Answers are in Appendix A2)
1. Is your Emergency Operations Center (EOC) located near the heart of the city? What is wrong with this location?
2. Is locating the EOC outside the city's downtown district sufficient?
3. Have several layers of fallback chain-of-command for the EOC, Fire Department, and Police been formed and communicated to all these groups in your city/county?
4. What factors may prevent or delay surrounding counties from lending emergency equipment to the bombed area?
5. Is it realistic to be able to wash radiation off a vehicle like the EOC Mobile Unit?

In the next chapter you will see how life skills and leadership help bring the city's communications back to life, which is a very important goal following the explosion of a nuclear weapon in your city. You will save many more lives if you can communicate. This story is called "There will be Heroes," and in it you will see what a nuclear terror attack on the city looks like from eight miles away.

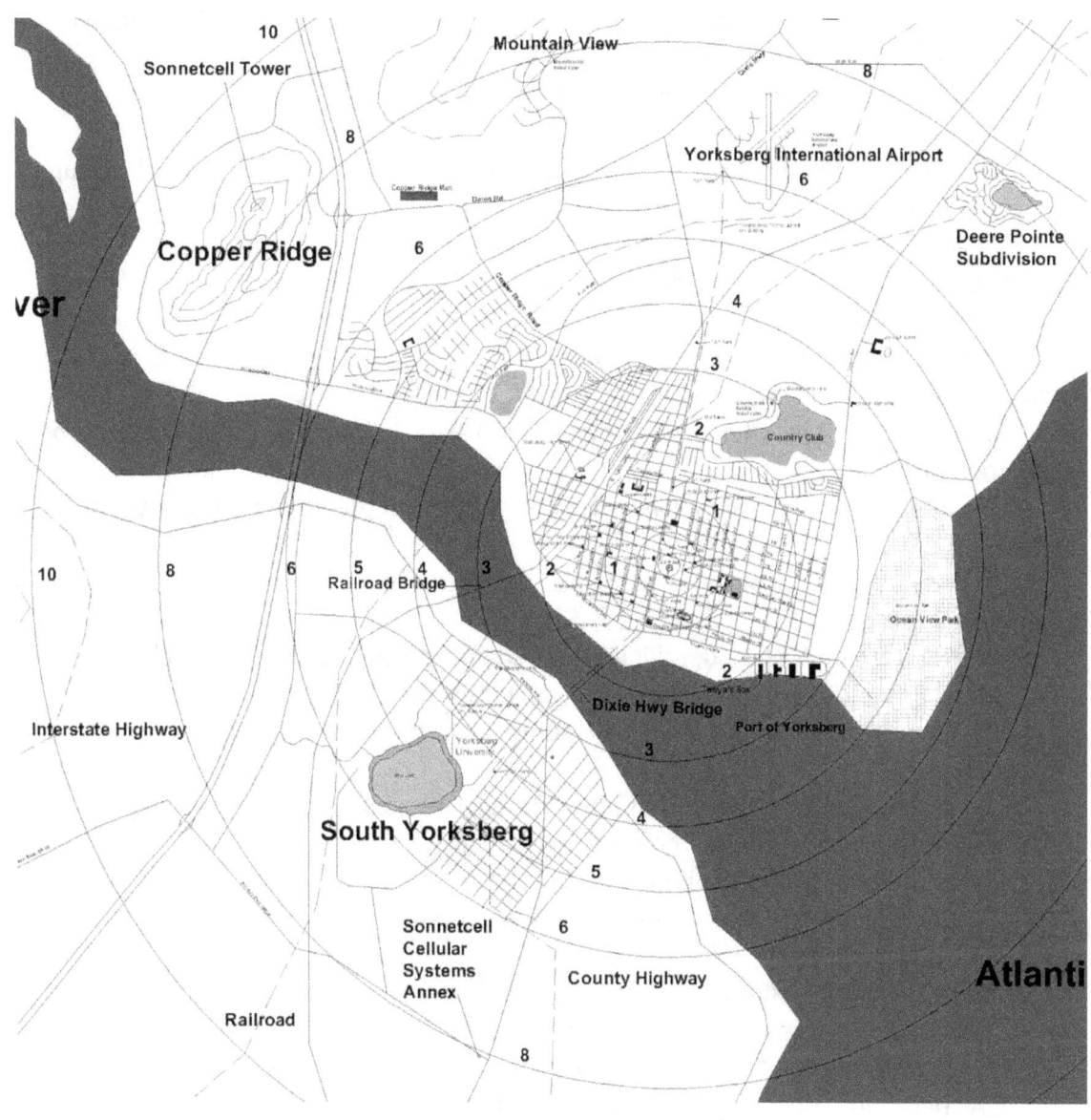

Yorksberg 8-mile view[53]

19 - Chuen "Bull" Ho – There will be Heroes (8 miles)

Bull Ho pulled up to Sonnetcell Cellular System's Yorksberg Annex and got out of his pickup, wincing at the soreness in his ex-Navy Seal legs as he walked up the steps.

How could a 35-year-old ex-Navy Seal get so sore from one weekend of camping with the Boy Scouts?

He shook his head at that sorry thought.

---

[53] Locate the Sonnetcell Cellular Systems Annex near the point where the county highway crosses the 8-mile ring. Follow the 8-mile ring up to Copper Ridge. These, and Yorksberg High School, are the locations important to Chapter 19.

Ho, you're getting old.

Opening the door he walked into the front office and Pam's cheerful greeting.

"About time you showed up," she said.

"One of the privileges of being in charge," he said.

"How was the camping?"

"Really nice. The weather was cold, but I was ready for that." He leafed through the mail to see if anything important was waiting for him.

"Ready? How can you be ready for camping in thirty-degree temperatures? I may be a simple office manager, but that does not make any sense to me at all. Give me a good, warm motel room anytime."

Bull laughed. "You don't know what you are missing. There are ways to prepare, and if you work at it, you can stay as warm as toast."

She shook her head, feigning disbelief, then added, "Jason's in the back. He's been asking for you."

"I'll go see what he wants. I've got a test to run and the guys are probably ready to start."

In the Sonnetcell maintenance shop in the back of the Annex he found Jason repairing a preamplifier.

"How's it going?" he said, taking off his coat and hanging it on the back of a chair.

"Hey, Boy Scout, welcome back. Did the kids wear you out?"

"Not while camping, but boy I have some new muscles this morning. I can't believe how sore my legs are."

Jason smiled. "Been there, done that. Things are going well this morning. Chad and Tom are up in the shack waiting. They are ready to go."

He pulled out his phone and dialed the shack.

"Copper Ridge Rat Shack," Chad's voice came back.

"It's Bull. You tower rats ready?"

"Sure are, boss. Just give the word."

"Okay, let me get the analyzer on. Who's going up?"

"That would be me," Chad said; "I lost the toss."

"All right, put Tom on and go ahead and start up. Work safe."

Bull waited and watched the clock while writing the report that would document this test. It had been forty-five minutes since Chad had started climbing up the tower. The phone rang.

"Bull," he said, recognizing the shack's number.

"He's done and the antenna is ready," Tom said.

"Okay, have him back down about 15 feet and then turn it on."

"Roger."

Bull saw the power spectrum analyzer's display light up a minute later.

"Looks good here. What's your SWR[54]?" Bull said.

"One point two," Tom said.

---

[54] Standing Wave Ratio. This is just a measure of how well the antenna is tuned to the transmitted frequency.

"Okay, Tom, tell Chad to come on down and pack up. Good job for a cold day."

It was a cold day, especially 150 feet in the air on a tower on top of a mountain, Bull mused. The winds are always a bit brisker up there than at sea level. They had been lucky. A few above-freezing sunlit days had assured there would be no ice on the tower. Sonnetcell tower rats do not climb on ice.

"Let me know when he's down," Bull said.

"Will do," Tom said.

A second later the room lights went out, briefly came on dim, and then went out again.

"Damn," Bull said, realizing he hadn't saved the last two paragraphs of his report. He looked at his cell phone. The signal strength bars indicated there was no cell signal.

Copper Ridge has lost power too.

"Thank you, Yorksberg Power and Light," Bull said out loud, with a hint of frustration in his voice.

"I guess it's time for a cup-o-java before the pot gets cold," Jason said.

Bull was half aware of Jason moving to the coffee pot when suddenly Peg burst into the lab, almost knocking the cup out of Jason's hand.

"Whoa horsy, slow down!" Jason said, as Peg swooped over to Bull.

"Did you see that light?" she said. "Just as the power went off the whole sky lit up." She headed to the side door and they followed her outside.

"Probably UFOs," Jason said, casting a sideward smile at Bull.

As Bull stepped out the door, the room lights briefly flickered on and then died into blackness once more.

Serious problem.

"Oh my God!" Peg said in her Jersey accent.

He looked to the north and felt a hard, singular puff of wind, which knocked Jason's Hokie ball cap off his head. The wind decreased, and then seemed to reverse for a second or two.

A loud, horribly deep rumble came from the direction of Yorksberg where Bull could see a mushroom-shaped cloud rising high over the city.[55]

Bull thought of his man on the tower, but he realized the tower was as far from the explosion as he was. So Chad would be okay. His next thought was for his family. He turned to Jason.

"Which way is the wind blowing?" he said with urgency.

"That way," Jason said, pointing south.

"No," Bull said, "that wind came from the blast from that explosion." He pointed at the city as he spoke. "I mean the wind up above us, say at 20,000 feet."

"I don't have a clue," said Jason. "Why?"

Peg had gone back into the building, retrieved a small disposable camera, and began taking pictures of the distant cityscape and huge mushroom-shaped cloud above it.

---

[55] John Hersey, in his book *Hiroshima,* tells of a fisherman some twenty miles away who recounted that "--he was nearly twenty miles from Hiroshima, but the thunder was greater than when the B-29s hit Iwakuni, only five miles away." The fisherman saw the flash and described the noise as a "tremendous explosion."

Bull thought out the situation. "Jason, go get the portable generator out of the service van. Set it back here and run an extension cord inside and power up your computer. Let's see if the internet still works."

As Jason ran to the parking lot, a thought crowded into Bull's mind and gave him a twinge of fear in the pit of his stomach. He had not felt that for many years, and it caused him to run to the south end of the Annex and scan the southern and western horizon.

"What are you doing?" Peg said when he returned.

"I am looking for other mushroom clouds, but, thank God, it looks like we only have the one over Yorksberg. If this was the start of a nuclear war, there should be other targets hit—we'd be seeing several mushroom clouds from this vantage point."

"Oh," she said, "I never would have thought of that."

A few minutes later Jason had the portable generator humming, and Bull clicked to a National Weather Service site and pointed at the screen.

"Upper-level winds over Yorksberg are trending northeast. We are okay here," he said.

"What about your family?" Jason said.

"They are at home up in the Hidden Valley Subdivision—I hope."

"Where is their school?"

"Homeschooled, thank God," Bull said. "I just hope Amber didn't go shopping downtown."

"What do you mean? We are okay here." Jason said, more serious than Bull had ever heard him.

"That looked like a nuclear explosion. If so, that cloud we saw is full of highly radioactive dirt. The heavier stuff will fall back to the ground in the city. It can kill the people it falls on if they don't shelter from it or leave. The upper-level winds will carry it away from us I think."

"My God! My son's at Yorksberg High!" Peg said. Bull watched as she picked up a desk phone.

"Got a dial tone," she said, and dialed. Bull figured she was calling the school's number.

"No ring, no busy signal, no voice mail, nothing," she said. She tried again and then hung up.

Bull took the phone and dialed home. It rang four times before he heard Amber's sweet voice.

"Are you all right?" he said.

"Yes, the boys and I were outside, looking at the cloud. Is that what I think it is?" Her voice sounded strained.

"I think so. Listen, toss the kids in the car, make sure the house is closed up tight, and head for Mom's place. I'll meet you there."

"What about the kids' clothing?"

"Pack light and don't take too long. You don't want to take the chance that the cloud will drop radiation on you. Just go—checkbook, credit card, and go."

"Okay, I'm gone—I love you, Bull."

"I love you too. I'll see you at Mom's. Bye."

He wanted to leave immediately to join Amber and his kids, but Peg's obvious distress bothered him.

Seals never leave a man behind.

He turned to Peg. "Let's see if we can get your son out. Jason, get the 15-passenger crew cab and follow me. I'll drive the van with Peg. Let's make this a quick in and out."

Grabbing a couple of bottled waters and some white rags from the scrap bin, they loaded up.

On the interstate they proceeded north across the Taconic River Bridge. He noted there was no visible damage along the way except for a truck turned on its side near the southern approach to the bridge. It had been carrying cantaloupes and had broken open when the truck landed on its side. Hundreds of the juicy spheres were scattered about. Several had been run over.

"It's an exodus," Peg said. Cars were bumper to bumper, fleeing the city on the southbound lane of the interstate. "Are we going into something dangerous?" Peg said as they crossed the river.

"Well, sort of," Bull said. "Downtown will be hell on earth and very dangerous, and the school is somewhat north of downtown, and that's the wrong direction."

"What do you mean?"

"That cloud drops its crap on the ground it blows over. Some radioactive fallout may be raining on the school."

"Will it hurt us?" Peg said with concern apparent in her voice.

"Yes, but we won't stay long enough to get sick; at least that's my plan."

Access to the High School, located on 8th Street, is down Riverside Drive from the interstate.

The Riverside Drive exit just north of the river took them to 8th Street. There he pointed out signs of the explosion, damage similar to what they might have seen following a strong thunderstorm: broken trees limbs, paper debris of all kinds here and there, and some roofing tiles in the street.

Near the high school there was a smoky haze in the air, and he smelled smoke. Once parked at the school, he wet a rag and tied it around his face so that his nose and mouth were covered. The others followed suit and then they walked toward the front of the school.

The high school looked untouched at first, but as he got closer he could see the wall of the gym that faced the downtown district had been blown in, and the gym's roof had collapsed on one side. Some windows were missing in the main school building. Many students and faculty were in front of the school and, a surprise to Bull, there were buses parked out front, some filled with kids, some half empty, and some leaving the loading zone.

"They pre-position the buses at 2:20 to have them ready for the 3 p.m. dismissal bell. They must have been on the way when the bomb went off," Peg said, scanning the crowd for her son.

Bull ran to the lead bus's door and signaled for the driver to stop and open the door. "What's up, Mister?" the driver said.

"Are you going to run your normal bus route?" Bull said.

"Was planning to, but I am not comfortable with that." He lifted one finger from his grasp of the steering wheel and pointed toward the city.

"Park it for a moment, and come with me," Bull commanded. He felt as if he was leading his team again. He walked over to a group of adults who looked like school staff.

They were having a discussion on the lawn, with the distorted mushroom cloud spread out high above them and across the sky to the northeast. The people in this group appeared to be arguing.

"We haven't accounted for everyone yet."

"I know that," a lady said with some exasperation. She wore a tag that said "Counselor." "We don't have any way of accounting for all the students. You heard what the fire inspector said; we need to get out of here."

Bull's bulky, muscular frame usually elicited attention, and it did so here. As he walked up to the group and spoke, all eyes turned to him. He sensed a group without direction.

"Where is your Principal?" he said.

A lady in a pink dress spoke up. "He went downtown for a meeting with the school board. He left Vice Principal Durey in charge." Bull heard a tone in the lady's voice that suggested something was wrong, and another staff member confirmed it.

"Mr. Durey went to the gym to watch the basketball team practice, and was killed when the wall fell."

A woman in PE shorts and a blue-and-white tee shirt that said "Yorksberg Terriers" spoke up next.

"We have to go through the school again. There might be others, especially in the rubble in the gym." Bull noted that on one side of her face her skin looked as if she had a mild sunburn.

"The fire department should be here soon. I can hear a siren," an older man said. They all heard it, far off in the distance.

Bull interrupted them. "Look, the fire department isn't coming. There are fires everywhere." He pointed to the city and their gaze followed his finger.

Bull quieted his tone and motioned for those staff close by to come nearer. "I am Bull Ho, ex-military. I have trained for this sort of thing and I need you to listen to me. Speed is of the essence. This dirt falling on us is from that cloud and it is highly radioactive." He brushed some dust off his own sleeve to make the point. He could see the bus driver who had followed him was listening.

"I see your buses are leaving. Why aren't these kids on a bus?" He pointed at the students standing around.

The group seemed to respond to his leadership.

"Those are the kids with no cars, and they're not assigned to a bus route."

"Then get them on a bus, any bus. You must use your buses to get them out of town. Don't let any bus leave with empty seats until everyone is on board." Looking at the bus driver he added, "And do not run your regular routes anywhere north of the river. The kids' neighborhoods are likely a death trap."

"I'm not sure we are authorized to do that, Mr. Ho." He turned to see a lady who had a pin on her blouse that said "Attendance."

Bull spoke quietly again. "I know this is out of your comfort zone, but the school board and your Principal have been vaporized downtown, your Vice Principal is dead, and you're about to send the kids to their homes, which by now are highly radioactive due to fallout. Three months from now when you're called before the judge and asked why you sent the kids into deadly radiation, what are you going to say?"
The group did not answer.

Bull continued. "We just came up the interstate. Thousands of cars are leaving the city. They know, and they are leaving until the authorities can survey the city and let folks know where it's safe and where it's not safe. If you send the kids to safety, you'll be heroes."

"I think he's right," one of the men said.

"Okay," Bull said, before anyone could object. "Here is the plan." He made it up on the fly. "Driver, go to each of the buses and tell them to follow your lead and to forget running their regular routes. When everyone is loaded up, lead the pack to the interstate and go south. And if you can, contact the buses that have already left and tell them what we're doing. Direct them to get out of town too."

Then he said, "Where are the injured?"

"We sent them to the hospital in any car we could find. We couldn't get 911."

"Isn't the hospital closer to the explosion?" he said.

Again there was silence, and he continued. "Look, the hospital will have the good sense to send those folks to the University Hospital south of the river or out of town. Do you have more people in the building?"

"Yes," the gym teacher answered. "A group of the men are in there now searching room by room."

"Those of you who want to leave in your own cars, go. Head west and south. Bus driver, make sure no student is left behind. They can join up with their families later. If there aren't enough buses, take someone in your car. Get away from the city," he said. "The rest of you follow me."

That speech worked and the crowd of staff, parents, and bus drivers began separating and moving to their vehicles.

Bull looked at his watch. They had been in the radioactive fallout for several minutes. He bent over and brushed the sand out of his hair and off his shoulders.

He walked into the school with Jason, Peg, and seven of the school's teachers. At Bull's direction, they worked in pairs, running to the far end of the hallways and working their way back to the main entrance, searching, and calling for everyone to get out. When Bull reached the entry way, in a matter of moments he was joined by the other searchers. A man in a coach's shirt said, "We located the other searchers and brought six students out to the buses, one with minor injuries from falling bricks in the gym."

Thanking the man, he turned and saw Peg approaching with two girls, one who had obviously been crying.

"They were in a restroom," Peg explained. "One can't see well, some nasty eye injuries, and the other was helping her. She also has some cuts on her back from a window that broke."

"Okay, get them on a bus," he said, and then turned to the searchers standing nearby. "Take me to the gym."

The collapsed gym, illuminated only by daylight coming in under the collapsed edge of the roof and a few high windows on the side that had not failed, looked like a gloomy, dusty cavern.

Bull could see the body of a man lying apart from the fallen mass of bricks and covered with a sheet. This was the Vice Principal he surmised, and noted the poor man had just been caught by the falling bricks. A trail of blood on the gym floor from where his body had been dragged free of the rubble to its present location told the story. The thought occurred to Bull that if the man had been standing ten feet to his left, he would have been spared.

"Does anyone know how many people were standing along this wall when it fell?" Bull said.

No one knew.

Bull could tell by the amount of rubble that it would take several hours to make any headway at uncovering more victims, and the stability of the rest of the wall and the ceiling looked shaky. Another brick tumbled to the floor with a crash even as he considered these thoughts.

One of the men stepped forward. "I am Cal Watkins, the shop teacher. I have an electric lift back in the shop. It can move lumber. We could move bricks with it."

"Thanks," Bull said. "I hate to say this, but I think we need to leave the area. We have no way of knowing how strong the radiation is here, and it's possible that we could get too much in an hour. We could all lose our lives trying to save some dead people. Let's call it over, and assemble out front."

"There's a radiation meter in Mr. Horton's science lab," one of the men offered. "I'll go get it."

Bull did not want to wait any longer, but conceded.

The man returned shortly with the device and announced it did not work.

Bull accepted the device and looked it over. He had been handed an old Geiger counter similar to ones uranium prospectors use when searching for uranium deposits. When switched on, its meter read full scale and the small speaker on it was silent.

"It's either broken or there's too much radiation here for it to measure the amount," Bull concluded. "Let's get out of here."

With all the students and faculty loaded, Bull sent the buses down the road. And then he and Peg, with a few students in the back of the van, were on the way.

There were still vehicles on Riverside Drive, all jumping on the interstate, moving slowly but steadily. When Bull finally reached the interstate highway he went south.

"Sorry we didn't locate your son," he said to a very quiet Pam. "Chances are good he made it out. There were a lot of kids on those buses, and we know some left earlier. He'll turn up later."

"I hope so," Peg said quietly. Bull could see tears on her cheeks.

Fifteen miles down the interstate Bull's cell phone rang.

"Must be the area-six tower to the south of Yorksberg," Bull said. He could hear several of the students getting on their phones. "Hello."

"Where are you, honey?" Amber said. "We are about halfway to your mother's place."

"I'm okay, sweetheart. Just a bit of a delay. It will be some time before I get there. Jason and I have a little project to do."

After ending the conversation with Amber, Bull called Jason's cell.

"After we drop these students off, we have to get Sonnetcell customers back in service."

"I'll call Taconic Power and Light," Jason said. "Perhaps they have a portable generator we can use."

Analysis of Chapter 19

"Bull" Ho is included in the sequence of vignettes of the lives of certain citizens of our fictional Yorksberg not because he was close to the explosion. He is a survivor like many who read this book will be. He is included because he was eight miles from the explosion, and you need to know that most people in the city will survive.

His actions are not entirely commendable, however, because he risked his life and the lives of others. "Bull" knew the facts and the danger and still chose to go into the city for the sake of another's life. There will be people like Chuen Ho in whatever city the terrorists hit.

The author has placed him eight miles from the explosion so readers who live some distance outside a city can learn through Bull's experience what they may see and hear if their city is hit. At this distance the blast wave and heat of the fireball are so diminished it is unlikely there will be any damage to property. The only direct danger at this distance is retinal injury if the atmosphere is particularly clear and a person happened to be looking directly at the point of the explosion when the bomb went off. Fallout from the Yorksberg bomb went north, leaving South Yorksberg clean and usable.

In Yorksberg there are several cellular phone companies, and all of them except for Sonnetcell had their antennas on the top of the large buildings downtown. From that vantage point they could reach the entire Yorksberg area with good signal strength. By selecting the right antennas, they were able to communicate with cell phones for many miles up and down the interstate, far enough so that travelers never lose their signal as they approach and then depart from the Yorksberg area on the interstate. The company Bull works for is a latecomer and elected to construct a tower on Copper Ridge west of the city. This gives Sonnetcell Cellular better coverage than the other companies, but at a significantly higher cost of installation and maintenance. They have the only cell tower that survives the nuclear attack.

Many cell towers have 2 to 4 hours of backup battery power. Some also have a generator and stored fuel on site. Sonnetcell had plans to install a generator but had not yet done so at the time of the attack. When the downtown cell towers were eliminated by the terrorist's bomb, and the electric power feed to the Copper Ridge area failed due to the damaged power system, Yorksberg lost all cellular communication.

City emergency planners should consider the cellular service in their area a vital part of emergency operations for large-scale disasters. A survey should be performed to determine the placement of the towers. Are they all in one general location? What is their coverage? Can they all be eliminated with one bomb? And which towers have 2-hour backup battery power, 4-hour backup battery power, generator backup power, or none?

In addition, consideration should be made of having a portable cellular receiver and transmitter that can be set up on a hill or flown in an aircraft over the devastated area if all other service is knocked out. Cellular companies may be willing to set up such units, perhaps regionally, to be deployed to a disaster area. They may be willing to provide this gratis for the service of their customers.

Peg saw the flash of the bomb's explosion as a "strange light" outside her office window. Electric power was affected instantly, but at eight miles from John Jay Plaza it took about forty seconds (five seconds per mile) for the blast wave to reach the Sonnetcell building. At that distance the blast wave did not have enough power to damage anything, but was able to provide a puff of wind to blow Jason's loose-fitting ball cap off his head.

The blast wave is actually a huge pressure-wave in air. All waves have a peak and a trough. At significant distances from the point of a nuclear explosion this wave-like nature of the blast wave can be experienced, as it was for Bull, Jason, and Peg. First a strong "puff" of wind came by them (the peak), followed by a reversal of the flow of air (the trough). This is actually a suction of air back toward the direction of the point of the explosion. Then the flow of air tapers off and may even flow outward again for a short time.[56]

The duration of the blast wave is about 1.4 seconds for a bomb the size our fictional terrorists used. Bull, Jason, and Peg do not hear a "boom" when the wave goes by. A "boom" or "pop" or "bang" is a very short phenomenon. The magnitude of the nuclear blast wave and the scale (8 miles) make this a huge wave of air with a frequency approximating less than one cycle per second. Humans cannot hear sounds much below 20 cycles per second, so the blast is not heard as much as it is felt. But following the passage of the wave, all the other sounds such as falling debris, crashing buildings, and echoes of the blast wave passing through the city are present. This is the distant rumble that Bull, Jason, and Peg are able to hear.

Bull showed concern about his "tower rat" (technician) up on the Sonnetcell Copper Ridge tower, but he need not have been concerned. The tower is also about eight miles from downtown. The blast wave proceeds out from the point of the explosion equally in all directions. So the tower experienced a blast wave not any worse than what Bull experienced. We will see this in the Chapter 20 story of Kasey Tellure called "Belief is not Enough" where we will see the explosion through her eyes high above Copper Ridge.

Bull's experience and training for survival from nuclear weapons is first evident when he asks Jason which direction the wind is blowing. Many folks think the wind blows only in the direction they see it blowing on the ground, but this is almost always wrong. The wind blows in different directions at different altitudes. After a nuclear explosion the winds at moderate levels, and to some extent high levels, will determine the fall of radioactive dust in the first one hundred miles from the explosion point.

From his vantage point, Bull could not determine which direction the mushroom cloud was moving. If it had come south it would have passed over them and they would have been in danger of receiving radioactive fallout at the Sonnetcell Annex.

Bull knew they had no electric power. Why then did he try the internet? The answer is he knew both the phone and cable utilities often have their own independent electrical backup systems. You may have noticed your house phone continues to work even when the power in your home is off. You can't see that the internet is also available when commercial power goes off because you need commercial power for your computer and modem, but it is there, unless the lines have been broken or your internet provider was too close to the explosion point.

Bull used a portable generator to power up a computer and found the internet connection still worked. Peg later found she had a working phone with a dial tone, but the

---

[56] *The Effects of Nuclear Weapons*, Samuel Glasstone and Philip J. Dolan, United States Department of Defense, 1977, Sections 3.11 through 3.16

lines could not connect her to the high school. Survivors in the city should keep this in mind. Even though power may be off, the phones and internet may allow communication with folks outside the damaged area. That proved true when Bull reached his wife in the Hidden Valley Subdivision. Phone lines were down in the city, but in certain suburbs of the city they were still operating. This is because the phone system is set up with a variety of switching stations and lines.

Notice that although Amber Ho, Bull's wife, lived fifteen miles from the point of the explosion, he asked her to evacuate the area. This is because Bull had seen the fallout contour lines around test shots and knew radioactivity could fall that far from the blast even if it was upwind from the blast. So as a precaution he sent them to a distant, safe place.

The decision to go to the school and rescue Peg's son was not a good decision for various reasons, which have been listed below. Some of these may apply to you if you are thinking of going toward the blast zone to fetch someone out:

1. Bull did not know what damage, what barriers, what obstacles he would have to get through to reach the school and get out of the city again.

2. He did not have any radiation instrumentation and therefore could not know how much radiation damage they would be subjected to.

3. He had no way to know the condition of the school and the kids. They might have already been evacuated when he, Jason, and Peg arrived.

4. The chances were good that the traffic would be in a huge snarl and that he would get trapped in it, perhaps never reaching the school. There is the danger of driving into an area with dangerous radiation levels, and then being stuck there by traffic jams. Your notions of good will could kill you.

5. Local authorities may have prevented him from entering the area.

6. He was betting his life that his vehicle would not break down and strand him in an area subject to dangerous radiation levels.

All these traps will be hindrances to those trying to get across town to pick up their children or perform some other act after the explosion. A better way would be to prearrange with your children a "safe place" to meet at or call. This will give both the child and yourself the freedom to run from the radiation danger, knowing everyone will attempt to make contact and join together later. This could be difficult for the younger children, but it can still be done. Consider a locket or a bracelet containing the relevant emergency contact information.

On the way to the school, Bull's group passed a truck turned on its sides along the interstate highway. This is one of the large tractor-trailer rigs so commonly seen on our highways. At the time of the explosion it was approaching the interstate bridge over the Taconic River about six miles from the downtown area. At six miles the blast wave overpressure had dropped to less than a quarter of a pound per square inch. That is not much, but remember the side of the truck facing broadside to the approaching blast wave offers a 12-ft by 53-ft surface for the wave to hit. That's 636 square feet of surface area, or more than 91,500 square inches. So the force felt by the big rig when the ¼-psi (pound per square inch) blast wave hit was about 23,000 lbs or eleven tons of sudden "push" trying to topple the truck over. This is a short duration push, and at this distance from ground zero, the dynamic pressure is small. So it is not likely the truck will be toppled. But, depending on driver skill and reflexes, the total load weight and distribution in the trailer, and driver distraction caused by the rising mushroom cloud, each truck will respond differently. For the sake of presenting the possibility of the blast wave overturning a truck, a truck going over on its side was added to the story.

The effect of pressure on a surface area is why a 1-psi blast can blow a window or a door out of a wall. Consider a glass window 3 feet by 4 feet. That's 12 square feet of window, or 1728 square inches. A 1-psi blast wave pushes instantly against the window with a force of 1 X 1729 = 1729 lbs. How many windows in your house could withstand a sudden push of almost a ton?

Bull finds people at the school on the verge of doing the wrong thing, (i.e., sending the kids home on the school buses). They have the buses loaded, some have departed, and others are about to roll, but there are injured and missing and the staff feels responsible for the safety of the students. With the Principal and Vice Principal dead, the remaining staff members have no real leader. Bull is able to provide that leadership.

Remember that we emphasize survivors because we are trying to counter the destructive myth that living through a nuclear bomb explosion is hopeless, and that therefore we do not need to prepare for it.

It is true that thousands will not survive. This will leave holes in the normal fabric of the society that were once filled by leaders (the Principal, for example) whose wisdom, judgment, and authority are especially needed in a time of crisis. This is the experience of the staff at Yorksberg High.

Consider what would have happened to the children who attend Yorksberg High School if they had been bussed to their homes under the fallout. Within a few minutes or hours, depending on the location, they would have received a lethal dose of radiation.

There is another related area of concern, and that is the lack of communication between the parents and the schools. Will parents increase their exposure to radiation by staying in the area, waiting at home for their kids, or by driving to the school to pick up their kids? What will they do when they find the school empty? Perhaps they will drive back home, thinking their kids have just missed the bus, increasing their exposure once again.

The complexity of the situation will lead to thousands of people becoming sick and dying unnecessarily, people who would otherwise be perfectly healthy. The consequences of not planning ahead are enormous, but can be avoided for the most part with proper planning. First, school districts must plan to send buses out of town in the case of a nuclear attack, and communicate this fact to every parent and child. Second, authorities should quickly get on the remaining commercial radio stations and inform parents about what is being done. That all cars have radios is a big plus in this situation, and community leaders should use this to their advantage. Just think of the reduced radiation exposure to thousands of people that could result from just a simple broadcast listing where the children of each school were taken. This will not happen in a timely manner, however, unless these kinds of decisions are made ahead of time, written down, and shared with everyone involved.

Bull leads a group back inside the school to make one last sweep and to help stragglers they might find. He knows the fallout will be landing on the roof of the school, but the roof will keep the radioactive dust particles some distance away from them while they search, thereby providing some minimal level of shielding.

The scenario of the two girls in the restroom is a distinct possibility. Someone once asked this question at a health seminar: "Where do most heart attack victims go when they start feeling pain?" The answer is the restroom. A restroom is private and sickness is embarrassing. So the hurt girl's friend, unable to find the school nurse, has taken her to the restroom to clean up the blood and to try to remove some of the glass. They could have quite easily been left at the school by a panicky staff member who wanted to get away quickly. The girls were unaware of the situation and their lack of knowledge about the effects of nuclear explosions reduced their chance of surviving. In this sense, the searchers may have saved these two students.

Leaving people behind is a most difficult thing to do, but sometimes it is the only thing to do. Bull realizes there may be dead or injured under the rubble in the gym, and he elects to save as many of the living as he can by not staying and searching further.

Some of you reading this will say, "I would not leave them. I would work until I got them out to safety. I would give my life before I would leave an injured student." Many of us feel that way. But such action in this situation may only result in more deaths instead of just one.

In some large nuclear test shots, radiation rates of 3000 rem/hour were seen in the area of the explosion one hour after the event. If 500 rem will kill half the people exposed to that much radiation, how many minutes could Bull work in that exposure rate before he stayed too long? The answer is about six minutes (3000/500). In fact, the radiation levels around Yorksberg High School were much lower than 3000 rem/hour. Since nobody knew what the actual radiation levels were, wisdom says to go and not stay.

The Geiger counter brought to Bull by one of the staff cannot measure high levels of radiation. It is very sensitive, and can actually sense individual radiation particles as they pass through its detection wand, which makes it useful for finding low radiation sources or demonstrating radioactivity in the classroom. Large amounts of radiation, however, put the detector into what is called a "saturated" condition, where it can no longer count radioactive particles.

The fact that neither the school nor Bull had any radiation instrumentation made all of Bull's decisions risky. If they had a radiation survey meter, and saw the radiation levels were approximately 20 rem/hour they could have chosen to take that radiation exposure and work several hours digging through the rubble for survivors. City, state, and county rescue workers, as well as schools, should have radiation survey instruments to enable them to make intelligent decisions following a nuclear terrorist attack.

118

Driving south on the interstate, Bull eventually comes in range of the next Sonnetcell tower down the highway. While the explosion may knock out all local cellular service, survivors will do well to remember that a few miles up or down the highway may bring them within range of a cell tower that is still operational. Reaching such a tower may be possible from a high location also, such as on top of a local mountain that has line-of-sight reach to the distant cell tower.

By three the following morning, Bull and Jason had a Taconic Power and Light portable generator delivered up on the ridge, along with a TP&L crew to do the connections. Bull activated the Copper Ridge tower an hour later and any Sonnetcell phone in the Yorksberg area could reach up to it. For several days this served as the only cellular service in the bulk of the city of Yorksberg. Rescue workers, cleanup crews, police, fire, and hospitals all managed to find someone with a Sonnetcell phone to make firefighting, rescue attempts, and evacuating the city more efficient.

The use of a fixed-wing aircraft has the potential to be a high-altitude platform for cellular equipment. City officials might consider setting up such contingency equipment at an airport a safe distance from the city. This could be activated by trained folks to provide needed communication following a terrorist attack. The equipment should not be stored inside the city, for obvious reasons. If the airport is within 50 miles of the city, and the mushroom cloud drifts in that direction, officials may only have a few hours to get this aircraft up before fallout requires evacuation of the airport.

Much has not been discussed. Several of the bus drivers, who departed the school before Bull arrived, without clearly understanding the situation, took their kids home via their normal routes. The ones delivered north of the city to homes where the parents were clueless and stayed put, all eventually suffered from radiation exposure and many died.

The traffic jams on roads out of the city grew in difficulty as more and more people began to leave the city. Many people leaving the northern part of the city received large doses of radiation on the way out because of the long time it took them to get clear of the radioactive fallout. The traffic jams made police, fire, and fire rescue operations very difficult.

Consider the difficulty of locating temporary lodging within a hundred miles of such an attack. If you are leaving such an attacked city with no relatives to stay with, you might consider driving 300 or more miles before taking lodging.

You should know that many of the students from Yorksberg High School later exhibited symptoms of the radiation exposure they received at the high school, as did the staff who remained the longest time. Bull, Jason, and Peg were eventually admitted to hospitals for testing due to their radiation exposure. Each had received more than 150 rem of radiation damage and afterward exhibited moderate signs of leucopenia.[57] It took some months for them to return to near normal health, but all three lived out normal life spans following their recovery.

The flash-blinded girl found in the restroom survived but never fully recovered her eyesight in the damaged parts of her retinas.

Sadly, Peg's son never showed up. His remains were found under the collapsed gym wall in the school some months later by crews working to remove and bury radioactive debris. Heavy equipment was necessary to recover the remains, justifying Bull's decision not to try to extricate everyone.

Quiz on Chapter 19
(Answers are in Appendix A2)

1. When the electric power goes off, what electrically powered services may still be available?
2. Give four reasons why going into the city to check on someone is a bad idea.
3. True or false: Bussing the kids back to their homes following a nuclear explosion might not be a good idea. Explain your answer.
4. Is it ethical to leave injured or trapped individuals behind and evacuate if staying to help will cause you to receive a lethal dose of radiation?
5. True or false: a Geiger counter is a good radiation detector to have following an atomic attack. Explain your answer.

Sometimes what we believe is not enough. Sometimes our choices make the difference. So it is with our next citizen of Yorksberg. She has a terrible morning followed by a horrendous afternoon. She will survive, but it is really close. In the next chapter we will see how her choices cause her to fall out of the sky.

---

[57] Leucopenia is a condition that can be brought on by excessive radiation exposure. Leucopenia means the total number of white blood cells in the circulating blood is decreased from the normal 5000 to 10,000 per cubic milliliter to less than 4000. This condition weakens the immune system and increases the chance of an individual suffering a bacterial infection.

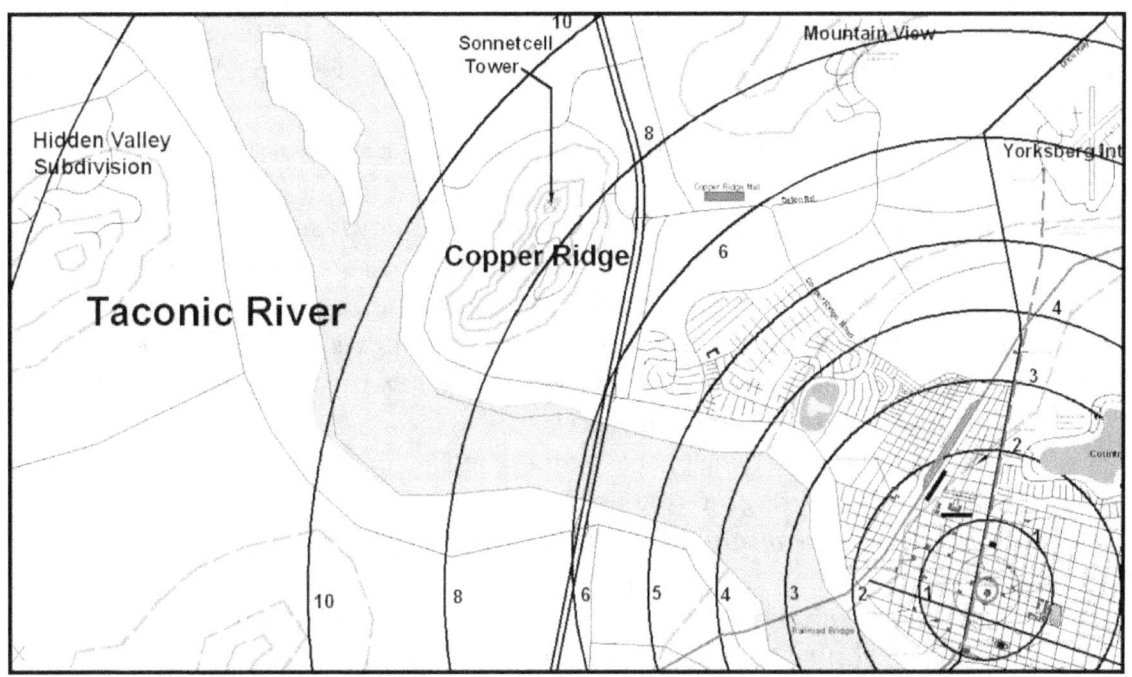

Eight Miles from Downtown to Copper Ridge.

20 - Kasey Tellure - Belief is not Enough (8 miles)

Kasey felt herself come up out of the fog of sleep like a drowning swimmer struggling for the surface with a desperate need for air. The odd noise that interrupted her slumber continued until she finally awoke into earthly reality, the noise resolving itself into her beeping alarm clock. *Oh my God, it's beeping and not playing music. I pressed the wrong button again.*

It beeped on, growing ever louder, guided by some whiz kid's demonic electronics, designed to gradually raise its volume until reaching a banshee crescendo guaranteed to wake even the dead... beep Beep BEEP!

Desperate to stop the approaching banshee, she thrashed her half-numb left arm out several times in a muddled effort to press the silence button, a kind of flailing, early morning whack-a-mole game she had played before. She was successful, but there followed a crash of glass on the tile floor.

Oh my God, my water glass!

She remembered now, placing the glass next to the alarm in case she became thirsty during the night. Sitting up, brain still half asleep, she swung her legs over the edge of the bed and then saw the clock.

Oh my God, it's seven o'clock! I'm late!

Realizing she had forgotten to set the alarm to her normal rise and shine time, she stood up quickly to make a run to the shower. A sharp pain in one foot stopped her.

Oh my God, the glass!

She sat down and pulled her injured foot up to extract a small glass intruder, grabbed a tissue, sopped up the small drop of blood leaking from her toe, rolled over to the opposite side of the bed, and then limped to the bathroom with the tissue toe-held in place, stripping as she went: pajama top; pajama bottoms; bra; and, with the drop of her panties, freedom.

Two minutes later she pulled the shower curtain back and froze. There was a spider on the curtain.

Oh my God, now it's a spider! I hate spiders! This day is sure starting out lousy.

She took a piece of tissue paper and caught the small arachnid in it, but as she squeezed the tissue so that it wouldn't unfold and allow the spider to run up her arm, she felt the spider's little body pop from the pressure of her fingers. She heard the pop, and the sound and sensation totally repulsed her. She quickly threw the tissue in the trash.

Oh my God, *I mashed it! Ohooo gross!*

She shook her hand, trying to shake off the feeling of that little body splitting wide open, its liquid inners squirting into the tissue.

I should have worn my amber-star amulet to bed.

A quick shower done and the idea of breakfast discarded for the sake of time, she began dressing and putting on the minimal makeup and bling.

Finally ready to go out the door, there was one more step to be taken. She knew she could not deal with the spiritual forces swirling against her out in the work-a-day world without her protective amber-star amulet.

Reaching the spare bedroom where her shrine to the earth goddess Minerva occupied half of one wall, she froze, her breath momentarily sucked out of her. The alabaster statue of Minerva had somehow fallen to the floor. Worse than that, Minerva's right arm, still holding a clutch of grapes representing fertility and abundance from the soil, had broken off and lay like a piece of a corpse next to the shrine table's cat's-paw-shaped leg. And the amulet was nowhere in sight.

Oh my God, my amulet! I know I left it hanging on Minerva's arm. It's gone!

She heard somewhat of a cross between a gasp and a screaming croak come out of her mouth, as her right hand now involuntarily reached for her upper bosom where the amulet always hung, there to radiate its crystal aura vibrations of protection around her. She felt her heart race and her hands were suddenly clammy. She had goose bumps down her back.

Oh my God! My power crystal is gone!

She remembered Guru Abnathenatheonon Dejavu telling her about the aura, and the dangers of going out without the protective amulet. *Who could have done this? The doors were locked, the...*

Her eyes fell on a small piece of white fur clutched in Minerva's stone-dead fingers on the floor.

Oh my God! *Snowball! That damn cat!*

"Damn cat, damn cat, damn cat," she said, louder and louder with each exclamation, and began looking for the little furry criminal with a vengeance.

You've gone too far this time!

She knew she loved her cute little angora, but this offense pushed way beyond cute. Kasey sensed being on the edge of losing it, and although she hunted the cat with retribution in part of her mind, another part hoped the feline would not be found.

"Snowball!" she sweetened her voice to attract the wicked little puffball. "Where are you, you evil kitty?" As she called the feline felon, she combed the apartment room by room looking for the cat or the amulet, half expecting to find them together. Then another thought came and she started going over it in her mind.

Oh my God, would a cat eat an amulet? What can I do to get the amulet out of the cat?

At that moment she realized she had a claw hammer in her hand and couldn't remember when or where she had picked it up. Fearful for her cat, bad as it had been, she set the hammer down.

I hope she didn't eat the thing! I can't afford to wait two days for it to reappear and I certainly can't afford a vet.

None of her ideas about separating cat and amulet resonated as very pleasant, but considering what the cat had done, she had some satisfaction in the thoughts.

Finally, looking behind the commode in the spare bathroom, she spotted the amulet, under and behind the toilet tank, glowing its dim amber light through a fog of dried cat saliva and clinging dust-bunnies.

Armed with a clean amulet around her neck and a hastily packed sack lunch, she opened the door and stepped out.

I hate being late!

Then the cold air hit her in the face and washed under her unbuttoned coat, chilling parts of her that should never be cold.

Oh my God! Why does it have to be so cold!

Arriving at work, late again, she entered the Channel 5 News building and passed by the receptionist. Beverly smiled at her and gave a knowing tap of her finger on her watch.

"Good morning, Kasey," she said aloud, and then whispered "Bridgett has already been looking for you."

"Oh great," Kasey replied. "I hoped to have some time for a bagel and a hot cup of coffee before she sent me out on a spot."

"I think she has a couple of jobs waiting for you. You might want to see her right away. And Good Morning, Kasey!"

"Oh, sorry, Bev. Good morning to you too. You can't believe the morning I just had."

Walking to the elevator, she entered and punched the button for the fourth floor. Exiting the elevator, she stopped for a moment to look out the fourth-floor window at the Plaza below.

John Jay Plaza held a ring of yellow school buses parked around the fountain reflecting pool. There were no children in sight and she figured they were probably in the museum. Patches of un-melted snow were slushed up in heaps around the plaza where the weak winter sun had failed to remove them.

The buses, and the thought of the children they carried, hurt her deep inside, but she could not take her eyes off them.

Two years of my life wasted loving that man.

She remembered the awful breakup, their child, the other woman, the abortion... and she turned away from the window with tears in her eyes and her nose stuffing up.

Why didn't they tell me about these regrets?

Calling up a reserve of strength, she stifled the cry that begged to come out, and tried to ignore the pain. Those memories were in her past and she wanted them to just go away, just like the small patches of snow on the plaza below her.

Just go away.

She yearned for the day they went away and life became warm again.

By noon she knew she had two assignments she could choose between. She could either do an interview covering an overnight robbery, at the park in the frigid wind, or she could ride in the News 5 helicopter to do a spot on a new cellphone tower improvement. The cold wind made her choice easy.

So at 2:15 she grabbed her jacket, and, script in hand, walked out onto the roof of the Channel 5 building. She found Eagle 5, Channel 5's eye-in-the-sky, sitting on the rooftop with its engine running, blades whirling up a minor windstorm, and the pilot and the cameraman already seated. She ran out across the roof, doing the obligatory helicopter approach hunch-over, and scrambled into the door held open for her. Amid wind and noise, she settled into the back seat of the chopper. A quick glance into a small pocket mirror revealed every last primp of her hair... gone.

From her seat just behind the pilot and next to a door, she could see out an oversized window to her left, an arrangement she knew allowed the cameraman, seated in front next to the pilot, to unbuckle his seat belt, turn around, and get a nice shot of her and the view out the window. She would provide the gab, and he would provide the video for the 6 p.m. news audience.

The helicopter engine increased its powerful whine and the craft rose abruptly. Her stomach spoke a few words of primitive nausea when the wind coming up over the building buffeted the machine up and down, and then they swooped off toward the south to avoid the multiple high-tower buildings downtown. There were several other sudden drops amid the turbulence over downtown, but once they gained some altitude the ride smoothed out. She relaxed a little and tried to read the script again.

Looking out the window, she realized the pilot was taking them over to and up the Taconic River. *I can see for a hundred miles. This view through the crystal-clear, cold, winter air is so beautiful!*

The view is spectacular, Chad thought, looking out across Yorksberg and the river from his perch 150 feet up the Sonnetcell tower located on Copper Ridge, 8 miles west of Yorksberg. He was cold, and glanced at his watch: *2:15.*

"Shoooweee it's cold up here today," Chad said. "It's colder than a witch's... ah, belt buckle."

"As a twenty-eight-year-old, happily married father of four, you had better be staying away from witches," Tom said.

So what's the wind speed up here?" Chad said.

"Wait one."

Chad knew his buddy below in the tower's warm equipment shack was walking over to the weather panel. A moment later, Tom's voice came up on the radio. "Wind speed is hovering around nineteen miles per hour and the temperature is 33 degrees Fahrenheit. Nothing that an old tower-rat like you can't handle."

Chad smiled. Any other day the roles might be reversed; besides he had dressed for the cold. He had warmers in his pockets, thermal underwear, a wind-breaking parka, and was timing his climb in order to limit how long he was up. He could sense it was time to go down, but had one more thing to do and then pray the test results would not require him to fix something.

He secured the last cable onto the new antenna and then radioed Tom some 150 feet below.

"Okay. The last connection is secure. The anti-vibration collet gave me some trouble, but it's now in place."

"Wait one," came the call back from the tower's equipment shack. And then a moment later, "Clear the antenna, Chad. Let me know when you are clear and we'll power up."

"You got it."

He immediately began maneuvering down the ten feet or so and stopped to move his safety lanyard "A" from the slide rail above him to the slide rail on the section of tower he had climbed down onto. Then he repeated the action with safety lanyard "B."

Never compromise when it comes to safety.

He often thought of his kids as he carefully disconnected and reattached these lanyards. He then continued his climb down another ten feet or so. This was ample distance from the powerful antenna above him. Most of its power would be directed out over the city.

He noticed a helicopter approaching the tower some quarter mile away. He could see the numeral 5 on its side.

He keyed the radio again.

"The rat's clear of the pattern. You have a 'go' to test." Then he added "I got a whirly bird going around the tower. Looks like a News 5 chopper."

"Smile, you're on camera. Bull said the company let the news folks know about the tower work. He said they might be out."

"For God's sake, why?" Chad said. He waved at the chopper.

"Free publicity," Tom replied. "You're going to be a TV star on the news tonight."

"There he is!" called out the cameraman, pointing at a tiny dot high up on the cell phone tower on Copper Ridge. "Damn, that has to be a cold job."

Kasey stretched forward to get a glimpse of the man. They were rapidly drawing closer. The pilot brought them around the end of the ridge at about the same height as the man on the tower.

She knew the plan. They would take up a position for the shoot on the north side of Copper Ridge, allowing them to capture both the man on the tower and the city in the background.

This is perfect. This will be spectacular in high definition!

Kasey felt excitement and a sense of joy for the first time this day.

This is why I became a reporter, for times like this!

The clear cold air made the city and the distant ocean stand out, and she knew it would make a good high-definition backdrop for the tiny figure of a man high on the metal tower. She also felt good about the positive exposure this piece would give her.

Chad realized Tom must have left his radio on transmit because he could hear the voice of Sonnetcell's tower's engineer on a cell phone probably lying near the radio's mic.

"Okay, Tom, it looks good down here. Tell Chad to come on down and pack up. Good job for a cold day. Let me know when he's down."

"Thanks, Bull. Will do." Tom's voice then came through their portable point-to-point radios. "Icicle man, Bull says come on down. Hot coffee waiting."

Chad took a moment to enjoy the view from his high perch. The bright, winter sun gave the entire landscape an emphasized relief. It was downright beautiful. Through the clear air he could see the city eight miles away, the broad sweep of the Atlantic Ocean, and the fat meander of the Taconic River as it finally met the sea.

The News 5 chopper hovered due west of him and had moved a little too close for comfort. They were obviously filming him with the city in the background. He could see the pilot clearly and a person in a rear seat who waved at him. She had a microphone in one hand. He watched them jockey the helicopter around. It dropped down a bit and then cautiously moved in closer.

Chad leaned out on his safety harness with one hand on the tower and the other waving at the film crew.

As the pilot took them into position, Kasey saw the man waving on the tower. She waved back, wondering if he could see her. He looked dressed for an Alaskan adventure, with his puffy padded coat, climbing boots, parka-like hood, and gloves.

"Okay, ready," the cameraman said. "Take one."

"This is Kasey Tellure, Channel 5 News, reporting from Eagle 5, our eye-in-the-sky," Kasey began into her partially memorized script. She enjoyed being in front of the camera.

"Cut," the cameraman interrupted. "Drop us down a bit," he said to the pilot. "The guy on the tower has the city behind him and it's hard to make him out in the clutter. Try putting him with the ocean behind him. We can still get the city and he will stand out like a bug splattered on a windshield."

"Will do," the pilot said, and readjusted their position.

"That's it. Perfect. Ready, Kasey?" The little red light on the camera indicated it was already recording.

"Go," she replied.

"Ready. Take two."

"This is Kasey Tellure, Channel 5 News, reporting from Eagle 5, our eye-in-the-sky. We are high above Copper Ridge just north of Yorksberg to show you a man who is going to make a difference for many of you, in spite of freezing cold temperatures and wind. That's him hanging on that tower, Sonnetcell Tower Technician—"

At that instant she saw the interior of the helicopter illuminated by a bright light coming from behind her. She saw the pilot and cameraman wince and saw the camera's automatic aperture close down. "What the hell?" said the cameraman.

"Keep recording! Keep recording!" yelled the pilot.

Kasey, completely thrown off her script, turned and looked at the city. A huge white-hot fireball rolled up into the sky above the distant city. It dimmed to yellow-orange brilliance and finally to an angry orange-red as it rose. She watched, spellbound, for a full fifteen seconds until all the color had gone out of the cloud.

"Oh my God," she said, her voice a whisper.

Chad was surprised to see the very air around him light up. It was so bright that the reflection off the chopper left a momentary after-image in his vision. He swung around and looked back toward the city to see where the light was coming from. The sight took his breath away. The entire city, the harbor, the river's mouth emptying into the ocean, and the wide expanse of the Atlantic Ocean were temporarily overshadowed by a ball of brilliant light, too bright to look at, rising up out of the downtown district of Yorksberg. Spellbound he watched it rise. He could now see the ball of light as a roiling mass of hot gases changing from white hot to yellow, then orange, and finally streaks of glowing red swirling upward in clouds of reddish gray smoke. Within fifteen seconds it had dimmed out and assumed the wicked shape of a fast-rising mushroom cloud. The city had become one huge dust cloud of smoke and haze. He released an uncontrollable explicative, wondering if he had just witnessed a quarter of a million people die.

Suddenly Kasey's world went out of control. The helicopter pitched over and began a precipitous, spiraling drop that left her stomach in her throat. She tensed as the engine roared, but the craft only increased its dizzying spin.

With the ground hurtling up at them, Kasey only had time to whisper, "Oh my God, help us!" her protective amber-star amulet completely forgotten.

Chad noticed a faint, perfectly circular ring of disturbance moving outward from the city across the river, and then the tower jerked violently, knocking him free. He fell only as far as his safety lanyard friction stop allowed, but the fall scared him and the stop at the bottom hurt when he banged up against the tower a couple of feet below his perch, glad he wore a helmet under the parka hood. He grabbed the tower while cursing the fact that he let himself get distracted.

My first fall of my career. Damn that's embarrassing, and all caught on camera.

That thought caused him to look back at the helicopter. Then he heard the sound of a straining turbine engine and saw the machine falling and spinning out of control.

He hit a guy wire. That's what knocked me off. Looks like he lost his tail rotor.

He watched as the pilot made a partial recovery just before impact, but it sure looked like a rough crash.

"Brace yourselves!" the pilot yelled at the last instant. Kasey saw the cameraman desperately trying to get his seat belt on, but before he succeeded they hit with a bone-jarring crash and then a violent, tumbling, downhill roll with rotors flying off and metal coming apart amid the dust, the rocks, and the cold.

Chad pulled out his radio. "Tom, the copter has crashed. Call 911." Tom's response came after a slight pause.
"Lights are out and the phone is dead. Come on down."
It was suddenly very quiet high on the tower. At that moment Chad felt a strong, quick gust of wind pass by, followed by a deep, rumbling roar from the city. He guessed that singular, strong puff of wind had come from the event in the city. He looked back at the city and could see the long dark shadow of the tall black and reddish-gray cloud stretched high into the sky. Its upper reaches were beginning to drift north. A shiver went down his spine as he glanced over at South Yorksberg where his family lived, and he prayed they were safe. He rapidly climbed down the tower, connecting and disconnecting his two safety lanyards as he went, thinking of his family and the people in the helicopter.

The first thing to reach Kasey's awareness after the crash was the cold. It was so cold. Then she noticed the ache in her legs, distant at first and then growing into a white-hot pain more intense than anything she had ever experienced. It hurt so much she could hardly draw a breath to scream, but she did scream, over and over again until only a gasping moan came out. Terrified by the pain and the cold, she saw evidence of fire, its light flickering up and around the far side of the wreck of the helicopter's cabin.
Oh my God. How can it be so cold with all this fire?
She tried to release her seat belt but could not find the release mechanism. Each effort sent waves of pain through her, forcing her to remain still, all the while knowing she had to get out. She yelled for help and looked for the pilot. She could see him slumped forward, still strapped in his seat, his helmet gone. The cameraman she could not see, but his seat was now becoming engaged in the fire.
Then someone yelled for her to unbuckle, reached in, and released the seat belt strap. The next thing she knew she was being pulled out of the wreckage. The pain in her legs as they dragged across the wreck of the door set her to gasping and moaning. A moment later, lying on the cold, hard, jagged rock hillside and looking up into the sky, she reached for her protective-amber amulet on the chain around her neck... and found nothing. Her mind reeled in a confused miasma of fear and cold and intense pain.
Damn cat! Damn cat! Damn cat!

When Chad reached the wreckage, he found Tom there with someone he had pulled out of the burning machine.
"The pilot and cameraman are dead. Tom said.

He could see a woman lying at Tom's feet, obviously in great pain, moaning and crying. Her right arm appeared burned and her hair looked like a singed mess.

"I think both her legs are broken," Tom said. "She keeps saying something about a cat."

Chad tried his cell phone but got no signal. He wished he had called from up on the tower. Up that high he might have reached into the next cell down the coast.

"What happened?" Tom said, pointing at the smoking, fire-dappled city and the awesome black and gray cloud drifting far to the north.

"Looked like a nuke to me. Only thing I know that would be that bright."

Tom said, "There's a tarp in the truck. We can use it as a stretcher... unless you have a better idea. And we will need something to immobilize her legs. Give me your jacket; this lady is not dressed for the cold."

"I vote we wait for the EMTs. I don't like the idea of moving her." Chad doffed his jacket and tucked it over and around the woman.

"You think we can raise EMTs after that?" Tom pointed at Yorksberg.

"I guess not. I could drive down and find someone."

"Something tells me that will be slow also. Could we hit another cell from up on the tower?"

"Don't know how big this is. Maybe the other cells are down too." Chad paused. "Oh crap, I'm going back up. We have to do something." Before Tom could say anything else Chad sprinted up the hill.

He ducked into the equipment house and basked momentarily in its warmth. His cup of coffee, lukewarm, still sat on the table. "God bless you, Tom," he said, dumping a load of sugar in it; and, without stirring it, drank it quickly; grabbed Tom's jacket, and started back up the tower. He climbed as rapidly as he could and about halfway up tried the cell phone. There were no signal strength bars.

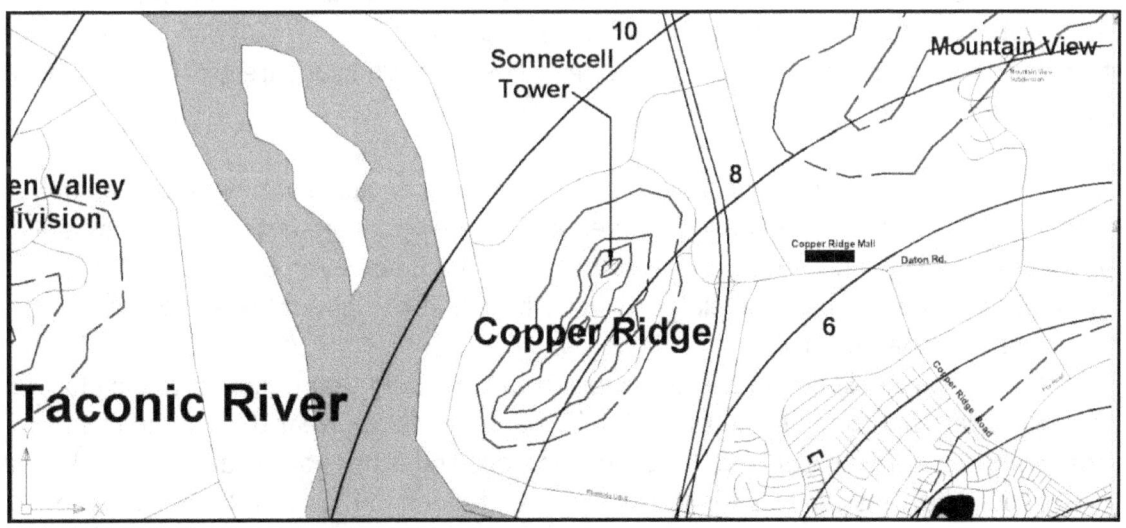

Copper Ridge Close-up

"Can you hear me now?" he mumbled with caustic humor at his situation. He climbed another 35 feet, stopped, and turned the cell on. *Bingo!* he thought, seeing the signal strength, and pressed 911. "Busy," he said under his breath. "I should have figured."

What could he do? He considered his options. He could wait there and keep trying, or climb down and drive off the ridge to get help. He decided to go down. Most likely the 911 system would continue to be clogged with folks reporting the big explosion.

As he reached the bottom, he saw a car turn off Copper Ridge Road and start up the gravel road to the top of the hill. Perhaps someone had seen the chopper go down. Chad whistled loudly and pointed down the hill. He yelled, "Car coming!"

A few minutes later a Yorksberg police car drove up and stopped next to their truck with a spray of gravel and dust. A patrol officer and a man in a gray hooded coat got out.

"News helicopter caught a guy wire. One survivor. Can you get some EMTs up here?" Chad yelled.

Analysis of Chapter 20

Kasey is another person who by fortune or fate, or the protective power of amber for those who believe that sort of thing, managed to not be where the one-hundred-million-degrees Fahrenheit surprise could reach her. Within a tenth of a second of detonation, the weapon's fireball had expanded to within 400 feet of the very window Kasey had looked out of and seen the school buses. Everyone in the building died instantly from enormous overdoses of radiation, but they had no way of knowing this could happen since the building and everything in it was blasted to pieces and flung city blocks away before any symptoms of radiation damage could be felt.

Indeed, fifty-three years later, a crystal paperweight Kasey had left sitting on her desk would be found by some children playing in a downtown park off Clay Avenue, its glass turned an odd yellow color by the intense gamma radiation exposure it had experienced so many years before.

Chad and Tom survived the attack on Yorksberg because of their location 8 miles from the event. Tom never knew it happened since he had been inside the equipment shack at that time. All he knew was the power went off. Chad, however, had seen the whole thing. From his vantage point we can claim he was within line-of-sight of the explosion point, so let's consider what he saw.

Chad was looking 180 degrees away from Yorksberg at the time of the explosion. He later reported that for an instant the air all around him lit up. Near the ground the atmosphere contains natural dust, pollen, aerosols, and other particulate-like smoke that can reflect light. This can be seen when the sun is hidden behind clouds and "rays" of sunlight stretch from holes in the cloud cover to the ground. This is just sunlight reflecting off the airborne particulates in the atmosphere. At high altitudes or after a good rainstorm there are fewer particulates in the atmosphere and "sun beams" are dim or not seen at all. From Chad's perch high above the ridge the air was fairly clean. But there were enough particulates in the air around him to make the air appear to light up when irradiated by the intense light from the terrorist's bomb.

The perceived brightness of a light depends on the size of the glowing element and the temperature of the glowing material. The light's color also changes with temperature in a complicated way, tending toward the red when not so hot and toward the blue end of the spectrum when very hot. During the first 1/1000th of a second of the bomb's explosion, the temperature of the bomb's material exceeds the temperature of the gas in the sun. In fact, it is so hot at that time that much of the "light" that comes out is in the form of X-rays. These X-rays are so intense they instantly heat a large volume of the surrounding air to white-hot incandescence. Within 1/10th of a second, the heat from the explosion formed a fireball of white-hot gas about two football-field lengths in diameter.

So Chad saw the flash reflected in the air around him. But he also reported the light reflected off the helicopter left after-images in his eyes.

After-images are those white spots you see in your field of vision after looking in the direction of a flash photograph. No eye damage is done, but the photochemicals in the eye's retina are temporarily depleted, leaving "spots" in your field of vision that seem to move with your eyes.

By the time Chad turned around to view the city, almost 1.5 seconds had passed. The fireball had expanded to about 900 feet in diameter (3 football-field lengths) and had begun to rise.[58] But even then the light the fireball emitted was too bright to look at directly.

Chad observed a circular ring moving across the river and centering on the point of the explosion. This "ring" is caused by the spreading blast wave from the explosion. As the blast wave travels over a body of water, the sudden pressure changes on the surface of the water are visible as an outward-expanding circle. This phenomenon can be seen in historical videos of nuclear tests conducted near or in bodies of water.[59]

Chad is naturally concerned for his family. They live in South Yorksberg more than three miles from the point of explosion and upwind from it, which suggests they will be okay. There is a possibility that some fallout may drop on South Yorksberg, depending on upper-level winds and the spread of the mushroom cloud as it rises. Rough dose-rate contours for early fallout from a 2-megaton explosion indicate the presence of radioactive fallout between 5 and 10 miles up wind of the blast.[60] The 2-megaton explosion is one hundred times the explosive power of our Yorksberg bomb and fallout effects at Yorksberg

---

[58] The fireball rises for the same reason smoke rises over a fire. When gases are heated, their density, or weight per unit volume, decreases. The hot gases are like a bubble under water. Since it is very light compared to the surrounding water, the surrounding water tries to rush in and fill the bubble, forcing it to move up to the surface. Likewise, the nuclear fireball is huge and hot, but it also has a density lower than that of the surrounding air, which rushes in, lifting the ball of fire up into the atmosphere.

[59] Search the internet for "nuclear test video" and then watch the ocean tests. You will see this expanding "ring" in some of the movies.

[60] *The Effects of Nuclear Weapons*, 3rd ed., U.S. Department of Defense, 1977, Figure 9.86a. Note that the wind speed is the same as that of our fictional Yorksberg event.

may be assumed to be less proportionally. Wisdom would direct Chad's family to evacuate the area until authorities can declare it safe.

Don't miss that last sentence. If you are within 10 miles of a nuclear event, even if the mushroom cloud trends away from you, it would be wise to evacuate until you know it is safe for you to stay. The alternative is to have radiation-detection instruments you can trust and then evacuate only if fallout appears in your area. Remember that for months following such an attack, changing winds may transport radioactive dust from the contaminated city into your neighborhood many miles from the blast site. So prepare and take action accordingly. It is likely an attack on your city will displace huge numbers of people from totally undamaged neighborhoods for as long as several years. Have a "go-pack" ready. This bag will contain your important papers and documents, everything you will need to establish a new residence somewhere. You want it ready to grab and run without taking time to try to put it all together.

We need to comment here that the bomb the bad guys use may give a larger yield than the 19-kt weapon in the Yorksberg stories. The differences in the effects of a 5-megaton explosion and a 19-kt explosion are enormous. The fireball of a 5-megaton explosion, for example, would approach 2.8 miles in diameter.[61]
Survivability at a given distance drops with increasing weapon yield. It must be said, however, that the larger weapons simply move the zone of survivability farther out. But the area between mileage rings increases the farther from ground zero, so the larger the bomb used, the *more* people will find themselves in a zone that requires survivor knowledge and help to recover. So we should not give up and not prepare to survive just because the bad guys may bring a bigger weapon. Such thoughts should prompt even those living miles from a tempting target to read this handbook and prepare.
Fortunately, larger weapons are much more complicated. They are difficult to get, much heavier, harder to transport and hide, and easier to detect due to their larger quantity of fissionable material. Since the purpose is terror, which is produced with either a small or a large weapon, we expect the bad guys will elect to use a smaller weapon. Remember that what they use is not nearly as important as what the survivor knows.

Aircraft colliding with tower guy wires is not an uncommon accident. In our story the pilot is looking directly at the explosion and caught this light on his retinas. It was unfortunate timing to have been looking at the buildings downtown when the blast went off. He averted his eyes quickly, but even eight miles from the explosion his eyes were damaged and he was left partially blinded. In the few seconds that followed, he attempted to look back at the rising mushroom cloud, using the part of his eyes that had not been flash blinded, but was unable to see it clearly. During this time the helicopter, already too close to the tower, drifted down and in toward one of the upper guy wires. When the pilot finally realized he had drifted, he pivoted the aircraft to fly away from the tower and his tail rotor came in contact with the steel cable. Without the tail rotor to compensate for the

---

[61] http://space.au.af.mil/primer/us_missile_systems.pdf

helicopter's main rotor's torque, the whirly bird then descended in a death spiral to the hillside below. The pilot was killed on impact, the cameraman was knocked unconscious and died in the ensuing fire, and the female news reporter (Kasey) was pulled from the wreckage by our tower technician Tom.

So here we have two killed and one injured without being touched by nuclear radiation, heat, or blast. Are the terrorists responsible? You decide.

Kasey Tellure was more than eight miles from the explosion, and yet it almost cost her life. There were many others far out of danger, who were hurt or killed by the bomb. All their stories, although offering useful knowledge, will not be told here. Examples include several chain-reaction accidents on the freeways, where folks surprised by the light and the mushroom cloud instinctively slowed down, only to be rear-ended by other distracted drivers behind them. A man mending his roof in nearby Morgensport, surprised by the cloud, watched it roll up into the sky above Yorksberg and managed to fall off the roof. This resulted in severe hip and back injuries that were with him for the rest of his life. If the bomb ever comes to your city it will touch people even outside the city.

Chad is about 8 miles from the blast. The shockwave travels about a mile in five seconds, getting weaker and weaker as it goes. Thus Chad has plenty of time to get back on the tower and observe the helicopter crash before the blast wave arrives. It is just a puff of wind at this distance. Curiously, Chad and his supporting engineer, Bull Ho in South Yorksberg, are the same distance from the blast and both feel the blast wind at almost the exact same time. The deep rumbling roar Chad hears after the puff of wind passes is typical of large explosions heard at long distances.

Chad and Tom's dilemma about what to do for the injured newscaster is something that will be repeated time and time again in the zone of survivors. In an attack like this, thousands of people will receive physical injuries that other non-medical folks are going to have to deal with.

Who do you call? The phone system may not work and even if you can call 911, chances are it will probably be inundated with emergency calls. Once you get through there may be a long wait before emergency personnel can get to you. Chad and Tom ended up driving the woman to a distant hospital. Think about what they would have encountered in terms of the status of local Yorksberg hospitals, traffic pouring out of the city, clogged interstate lanes, contamination checkpoints, etc. Like most folks he probably would have gone south on the interstate. The best choice, however, primarily because so few will think of it, would be for him to head west on Riverside Drive away from the interstate and from Yorksberg and follow state roads to the nearest county hospital. The trip would avoid traffic jams, it would be quicker, and he would likely find the hospital not yet swamped with injured and dying.

You need to think about these things before the event. Where are the hospitals within 100 miles of your city? Do not count on using the hospitals within your city or even within your county. Get maps and mark routes to those hospitals. This should be easy using internet sites such as Google Maps. The author was able to immediately get hundreds of hospitals in his state listed on the screen using this site by simply plugging in the word "hospital" and the name of the state. You will have to filter out the many animal hospitals that will come up in the search.

Quiz on Chapter 20
(Answers are in Appendix A2)

1. How long did it take the blast wave to travel eight miles?
2. Can the flash of a nuclear explosion hurt your eyes eight miles away?
3. When a bomb explodes near a body of water, sometimes a circular ring can be seen expanding out from the point of the explosion. What causes that expanding ring?
4. Should you evacuate if you live in the city many miles from the explosion and the mushroom cloud blows away from you?
5. What is the most important thing you can believe if the terrorists explode a nuclear bomb in your city?

The next chapter will be a change of pace. Instead of looking into the lives of people in or near a big city, we will drop in on a family a long way from Yorksberg. Perhaps you live many miles from a potential target for nuclear terrorists. Do you feel safe? Are you really safe? There might be dangers lurking there that you would not imagine. Amiee Moller finds out the hard way. She is a small, meek, gentle lady who meets a pack of human wolves. Read her story in the next chapter that we call "Gentle as a Lamb."

Meek Amiee – Gentle as a Lamb

21 – Amiee Moller – Gentle as a Lamb (150 Miles)

Glennis Annette Lowsly stood on the porch with a huge grin on her face, and for a few seconds Amiee just stared, wondering if she was supposed to know this person.

"Hello, Mum," the young lady said.

The British accent gave it away, and Amiee took in a sharp breath. "Glennis? Is that you?"

"Yes, Mum. I surprised you, didn't I?"

"Oh my gosh, it's been so many years and you've grown into a beautiful young woman." After a warm hug she said, "Please, come on in."

Amiee moved some magazines from a chair and indicated her visitor should sit down.

"Mrs. Moller, before I sit I need to ask for your help, and my ride, Darcy, is waiting for a yea or nay. I'm on my way back to medical school and she can't take me any further. You were so hospitable to me during my stay with your family, I thought you might let me spend the night and fetch me to the Rainelle bus station tomorrow. Don't worry; if nay, I can take a motel room just up the road."

"Of course you can stay. I would be thrilled to have you here. We have some catching up to do! Please let Darcy know."

She watched Glennis run out to the car, get her suitcases out, and give the driver a hug.

She has really filled out. She is so beautiful.

"Glennis Annette Lowsly," she rolled the name across her tongue.

I always thought her name sounded like British royalty.

"Who is that?" said Mark, walking up behind her.

"That is Glennis Lowsly. She was our foreign student guest years ago, before you were born."

With hot cups of a dark, aromatic tea, Amiee listened as Glennis spoke of her family in Aylesbury, England, about her struggles in medical school, and about her trip to Savanna with her friend Darcy.

"You lived in Rainelle when I was here before," Glennis said. "I stopped by your old house and found you had moved out here in the country. We almost gave up looking for you."

"Ron and Grandfather Moller built this house while we lived in Rainelle, and we moved in about the time Mark was born."

Glennis continued. "We came up state highway 192 from Yorksberg, a very beautiful route. To be honest, I didn't think of you until I saw Rainelle on the map."

"Well, I'm glad you looked us up."

"Your husband won't mind? He worked at a nuclear power plant as I remember."

"Tawny River Unit 1, and no, he wouldn't mind at all, but he is not here. He was called up with the National Guard and is overseas. He has been gone nine months and thirteen days."

"Wow, that must be hard on you," Glennis said.

"At times, especially like this morning. He didn't send his usual email, and that always scares me." Amiee felt moisture coming into her eyes.

"I'm sorry," Glennis said; "I didn't mean to bring up such a subject. He will write soon; there could be a thousand reasons why you didn't get a message from him."

Amiee accepted a warm hug from Glennis.

After lunch Amiee sent Glennis off to the local market for some things the Moller pantry needed, and began cleaning house. An hour later she began to vacuum the floor to the music of her favorite country western radio station. As the singer wailed "Baby, that horse is dead and my saddle is cold," she heard Mark yelling from his room.

"Mom, can you turn that down? I can't concentrate!"

She stopped the vacuum and turned the music down.

Sometimes those two work so quietly I forget I'm homeschooling them.

"Sorry, sweetheart. Let me know when you're done," Amiee said.

"You didn't have to stop vacuuming," Mark said. "It's the words in the music that make it hard to read."

"That's all right. I have some other things I can do."

Like check the email for a message from Ron. I do miss that man.

Glennis returned, packages in arms, and Amiee helped her in.

Amiee looked at her watch and calculated the time overseas, and then sat down at the computer and checked again.

"Nothing yet?" Glennis said.

"Yah, Ron's pretty good about writing each morning over there, but he missed yesterday. I think I live for those 'you got mail' tones. The carpet in front of my computer has become my very own widow's walk."

The computer chimed "mail" and Amiee jumped.

A glance told her this one was from another of her homeschool family friends, Doris. Disappointed, she opened the email and read the chatty news.

"Is that Dad?" Mark called from his room.

"What did Daddy say?" chimed in little Megan, as she wandered into the room, rubbing her eyes.

"Awe, honey, did the computer wake you up?" Amiee hugged her littlest and stroked her hair. "It was Doris, not Daddy." She said this loud enough for Mark to hear.

Amiee turned to Glennis. "The fact that vacuuming and country western music can't rouse Megan from her nap, but the 'mail' chime can, speaks volumes of the hole Ron's absence has left."

"I hope he writes soon," Glennis said.

Amiee looked at her watch. It was 2:30 p.m. At that moment, the computer-chimed mail was arriving and Amiee opened it.

"It's from Ron!" she said.

He is still alive.

Her heart leapt with anticipation! The instant she clicked to open the email, the electric power went off, came back on, flickered, and then went out completely.

"Noooo!" she cried, looking at the dark screen.

"What happened?" Glennis said, looking around the darkened house.

Amiee felt as if someone had just taken something precious from her. She knew the email would still be there when the power came back on, but it still hurt.

Amiee made herself busy with Glennis, preparing a salad and trying to be patient.

"Does the power go off often?" Glennis said.

"No, it's really pretty steady. It usually only goes off when there's lightning around."

When power did not come back on after ten minutes, she called the local power utility to report the outage and received a recorded message.

"Due to emergency conditions," the artificial, recorded female voice said, "the power outage you are experiencing is widespread. Please be patient. Power will be restored to your area as soon as possible." The voice continued and then the line went dead.

Amiee, staring at the phone in her hand, tried to get a dial tone with no success.

What the hell is going on?

The first thing that came to her mind was that there must be a problem at the Tawny River Power Station, so she walked over to the television and turned it on. Instantly she felt silly. There was no power.

Glennis smiled. "I've done that myself."

"Mark," Amiee called out. "Where is your portable radio? The little blue one?"

"The battery is dead." His answer came down the hall from his bedroom.

"Follow me and I'll let you in on the Moller family secret," she said to Glennis.

She took Glennis down the stairs to their basement.

"I would never show this to non-family, but you're family as far as I'm concerned."

"Why thank you, Mrs. Moller," Glennis said, looking around the wood-paneled family room.

"Please, call me Amiee, and don't tell anyone what I'm going to show you."

She walked to one the end of the basement where a beautiful, old, floor-to-ceiling China cabinet stood. She pushed it sideways and it rolled away to reveal a doorway.

"We call this the cave," Amiee said.

"A secret room! How very interesting."

Then she opened the door and entered.

"This cave was the creation of Ron, largely inspired by Grandfather Moller, when they built this house."

"Do you mean cave like underground? This isn't just another room under the house?" Glennis said.

"Right. Ron's dad is of Jewish ancestry, and as a lad he survived the holocaust in Europe when a Christian family in France hid his family behind a wall in the basement of an old farmhouse."

"I've heard of that sort of thing."

"After the war, Papa Moller came to the States and was deeply involved in civil defense in the 1950s and early 1960s. When he realized his son was going to build a home near a nuclear plant he convinced Ron to add this extension to the home, and to hide it. Thus the China cabinet and hidden door."

"This is amazing," Glennis said. "I've seen shelters in England, but not this nice. You have bunks too."

"And camp toilets, ventilation, games, food, and three feet of dirt overhead. I always thought it was a bit of a waste of money."

Inside, she switched on the lights without thinking and laughed at herself again.

I've got to remember the power's off.

She felt around for the flashlight she knew was stored near the entrance, and used it to find the portable, shortwave radio. Sliding batteries in, she switched it on.

"Marky!" came her little one's excited voice from the basement stairs. "Mom's in the cave!"

Amiee could hear Mark coming down the basement stairs two steps at a time.

I wish he wouldn't do that.

"What are you doing, Mom?" Mark said.

"Shhhhh, listen." She had tuned the radio to a local radio station. The voice from the radio was in the middle of a sentence.

"...there are presently no estimates of the casualties from the Yorksberg explosion. Officials are still investigating the site; however, we can say that according to some sources it would not be a surprise if at least a half a million people have died."

"What?" Glennis exclaimed. "We just drove through there."

Amiee was holding her breath. The man's voice continued describing the emergency actions being taken to help the city. Finally he said, "For those of you just joining us, there has been a large explosion in downtown Yorksberg. The cause is not known at this time; however, video taken by a television news crew; the large, damaged area; and the presence of large amounts of radiation, suggest this was a nuclear explosion. It is not yet known whether this is a terrible accident or a terrorist act. One moment."

He paused, and they could hear voices in the background and the rustle of paper.

"I have just been handed this official announcement from the Governor's office and the Federal Emergency Management Agency. Due to radioactive fallout from the Yorksberg explosion, everyone living within 300 miles north of Yorksberg should immediately begin to evacuate to the west. If you live in or within 60 miles of any of the following cities and towns, you must evacuate to the west as soon as possible."

He then read an extensive list of cities and towns, which, Amiee noted, included Rainelle.

"God, I wish Ron were home."

What would he do? She could pack up and go, or she could stay. She was struggling with these and many other thoughts when one of them came to the front of her mind. Ron and Grandfather had built the hole for just this sort of event. Unlike her neighbors, she had a choice. She could stay and be safe, and that, she concluded, was what Ron would probably do. Her decision made, she called out to her littlest.

"Megan," she said, "would you go upstairs and get Mommy's coffee? Bring it down here and please don't spill a drop."

"Okay," Megan replied, always eager to be Mommy's helper.

After Megan left, Amiee said to Mark, "Someone has blown up Yorksberg and radiation is coming here. We are going to have to live in the cave for a while."

She was afraid this announcement would scare Mark, but, oblivious to the danger, Mark responded as if he were a boy just going camping. "Cool! Can I fold the bunks down?"

"Later. Right now I want you to find the radiation instruments. Do you know where they are?"

"I'll get the lights on too," he said.

Amiee and Glennis followed Mark around as he activated a couple of gel-cell rechargeable batteries, checked to see the two solar panels in the back yard were clean, and turned on the 12 VDC lights in the cave.

"Dad showed me how to do all that," Mark told Glennis.

After checking the small electrical panel, Mark announced formally, "The batteries are good and there is power coming in from the solar cells. They are working okay for this late in the day." Amiee could hear the soft whisper of a small battery and solar-cell-powered ventilation fan at the back of the shelter. She smiled and gave Mark a hug while winking at Glennis.

"Having Mark here is like having a piece of Ron at home," she said.

She watched Mark dig out the radiation instrument his dad had stored, and a moment later Megan came into the hole with the coffee held carefully in both hands and walking very slowly.

"I got Vanessa too. Can she stay in the cave with us?" She clutched her favorite doll underarm.

"Of course," Amiee said smiling. Having the kids around was actually helping her cope. "Glennis, why don't you go get what you will need down here."

"Okay. I guess we will rough it a bit. Any idea how long?"

"We'll let the authorities tell us," Amiee said as she pointed to the radio. "I'll take readings every half hour."

After they finished dinner, she tried a few phone calls to friends, which proved fruitless.

"Apparently most folks have already left the area," she said to Glennis. "I did reach my friend Doris, who said they have closed the public schools early and the buses brought her son home. They are headed for their cabin in North Carolina."

She held out her keys to Glennis. "Take my keys, and please move the car into the garage; then, if you would, come help Mark and me tape up all the windows."

A little after 6:30 p.m., four hours after the Yorksberg explosion, she saw the first rise in radioactivity. "It's risen from virtually nothing to a quarter of a millirem per hour," she said.

"Is that bad?" Glennis said.

"Having a husband employed at a nuclear power plant is the only reason I can answer you," Amiee said. "Fifty millirem per day is the safe dose a worker is allowed at the plant. Ron said you can get that much all year and it won't hurt you."

Six hours after the explosion she called out the reading taken at the front window. "It's 265 millirem per hour now. From now on I want you kids to stay in the cave. Take some toys and books down there."

Glennis' inquisitive look elicited a further comment. "Radiation damage adds up, and kids are more sensitive," Amiee said.

"Why is it safer in this shelter, Mom?" Mark said when she came back from one of her trips upstairs to take a reading.

"Well, tell me what you remember about what Dad taught you about radiation." She was playing the homeschool teacher role now, using questions to lead him.

Mark answered without hesitation. "He said that radioactive materials shoot out thousands of tiny, nuclear-sized bullets. Each little bullet causes a tiny amount of damage to our cells. He said they are like tiny paper cuts. A few don't hurt, but if you get too many, it will make you sick or you can die."

"You get an 'A' for that answer. Very good, Mark," Amiee said. She had not remembered Ron saying that until she heard Mark repeat it.

"Ask me a question," demanded little Megan, still clutching Vanessa.

Amiee struggled to think of a question Megan could answer successfully.

"Well, let's see. Do the little radioactive bullets fly really fast, or very slow?"

"Really fast!" Megan said with a smile and without hesitating.

"Right!" Amiee said. "You listened to your dad too, didn't you?"

"No," Megan responded, "he didn't say that really fast stuff. I just thought that if they went very slow they could never catch us." Megan said this matter-of-factly as if it were obvious.

Amiee looked at Mark and she and Glennis laughed. "Megan, you sure do think well," Mark said as a compliment. She beamed back at him.

Amiee looked to Mark and asked him a second question. "Name three ways we can protect ourselves from the little bullets."

Megan put her hand up and jumped up and down while saying "I know one. I know one. Let me answer!" Vanessa, forgotten for the moment, had fallen to the floor at her side.

"I can think of two. Let Megan say her answer first," Mark said.

Amiee pointed to Megan. "Go girl," she said.

"Daddy said one way was to use a shield. Like on Power Rangers. When they send energy balls at the Power Rangers, they stop them with their shields."

"Shielding," Mark said. "That was one of the ones I could think of."

"Correct," Amiee said. "This shelter is built out of extra-thick concrete. I watched your dad and grandpa pour it. The walls are 10 inches thick in front and on top, and you remember the little hill up next to the house in the back yard? Well that is 36 inches of dirt they piled up over us." She pointed up at the ceiling.

"So," Mark said, "the nuclear bullets flying really fast have to pass through 36 inches of dirt and 10 inches of concrete to get to us."

"And very few of them can get though, so we get much fewer of those atomic "paper cuts."

"You yanks do train your children well," Glennis said.

"The other one I thought of was distance," Mark volunteered. "If we stay far away from the radioactive source, we get hit less times."

"Right again," Mom agreed. "If this shelter were underneath a high roof that could keep the radioactive fallout away from the ground, then we would receive even less radiation."

"Okay," Mark said, "what is the last one? I don't remember."

Amiee pointed at her watch.

Mark seemed confused by this action. Then his eyes lit up. "Oh, time! Dad said the longer you are exposed, the more damage you get."

At that thought, Amiee's heart sank. She wished they had this conversation hours ago.

I made the wrong choice. By staying, I've increased the time of the exposure of everyone and drastically shortened the distance between the radioactive materials and their bodies. Huntsville would have been no exposure and a thousand miles away. But it's too late now.

She turned on the detector inside the shelter and it read 26 millirem per hour. That was 1.4 millirem per minute, or the nuclear plant worker's safe daily dose of 50 millirem every 35 minutes. The though made her skin crawl and she hated herself for deciding to stay. It had been a bad decision. She calculated the dose they would receive overnight and it came to more than 1 rem. Nowhere near making one sick, but still, it was unnecessary, and way too much for the kids.

They could make a run for it tomorrow, she considered. They might see a higher dose rate during the time it took to drive out of the fallout zone, but they would get that over the next few days if they stayed put, even in the shelter. Amiee made a strategic decision.

Tomorrow we will head for Huntsville.

About 2 a.m., with the kids asleep, she made a quick foray upstairs for another reading. As she expected, the radiation levels were falling, and from this she took some comfort.

After pulling the China cabinet across the entrance and closing the shelter door, she found her bunk.

"Is everything okay?" The British-accented voice came as a whisper across the shelter.

"Getting better," she whispered back, and then snuggled down into her covers and drifted toward sleep.

Amiee sat up in the bunk and listened, her heart pounding.

Was that a dream? Someone had broken glass in my dream.

She started to lie back down, but then she heard faint voices. They sounded as if they were coming from upstairs.

"Is your husband home?" whispered Glennis.

"No, that's impossible; besides, he wouldn't break glass to get in."

Heart racing, Amiee slid quietly out of her bunk and tip-toed to the door where she listened.

She could hear footsteps upstairs, and voices. Whoever it was, their loud voices said they obviously were sure no one was home.

"Who is it? Can you tell?" Glennis said.

"I think they're thieves. They must have decided to rob homes while everyone is gone. No police either."

"I wouldn't go out there. My dad says it's better to let them have everything," Glennis said, still whispering.

Amiee felt violated, but considered the kids. "I agree. It's best to let them have anything they want, as long as they leave us alone." She looked back at the two sleeping children.

She felt a threat to her kids and somehow this changed her. She went to a box on the top shelf and pulled down her and her husband's gun case. She worked the combination lock and in a moment had her 38-caliber revolver in her hands.

Glennis must have seen the gun. Amiee could hear it in her voice.

"What are you doing? I thought we were going to hide."

"Calm down. I'm just getting prepared. I doubt they will ever think to move the China cabinet, but I really don't know what they know about our house. Few people other than family members know about this shelter, but there is no telling what one of the kids might have leaked out."

Listening to the voices and the footsteps she thought, *It's just a matter of time before they come downstairs.*

It was quiet for a while, and then footsteps could be heard coming down the stairs, and then a man's voice.

"Hey, Buck, there's another flat screen down here."

Amiee placed her finger over her lips to signal Glennis to be extra quiet.

A fainter voice called back. "Bring it up. We got some jewelry from one of the bedrooms and Tank is on his way from the neighbor's. You are going to be surprised, my man!" There was a hint of excitement in his voice.

Amiee put her ear to the door to hear better, and then jumped back when the man in her basement opened the China cabinet door.

"Nothing but plates and glasses," she heard him complain, and then he began smashing the cabinet's contents onto the floor.

Amiee saw red and came close to charging out and confronting his sorry life. She felt Glennis' steadying hand on her shoulder.

Why would he do such a mean thing? Just go away!

A moment later she heard his footsteps crunching broken glass as he walked away, and then his steps ascending the stairs.

She relaxed a bit and took a deep breath.

A prisoner in my own home!

She heard the front door open and then what she heard stopped her breathing and sent chills down her spine. A girl was crying and pleading "Please. Let me go. Don't hurt me."

"Look what I found, guys. It's party time!"

"Damn, Tank. You struck it rich. Where did you get her?"

"Hiding in that last house we touched."

"Take her to the master bedroom," a deep voice said.

Amiee felt a wave of fear and panic flood over her. Horrified, she listened as the men argued over who was to have the girl first. She could hear the group of them moving down the hall upstairs and into the master bedroom. The girl was crying and pleading to be left alone.

Amiee was afraid more than she had ever been in her life, and her adrenaline was so high she was shaking. She was torn by her desire to help the girl and the need to keep her children safe. She heard the sickening sound of a blow delivered to the girl, who screamed, and then there was a thud when something hit the floor.

The men were quieter now, and this was worse because Amiee could not tell what was happening.

Amiee was not one to use cursing, but it came out of her mouth now, in a whisper.

"Don't do anything foolish," Glennis said. "We're safe here."

"And what about that girl?" Amiee said a little too loud. Glennis didn't answer.

Amiee reopened the weapon box, pulled out her husband's 10 mm semi-automatic, and grabbed an extra magazine.

A five-shot 38 will not be enough to settle this problem.

She could see the terror on Glennis' face in the dim light of the shelter's nightlight as she held the 38 pistol out to her.

Glennis shook her head. "I don't want it. My father said never to get involved in these things. I don't think you should go out."

"You stay here," Amiee said, her whisper full of fear and anger. She thrust the gun at Glennis and whispered harshly, "Protect my children. Take it!"

Giving her the purpose of protecting the kids seemed to affect Glennis, and she hesitatingly took the small gun.

"I am terrified," Amiee said, "But I've got to go help that girl. I'll close the door and roll the China cabinet back. If they come down here and open it, you just point the gun at them and pull the trigger. Do you understand?"

Amiee could see that Glennis was petrified, but she couldn't wait any longer.

She said a silent prayer of protection for her sleeping kids, rocked the 10 mm's slide back to set a round in the firing chamber, and made sure the safety was off.

With her finger along the side of the weapon as she had learned at the shooting range, she opened the door quietly, slid the China cabinet aside, and stepped out into the dark basement. With her free hand she closed the shelter door and slid the China cabinet back in place, cringing at the crackle of broken glass it made as it moved. Avoiding the broken glass and plates as much as possible, she moved to the stairway and crept up.

On the way up, her mind was racing, and she was conflicted about what exactly to do, not wanting to hurt anyone. And yet these strangers had violated her home and were hurting some girl in her own bedroom! Their actions enraged her.

The climb up the stairs settled her a little and helped to clear her thinking. She remembered Ron talking to her about how to confront an attacker in their home.

"Don't talk to them," she remembered him saying. "They will just wheedle a way to get the weapon from you. Remember they are in the wrong, not you; it is your home."

She considered just driving them out of her house and freeing the girl, a thought she found attractive, but behind this thought lurked a subtle discomfort.

Will they just go away, or will they come back, maybe with guns?

She knew there could be no peace after simply chasing the men away. With no police around and the men knowing where the girl was, she was certain they would be back.

So she resolved to do what she and her husband had talked about if Amiee ever had to defend their home from evil men when he was away. Ron's words, and his vivid imagery, came back. "Shoot to kill, two or three rounds in the center of the chest, fast, and with no conversation that could allow them to exploit you, gentle Amiee. In that situation you need to be a tiger, not a lamb, or they will kill you and roast you for their dinner."

"Gentle Amiee," he called me.

Amiee felt anything but gentle now. She could hear the girl crying and two men, obviously enjoying the activity, encouraging their brother on.

Reaching the top of the stairs, with her heart pounding and her face flushed, she took a deep breath and tried to consciously relax, and then carefully looked both ways before entering the hallway.

As she walked quietly down the carpeted hallway, she could see the bedroom door slightly open.

They have flashlights.

Now she could clearly hear the assault in progress. That sound, and the crying of the girl, and the blows whenever the girl resisted, removed all hesitation from Amiee. Hot anger took over and she moved as a machine to the door, snapped the pistol's flashlight on, and burst in.

The first thing she saw was one man at the head of the girl, holding her arms down. A second man was sitting on one of her legs, and the third guy was leaning over her. They all turned to look at Amiee in complete surprise.

Stance, sight, squeeze!

Boom! Boom! went the sidearm, and the man holding the girl's arms recoiled back against the wall behind him and slumped toward the floor.

As she moved the gun to the second man, his hand pulled a pistol from his belt.

Center of the chest, sight, squeeze!

Amiee pulled the trigger three times. Boom! Boom! Boom! Her ears were ringing, and the man, with a shocked look on his face, was falling backward toward the bloody drapes behind him. He fired once and she felt the air move as his shot passed by her right ear.

The third man was totally compromised, with no weapon and his pants down. He just had time to stand up and began to plead. There was no authority in Mr. deep-voice's words now. He was saying "Don't shoot; this is a big mistake, lady."

Don't talk to him! Center of chest, hold breath, squeeze. Boom! Boom!

Another may be in the house.

"How many were there in all?" Amiee shouted fiercely at the girl through clenched teeth.

"Only three," the girl said. "Thank God you came."

Amiee put her fingers to her lips to signal silence as she briefly checked each of the three men. They were all dead.

"Damn fine shooting," she said to herself to calm herself down. She was vaguely aware that she was still shouting.

Ron would be proud of me.

She got control of her voice. "Find your clothes and put them on. I have to check the house."

Ten-shot magazine. Only three rounds left.

Not knowing what else might happen, she popped the partially empty magazine out, pocketed it, and slapped in the spare magazine.

Warily, she walked through the dark house, all the while wishing her ears weren't ringing. She was having trouble hearing. As she started back to the bedroom, the girl came around the corner and startled her. Her hands were still holding the weapon in the combat stance she had learned at the range, and she was beginning to shake. She lowered the weapon to her side and began to breathe.

The girl came forward and they embraced. The girl cried in her arms and Amiee's shaking hands became a violent trembling over her whole frame.

"My God, my God, my God," she said amid tears. "I just killed three people."

Amiee was thankful that the girl became her comforter.

"It's okay, Mrs. Moller. It's really okay. You did the right thing. I am soooo glad you did what you did."

"I've got to sit down," Amiee said, and they walked to the living room

As Amiee sat down, the girl looked out the front window.

"There's their truck."

Amiee looked out the window.

"I didn't see anyone in it when they brought me in," she added. When she looked at Amiee, she said, "What's wrong."

Amiee was trembling and was leaning forward on the couch. "Oh my God. Oh my God," was all she could say.

The girl walked over, sat down, and hugged her again. "I am so glad you came to my rescue, Mrs. Moller. You did the right thing."

Both cried for a while, until finally Amiee said, "Just look at us. We are a mess," and then added, "How do you know me?"

"Mrs. Moller. I'm Becka. Don't you remember me?"

This set Amiee back, and she stopped wiping her eyes with a piece of tissue and looked at the girl's face. "Becka? Annette's Becka?"

"That's me," the girl said.

"I thought you were off at college," Amiee said.

"I was. My roommate dropped me off about 6:30 last night. She took off before I knew my folks were gone and the power was off. My cell phone is dead, so I just went to bed, expecting my folks to come home. Next thing I knew, one of those guys was in the house, pulling me out of bed."

"Oh, then you don't know about the radiation, and I forgot about it. We need to go downstairs."

"Radiation?" Becka said as they got up and started for the stairs.

"Yorksberg got bombed and this whole area is radioactive," she explained as they descended the basement stairs. "That's why your folks are gone."

"Bad luck. Rapists and radiation the same night," Becka said.

"Sit down over there." Amiee pointed toward a chair. "Excuse the broken glass. One of those idiots did that just for the fun of it."

"What are you going to do?" Becka said.

"I am going to have to survey you to see how much radioactive material got on you."

Amiee called out to Glennis and then rolled the China cabinet back and went in through the door behind it. She came out a moment later with the radiation instrument in one hand. She was still carrying the pistol in the other, and was followed by Glennis, also armed.

"Glennis, this is Becka, a neighbor."

She switched on the instrument, which buzzed angrily, adjusted the switch on the front, and moved the instrument across Becka.

"Well, best I can tell, your shoes are the only really radioactive part of you. Just leave them just outside the shelter door and come on in. Lots less radiation inside. We will be leaving in the morning. You better come with us. It's not healthy staying here.

"Yah, no kidding," Becka said.

"And no flushing toilets," Amiee added. "Dear God we could use a little flushing water and electricity."

At that moment the staircase light came on and Amiee heard the basement freezer kick on.

Becka looked at Amiee with amazement in her voice. "What are you, an angel or something?" she said with a smile. "How did you work that?"

"Wait a minute," Glennis said; "what happened to the thieves?"

"They are dead. I think you have a story to tell to your father now."

Mark's sleepy voice came from the back of the shelter. "Mom, was someone popping firecrackers? They woke me up."

Amiee smiled. "No, honey, go back to sleep. That was just the sound of the Second Amendment."

"The second what?" Glennis said.

At that moment Amiee's cell phone began ringing. Her heart leapt when she saw Ron's number displayed.

Analysis of Chapter 21

Any terrorist nuclear attack will affect people beyond the city limits. The impact on people living a long way from the attacked city depends on many variables. The actions those affected people will have to take to protect themselves and their families are therefore not exactly predictable; however, a general case can be made for what might be seen and what protective actions have to be taken.

What are some of the variables that affect people a long way from the terrorist's attack?

1. Energy yield of the bomb. If it is bigger in energy output, then more radioactive materials will be lofted and radioactive fallout downwind will increase.

2. Wind direction. The dust in the mushroom cloud will drift with the wind, and as it moves, tiny particles will rain out of it. The larger, heavier particles will fall first; the smaller, lighter particles will drift farther way before being deposited on the ground.

3. Wind speed. The longer the radioactive dust remains high in the air, the less radioactivity will be available to be deposited on any given site downwind. Also, a fast-moving cloud will leave less material on the ground under it as it passes over. In contrast, consider that if the wind speed was zero at all altitudes (not likely), then all the radioactive dust would settle back down on the city where the bomb was exploded.

4. Precipitation. Rain cleans the air, so if the radioactive dust cloud gets entrained in some thunderstorms that are producing rain, some of the radioactive materials may be washed down to the ground.[62]

---

[62] Note that in this case, the moving rainwater on the ground may wash streets and roof tops clean. This will concentrate the radioactive particles and may result in localized areas of extremely radioactive deposits, such as in roof gutters, street gutters, sewers, and anywhere else the contaminated water tends to pool.

5.   Ground or air explosion. A ground-level explosion produces more radioactive materials.

It is possible that you might have to evacuate your home for years, while another family that lives ten miles away may not have to leave at all. It all depends on the wind and the amount of radioactivity that falls where you live.

The amount of ground-level radiation that was written into this story was selected to be significant. You need to realize that even if the radiation dose rate is small at remote locations, the authorities may order an evacuation as a precaution. We wanted our sweet, gentle protagonist Amiee to have to make a choice. To complicate her choice, we gave her children, a husband away, a house guest, and a well-built and stocked shelter.

You will probably miss hearing about a nuclear attack only if you are where you cannot hear TV or radio, and if the cellular phone system no longer works. This is what happened to Amiee. She is far enough away that there is no visible light, no heat, no blast wave, or seismic wave effects to inform her that an unusual event has happened. Her first clue is the loss of electric power. This event, which affected her cellular service too, further isolated her from receiving the news. With a bit of luck, she lives far enough from Yorksberg that she learns about the explosion before the radiation arrived. It is possible that the radiation might start falling in your area before you learn about the explosion.

Amiee learned about the attack from the automatic phone message from the power company. They called it a "general emergency" to distinguish the problem from the more common local power interruptions due to lightning or equipment failure.

Local radio stations might be off the air too, and that is why Ron stored a shortwave radio in the cave. Shortwave radio signals travel a long way, especially at night. Using the radio, she was able to find a station that was transmitting.

Across the country, certain stations are designated emergency stations and are given a frequency that is their own, so that no other stations can interfere with them. These stations usually have emergency power generators and will likely be on the air. So you can only blame yourself if you do not hear of an attack.

Phone distribution centers have battery power supplies as well as generators, so your standard, wired phone will almost always be powered and able to make calls.

Amiee's choice to stay in their home shelter was not a good decision. Why? Because she had time to drive out of the area before the radiation arrived. She later realized she could have limited her kids' exposure to the radiation to zero had she left the area. Remember that the younger the person, the more sensitive to the effects of radiation they are.

Another flaw in her plan was the possibility of a car breakdown stranding them as they drove out of the radiation zone. Consider what might have happened to them in that case.

A shelter is good for situations where one does not have time to leave, such as if a dirty bomb is set off nearby, to hide in during a hurricane or a tornado, or if there is a general nuclear attack where many cities are hit and radiation is widespread.

Very few people build shelters into their homes when they build their houses. You will see tornado shelters in the tornado-prone Midwest states, but not much elsewhere. Here is what Ron did.

1. When the basement of the house was laid out, he included an extension of the basement, which was not under the roof of the house. He did this because he could cover it with dirt, which is a much better shield than the structure of the house. Basically it was a room added to the basement that stuck out into the yard. He provided for proper drainage around it so that water intrusion would not be a problem, and he used concrete and steel rebar to create a 10"-thick, poured-concrete roof, which was sealed to prevent water from entering. A layer of earth three feet thick was placed over this reinforced concrete, leaving a bump in the backyard that the kids played on. This provided a 46-inch barrier to radiation for the occupants of the shelter.

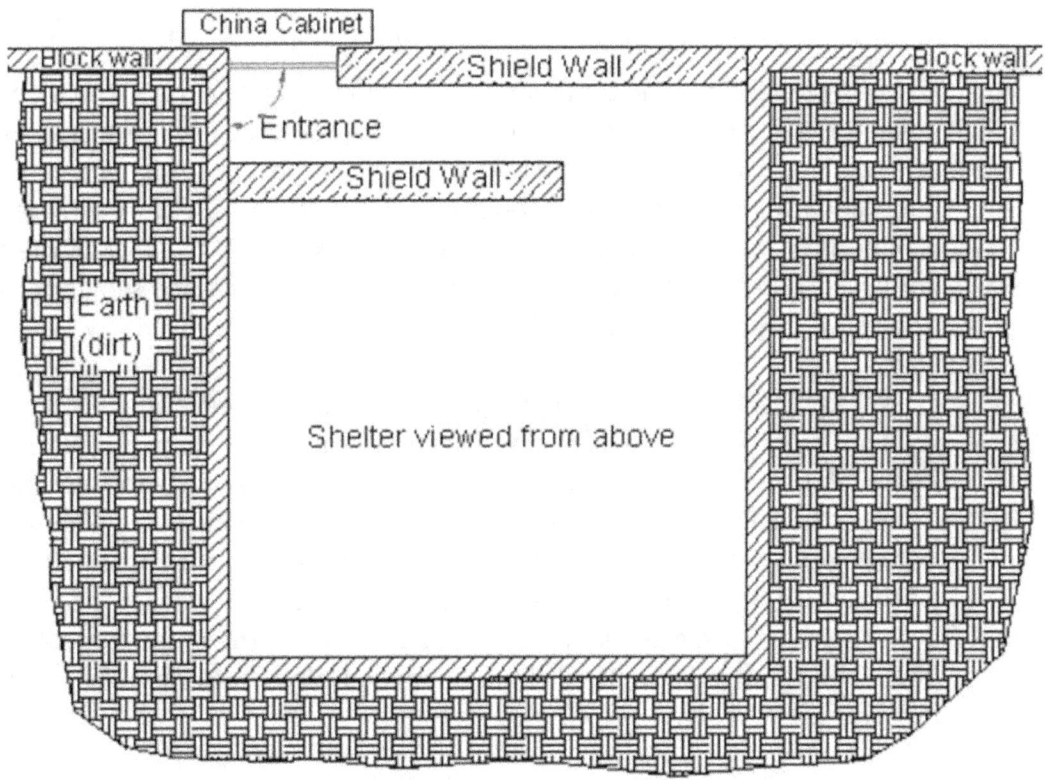

Amiee's Cave – The Shelter's Design

Ron chose to make the three outside walls of his shelter standard basement walls. There is no need to strengthen them as he did the roof and the entrance wall since there is no way for radioactive materials to get near them. The entrance wall, however, faces the interior of the basement where radiation dose rates may be significant, so he made that out of poured concrete because it is thicker and heavier than block.

He also poured another wall just inside the shelter entrance to create a barrier between the shelter occupants and radiation that might stream directly in from the basement through the relatively thin shelter door.

2. Ron and Amiee stored food and water in the shelter, books to read, and games for the kids to play.

3. A battery lighting system was installed, with an exterior solar panel to recharge the batteries.

4. A ventilation system was installed during the construction of the home. This included a small fan and a filter box. The filter box must be located outside the shelter because it will become highly radioactive as it removes contamination from the air.

5. Somewhere in the shelter there will be a small privacy curtain and a portable toilet for taking care of restroom needs. If the measured dose rates are small, those sheltering may elect to accept a few minutes of exposure to higher radiation dose rates and use the home's bathrooms. Flushing water can be stored in the bathtub and flushing can be accomplished by using a bucket to fill the back of the commode for flushing, or by simply pouring the water into the commode's lower bowl. Water should be conserved by not flushing after each use of the toilet.

6. Will a portable radio work underground in such a shelter? The answer is yes. It may not work well at the back of the shelter far from the door, but will pick up reasonably strong signals when near the door. To compensate for the shelter's radio signal attenuation, Ron installed a 20-foot-long piece of insulated copper wire when the shelter was built. It runs from the shelter up through the roof and up to the eve of the house. This is more than sufficient to bring in even weaker radio stations.

Note that Amiee did not store the batteries in the radio. It is better to keep them out of the radio or flashlight until needed, since batteries have a tendency to discharge or leak if not used for a long time.

7. The "bunks" in their shelter all look like army cots that simply hang flat against the walls until needed. When needed, the top portion is released from attachments to the wall and the "cot" rotates into the horizontal position. They are arranged one above the other, providing for efficient space utilization.

We can take a lesson about human nature from the events surrounding the hurricane Katrina aftermath in New Orleans, when the rule of law breaks down. There will always be those who choose to take advantage of others during times of crisis. Following a nuclear terror strike there will certainly be areas that are evacuated within which the fallout radiation dose rates are not high enough to scare off thieves and looters. Radioactive fallout provides the perfect situation: no people and no police! The only complication is that some of the merchandise may literally be "hot."[63]

Amiee undoubtedly would have let the three men abscond with her TVs, computer, and other valuables. None of those possessions are worth exposing herself and her children to the likes of such men. It is their choice to harm a neighbor's girl that drives Amiee into the risky behavior of intervening.

Could a petit, gentle homemaker successfully confront three adult men as presented in our story? The answer is yes. It happens all the time. The media tends to censor such news because of their prejudices against gun ownership, but the presence of a weapon in the hands of the intended victim often drives away those with bad intent. Most of the time, no shots have to be fired.[64]

Ron and Amiee took our forefathers' gift, the Second Amendment, seriously. They purchased weapons, learned to handle them safely, and to use them correctly within the law. Amiee was no novice. Surely some who read this will say she should have confronted these men, rescued the girl, and either called the police or let the men go. They need to remember it is not healthy to go outside and the robbers had chosen to take some radiation damage in order to gain financial advantage. The police would most likely not respond to such a call because they would have been ordered out of the fallout zones for their own safety.

Amiee is intelligent enough to know she cannot just save the girl and let the men go. For one thing, they will know both she and the girl have seen their faces and this meeting will be reported to the police. Amiee knows rape is an act of violence and the men doing it enjoy the violence and the dominance over the woman. If she saves the girl, she gives the men two women to try to dominate and to violate. It will be taken as a challenge by the men and they may use every trick they know to win this contest.

In fact, the leader of this group was planning to kill Becka after the three men finished with her. He had decided to beat her to death (he enjoys this sort of action) and then dump her body in the woods. That he had done this before should speak to you about his character.

Amiee knows these men are wrong, that she has caught them in a violent felony, and that she can leave no place for discussion. So with confidence and some fear, she does the right thing, the hard thing, the act that saves the neighbor's girl, which eliminates any

---

[63] If, following an act of nuclear terrorism, you find a really good deal on the street, it would be wise to wave a radiation instrument over it once or twice. You might find the "steal of a deal" was stolen from a fallout area.

[64] Sometimes shots are appropriate. Recently in Orlando, Florida, a father and his teenage daughter were in a hotel room. There was a knock on the door and when the girl answered, two men forced their way in at gunpoint. Motel robberies are common, but when they saw the girl their plans changed. They made the father lie down on the bed and one of the men began dragging the girl into the bathroom. Unfortunately for the bad guys, the father always traveled with a 45-caliber semiautomatic hand gun for self-defense, which was under his pillow. He killed the man standing guard over him and wounded the other man. The girl was not harmed. This true story was the inspiration for Amiee's story.

future legal action against her, and totally removes the threat of the men returning later. She kills, but she does not murder.[65]

If you think this discussion seems out of place in this book, then that says you have never been in a situation where the constraint of law and order has been removed. You have not learned that civilization is just a veneer, and that some people are nothing but constrained animals. Remove the constraints of law and civility and these folks, like the robber-rapists in our story, will revert to their true character, to the detriment of their fellow citizens. Even the "Good Book" speaks of this. Consider this passage from Jeremiah 17 (KJV).

> [9]The heart is deceitful above all things, and desperately wicked: who can know it?

> [10]I the LORD search the heart, I try the reins, even to give every man according to his ways, and according to the fruit of his doings.

Was Amiee injured by the radiation when she rescued the girl? Remember that the dose rate was about 265 millirem per hour earlier in the evening. Since the fallout stopped after the cloud passed over, it is likely this was the highest dose rate Amiee's home would see. If the incident with the three men took a half an hour, she received about 130 millirem of radiation damage, a harmless amount.

Even Becka will not see any outward symptoms due to her low radiation exposure.

This story points out that a large area downwind of the bombed city will be affected by only small amounts of radioactivity. These will be pretty much harmless, but per government regulations people in these areas will have to leave. For how long depends on the radiation level as time passes. The hardships caused by these evacuations will be enormous, and will disrupt life and industry far and wide.

Assume the 265 millirem (mR) reading was the peak radiation dose rate seen at Amiee's home. That was 6 hours after the explosion. Apply the rule of seven, and you get the following exposure per day at Amiee's home as time passes.

Time after the bomb	Dose rate at Amiee's home in millirem (mR) per hour	Total exposure per day
6 hours	265.0	6360 mR per day

---

[65] Murder – killing with malice and forethought. You think about it, you plan to do it, your intent is full of hatred and the desire to destroy the other or to gain something you want, and then you take action to take a life.

Killing – You do not want to do it, you have no malice toward the other party, you do not plan or schedule it, but you take the life in an accident or in self-defense. Taking the life of someone who is threatening to do great bodily harm or murder you, or someone else, is clearly killing, not murder, and that is why the law will not punish you.

42 hours	26.5	636 mR per day
294 hours (12 days)	2.65	64 mR per day
Limit per nuclear worker per day	2.08	50 mR per day
2058 hours (85 days)	0.265	6.4 mR per day

From this we can see the Mollers will not be able to return to their home for at least 15 days. Other homes that receive a greater peak dose rate will have to remain vacant longer if cleanup is not performed.

This is simplified somewhat, since there will be other issues that must be accounted for; for example, radioactive materials may be concentrated by nature, such as roof contamination being washed into rain gutters, producing local "hot" spots, and the presence of certain radioactive materials that the human body naturally concentrates. Some of these issues may preclude the children returning for several years just to be safe with their long-term health.

Although survival is not an issue far from the bombed city, it is obvious that the bomb's impact is spread much wider than just the city attacked.

Ron had been calling ever since he heard about the attack on Yorksberg. He was frustrated by the fact the cell system was down, but kept trying. The power was out because the PPF, simultaneous with the Yorksberg bombing, blew up several power substations to try to increase the chaos and suffering. It was one of those substations that powered Amiee's home.

As the whim of the wind and weather would have it, there was little or no fallout at that substation and the power company was on it like a scalded dog. The workers moved in portable equipment they had set up ahead of time for hurricane repairs, and with a few linemen volunteering to take some exposure by driving into contaminated areas and opening disconnects and line fuses at strategic points in the power grid, they were able to reenergize a large portion of the state the PPF had darkened.

Amiee, Becka, and the children did drive away the next morning and within 30 miles of her house they were clear of any fallout from the Yorksberg explosion.

Police were notified about the killings, and after an investigation, no charges were filed.

Part of your being prepared for a nuclear terror attack in your city or nearby is for you to take a trip to the nearest gun range and talk with the nice people you will meet there. You will be surprised by what you find. There you can rent a weapon to try out, and take some classroom training that will help you be like Amiee; gentle as a lamb and as dangerous to evil men as a rattlesnake. That is a good description of the word "meek," and doesn't the "good book" say it is the meek who will inherit the earth?

Quiz on Chapter 21
(Answers are in Appendix A2)

1. Why will the criminal elements in our society try to take advantage of a nuclear attack?
2. What are some of the variables that affect how people a long distance from the terrorist's attack will be affected?
3. If you live a long distance downwind from a nuclear attack, should you evacuate?
4. Aren't guns dangerous to have around kids in the home?
5. True or False: Radiation instrumentation is not necessary if you live far from a large city.

In our next story we will look into the lives of some people hundreds of miles from Yorksberg, and delve into the idea of a prepared shelter. All this death and destruction can be depressing, so since these boys are pretty safe, we'll have a little fun with them. You'll find that although they try really hard, these guys don't always seem to see clearly, so we call this story "Through a Glass Darkly."

The Sun Penetrates the Radioactive-Fallout Plume Miles from Yorksberg.[66]

22 - Luther Rheems – Through a Glass Darkly (250 miles)

Luther "Bug" Rheems sauntered up to his cherry-red Kawasaki Ninja motorcycle and rolled onto it with all the suave he could muster, thinking of himself as the cool rebel Wyatt in the movie "Easy Rider." He almost laid his bike over on its side when he sat down and had to fight it back to an upright position.

---

[66] Photo by V Blanchette

"Hooeee! I do believe you have had one too many, old Bug-a-roo!" said Clancy from his perch on his dusty-blue bike, churning out the deep, rich thrum-thrum-thrum only a Harley can make.

"Stuff it, you knothead," Bug shot back in his West Virginia drawl. He looked sideways at the bar's front window to see if Candy had seen his goof. As far as he could see, she had not been looking, and knowing this made him feel better.

He could see the bar's name, Shady Place, arching over the entrance, and every time he saw it he wondered what idiot gave it that name. There were no trees and no shade.

"That Candy, she sure keeps the bar full of old coots!"

"She sure keeps you coming back. Kept us both here for two hours and we got nowhere but a little buzzed by the establishment's fine fluids, ol' boy."

"You ain't got no argument there," Bug said, and he fired up his Ninja and sat listening to its sweet purr. He liked the Ninja, but really wanted a Harley like Clancy's.

That part-time job at the mill just don't pay enough.

He glanced at his watch.

"What time is it?" Clancy said.

"Fifteen after two," Bug said.

"You ready yet, cowboy? Or you want to sit and think about you-know-who some more?" Clancy said, still grinning.

"You sure have a mouth on you this fine afternoon. You took a few peeks yourself." Bug spit a used slug of Redman onto the parking lot gravel.

"That I did. Come on, partner. Let's find Scat. I'll bet you a one-eyed pirate he is over at the Drop In. See if you can catch me."

Bug watched Clancy pour petrol into his hog's mighty throat with a twist of his wrist, and then smiled as it sang speed back to him. Bug envied Clancy as the big bike went up the road. He could feel the acceleration and power in the sound that echoed across the nearby timbered hills. The roar of the Harley came back as a faint high-pitched lingering crash from the thick pine woods on either side of the road and up the mountain. He didn't try to catch Clancy. He just soaked up the sound.

A few minutes later Bug had the Ninja at 45 mph with the wind roaring past his head.

Damn that hurts my ears.

He wished he had worn his helmet, as the December air rapidly numbed his face. He caught a glimpse of Clancy's tail light several times and knew the kid was holding back and letting him catch up.

Pulling up beside Clancy's roaring machine, he grinned. Clancy grinned back and pointed at his own helmet and then at Bug, shaking his head. Bug passed back a bird and they both laughed. Such freedom!

They drove up to the Dew Drop Inn, another familiar rural watering hole he knew had a juke and a big-screen TV, but usually no young women. It would be warm inside, though, and that seemed to matter the most right now.

Sure enough, as they slowed to turn in, Bug could see Scat's battered old Ford F150 parked nose-to-the-road amid a few other cars. Bug liked Scat's predictability.

After their engines were shut off, Clancy said, "Why does that Scat always back in?"

"Scat always parks for the fast getaway," Bug said, warming his ears with his hands.

"Getaway from what?" Clancy said.

"He told me one time it's in case he kills the leader of a biker gang in a bar fight, or the communists come, or bird flu breaks out at the back of the bar. That's it; that's why he always puts his tailgate toward the establishment."

"Bird flu," Clancy said with a disgusted tone. "That boy's got bird flu of the brain."

They leaned their bikes over onto their kickstands, dismounted, and strode into the Dew. Sure enough if Scat wasn't at the pool table with Sharky. For Bug, the sound of Alabama's famous down-home guitar riff flowing from the juke and the sibilant-rich clack of ivory balls gave this place a real "homey" feeling.

"Wull, look what the cat drugged in," Scat said with a grin, laying on the hillbilly. "Dang, Bug, you look like wind-burn hell."

"He was thinking of Candy and forgot his helmet," Clancy said before Bug could respond.

"You're the one with lollypop on your mind," Bug said. "I'll bet you'll marry that gal someday."

"Them's fightin' words," Clancy said. "Keep that up and I will have to get Bubba to easy rider your butt."

Bug grinned. He knew "Bubba" as their boogie man, used as a threat in jest with each other.

"Hey you two. Pipe down. Al-Qaeda's done gone and got Yorksberg." It was old-lady Joan, the barkeep. She pointed at the television mounted above the bottles where those at the bar could drink and look.

"Unplug that juke for me," she yelled at no one in particular.

For ten minutes they sat transfixed, watching the news come in. The announcer's voice was calm and professional. "A nuclear bomb has gone off in Yorksberg at 2:30 this afternoon. Civil authorities are preparing to evacuate whole cities downwind." When they showed a film of the explosion shot from a helicopter, Bug looked over at Scat.

"It's finally happening, Scat, my buddy," he said with excitement in his voice. They both jumped up and ran outside to look south, followed by Clancy and half the bar's patrons. Sure enough, Bug could see a strange cloud above the horizon.

"Kinda looks like a big forest fire," Scat said with solemnness in his voice.

Bug had to agree. It looked black with tinges of gray against the late afternoon sky.

"Looks like it's coming our way," Scat said somberly.

"I always thought your survivalist crap was just crap," Clancy confessed.

Bug stood a little taller. "Well now you'll see. We're prepared, aren't we, boys?"

"You bet," said Scat, a gleam in his eye.

"Okay, you guys know the drill. Go get all your weapons and get 'em up to my shelter; only leave that dang 50 caliber at home, Scat. We don't have no room for that."

"What's the deal, Bug? You know you ain't got anything to equal it. That 30-06 pea shooter you call a rifle ain't worth nothing when the bad boys come. How are you going to penetrate an inch-and-a-half steel plate without my 50?"

"Scat, someday that thing's gonna kill you," Clancy interjected. "Besides, the only inch-and-a-half steel plate around here is in your ball-cap-covered head."

"You say what?" Scat shot back a little heated. Bug knew Scat did not like folks referring to the metal in his head, the result of a teenage motorcycle-riding stunt with no helmet.

"All right. All right," Bug said. "Bring the 50, but leave it in your truck. You can set it up when you hear Al-Qaeda's boys coming in their armored vehicles. Clancy, you fill the water containers and get them to Scat's shelter. I'll take care of the generator. Oh, and don't forget to fill your trucks. Gasoline's gonna be scarce I imagine."

"Ain't we forgetting something?" Clancy said.

"Candy?" Scat said.

"No, you moron. A woman in our shelter would be a disaster. We'd kill each other fighting over her. I'm speaking about the beer."

"Clancy's right," Bug said. "The little ice maker is already up there. I'll bring my small TV. Clancy, you bring the beer. Let's all assemble at Scat's. He's closer and we can put the food in his truck."

"Sure won't need any refrigeration for the steaks today." Clancy said, commenting on the air temperature while putting on his helmet.

"Okay survivors, let's move out. And don't let anyone know where you're going. We don't want no one crowding in."

"Keep your cells on, boys," Clancy said as he fired up his hog.

By the time he and Clancy turned off County Road 117 onto what barely passed as a dirt road it was already getting dark. Bug followed the familiar road's gentle meander a half mile uphill into the woods to a two-acre plot owned by his uncle Henry. He stopped on the top of the last hill and looked down on the small earthen shelter standing in a cleared area.

"Why did your uncle Henry give you this shelter?" Clancy shouted over the bike's engine.

"Uncle Henry was a survivalist himself, like us," Bug said with respect for his uncle's memory. "He prepared for this day for many years, 'being ready for the reds' he used to say. He exercised, got his blackbelt in Ki-fondue, bought gold and silver, and stored ammo and lots of survival food in his basement, but danged if the communists never got him. It was emphysema." He saw Clancy give him an odd look.

"You mean smoking killed him?" Clancy said.

"It's true," Bug said. "Cross my heart."

"I'll be damned," Clancy said while thinking of the pack of cancer sticks in his shirt pocket.

Bug led Clancy down into the hillside clearing and came to a dusty stop. Stepping off the bike, Bug felt the weight of his pistol on his right thigh. *A nice feeling carrying the weapon low and strapped down in special-forces fashion.*

Glancing at Clancy he couldn't see his carry, but knew he had his weapon in his belt under his shirt. "To surprise Al-Qaeda's boys," he had heard Clancy say.

"Ain't been up here in a spell," Clancy commented when the bikes were silent. "I see you got the roof done."

Bug admired his work: an earthen berm with a door and small window mounted in a heavy wood frame.

"Yep. Me and the bobcat put four feet of dirt on top. Took a couple of hours and made my lake bigger."

Clancy looked across to the lake. "Ain't no lake there." He pointed to a dry scraped section of a small swale about 100 feet from the berm shelter.

"Well, I didn't bobcat the dam yet. It will catch water someday. You'll see," Bug said.

Bug strode over to the berm shelter and fished out a key from the jangle hanging from his belt. He worked on the lock a bit.

"Durn thing is rusted shut," he said. He whacked the lock a few times and tried the key again. After fiddling with it awhile he stepped back.

"Now that just beats all. We spend all that time building this place and the blasted lock gets itself all rusted up."

"Shoot the sucker off," Clancy suggested with a mean tone in his voice.

Bug looked at him. "That only works in movies. The ricochet would probably kill you and I'd go to jail."

"Let me try." Clancy grabbed the keys. Bug felt himself dragged back to the door by the cable attached to the retractor on his belt.

After trying a bit, Clancy said with disgust, "That ain't the right key."

"What?" Bug said.

"Look, that's a Yomokito lock. You're trying to open it with a Shinloc key. Them are two different companies even if you can buy both their locks at Wally World."

In the fading light Bug found the Yomokito key and the lock snapped open.

Clancy opened the door and walked into the dark shelter. Bug pulled his made-in-China 21 LED flashlight out of its belt holster, snapped it on, and followed Clancy in. He played the light around the room, finding it just as he had left it. There were four bunk beds at the back, shelves scantily stocked with canned goods, two good chairs and a broken one, and a small cupboard. The walls were built log cabin style and the ceiling consisted of large timber laid horizontal and covered with earth. The place smelled damp and musty.

"Not bad," Clancy said appreciatively, pulling one of the chairs back from the table.

"Look out, a snake!" Bug yelled pointing the flashlight in his left hand below the table and quick drawing his 9 mm with his right. He filled the tiny cabin with the raucous noise of five quick shots from his weapon. "Boom, Boom, Boom... Boom, Boom." Not sure where the snake had gone, Bug ran out the door, leaving Clancy in the dark.

"God Almighty!" Clancy said out of the dark hole. "Are you crazy? You dang near killed me. Put that light back in here. I want to know where that snake went!"

His 9 mm cocked and ready with eight more rounds, Bug shined the light into the shelter as he approached the door. He found Clancy crouching on top of the table. Bug played the light across the floor.

"Well, I'll be jiggered," he finally said, "That ain't a snake." He leaned over and looked closer under the table with Clancy still perched on top.

"Sorry, buddy. It just a piece of rope we must have dropped last time we were up here."

Clancy got down off the table and recovered his ball cap. It had a bullet hole in the bill. "You dang near shot me in the head!" he said. "Look what a ricochet did." He held the cap up. "I never thought I'd lose my life over some stupid piece of rope."

Suddenly Bug heard a loud "Whumph" sound outside, the kind of sound he knew gasoline makes when it's ignited. He ran out with Clancy close behind to find his bike enveloped in flames. The bike's gas tank sported a neat 9 mm bullet hole, dead center.

"My bike!" Bug wailed as if his child had just died. He waved the gun around and yelled, "Do something!" As the fire got the tank hotter, the gasoline inside began spraying out through the hole, expanding the fire.

Clancy ran to his bike and with sheer brute strength rolled it away from Bug's cherry red inferno.

"Not that!" Bug screamed, almost incoherent. "Put the fire out!"

"Put the fire out?" Clancy said. "We ain't got no water."

Bug laid his still-cocked weapon on the ground and began scooping up hands full of dirt and throwing it, rather ineffectually, at the fire.

A half hour later he and Clancy were picking through the still-smoldering medical kit and supplies he had packed in his bike's pouches when Scat drove up in his pickup.

Scat walked up and said "Enemy contact?"

Bug said nothing. He had been thinking of the payments he would still have to make for this blackened skeleton of a bike.

"We had a little accident," Clancy said.

Bug, pining over his loss, watched Scat and Clancy unload a lantern and the TV from the truck, and set them up in the shelter. Then they began setting up the generator. When Scat asked Bug for the extension cord, he just silently pointed to twenty feet of charred copper wire still coiled on his blackened bike.

"No point in starting the generator, Scat said.

Sleeping bags, blankets, pillows, and beer were unloaded, and Bug thought these items gave the tiny shelter a warm, homey feeling. His friends coaxed him from pining over his ruined bike by popping a cold one for him. It took two beers before Bug felt as if he'd come back to life.

"You fellows just sit and relax," Scat said. "I got some more stuff to get. We can get the rest in the morning."

Bug saw him come back a few minutes later carrying an armload. He had a box of cereal, two cans of pork-n-beans, a shortwave radio, a yellow radiation survey instrument, and a pump shotgun. As he entered the shelter's dim light he suddenly flung everything but the gun to the floor and yelled, "Look out; there's a snake!" and swung the shotgun toward the floor.

"No!" yelled Clancy, jumping up and holding both his hands in the universal sign for "stop."

"It's just a rope!" Bug yelled simultaneously. The rest of what he said was lost in the loud, blasting roar of the shotgun. Ricocheting lead shot sprayed the whole inside of the cabin, several pieces stinging Bug's backside as Scat got off two quick shots.

"Dang it, Scat, you knothead! That's a piece of rope!" Clancy said. Yawning, Bug tried to stop the ringing in his ears, thinking the air in the shelter was now thicker with gun smoke than the OK Corral at noon.

"Rope?" a pleased-with-himself Scat said, picking up a very dead two-and-one-half-foot long timber rattler. "This rascal must have come in the open door while you boys rested."

"I gotta get me some air," Bug said, a shade paler, and walked out into the night. He heard the boys comment after him.

"What's eaten him?" Scat said.

"Long story," Clancy said. "And don't ask."

There was a single loud "boom" of a 9 mm outside the shelter and both men froze. Clancy looked at Scat and said, "My God, Bug's gone and shot himself over that dang bike."

They rushed out and almost fell over Bug, who was on all fours crawling around in the dark.

"Bug, you okay?" Scat said.

"Stepped on my own gun," Bug said. "Dang near blew my left foot off. Help me find it. The recoil kinda scooted it somewhere."

Clancy went for the light, carefully looking around the shelter floor before entering, and back outside with the light he found Bug's weapon. It had chambered another round and was waiting for someone else to step on it. He popped the magazine out and ejected the chambered round. He then gave all three to Bug.

"Put that puppy to bed before it gets us all. I think you got a commie gun."

Bug's face reddened. "Commie gun! This is a genuine Charltain Heston piece. Can't you see his picture on the grip, you dimwit!" He held the gun out toward Clancy.

"Calm down, friend," Clancy said. "I was just trying to be funny, and that's Charlton Heston, not Charltain Heston."

Bug looked at the inscription on his weapon and whispered reverently, "from my cold dead hands."

They reentered the shelter and turned on the shortwave radio to listen to the news. When the expert on the radio began to talk about fallout, Scat picked up the radiation instrument and dusted it off.

"Science teacher Johnson gave this to me in junior high," he said proudly. "It works too."

"What does it do?" Bug said.

"This here is a Geiger counter. You know, one of those things that prospectors carry to find uranium. It can detect radiation." He switched it on and out of a small speaker came a stream of tiny clicks.

"Is it counting?" Clancy inquired.

"Yep," Scat said. "Each click is a particle of radiation passing through this wand." He disconnected a silver metal tube from a clip and waved it around. The counter went "click, click click, click, click."

Bug appeared alarmed. "You mean there is radiation in here?"

"Not to worry, Bug-o-buddy, Scat said. "It clicks like that in Mr. Johnson's classroom too and it clicks like that at my place. Johnson called that natural background radiation. It is harmless. It comes from the sun and the rocks and the birds."

"The sun's done set and I don't hear any birds," Clancy said.

"Be calm," Scat said. "This amount of radiation won't hurt you. Mr. Johnson said so."

Putting two and two together, Clancy said, "So, if that Yorksberg fallout gets here it should click more. Right?"

"That's what I think" Scat said. "Let's check outside."

No sooner were they outside than the counter's little clicks sped up into a constant buzz. "Holy crap. It's already here!" Bug said in fear, and all three ran back into the shelter.

"Keep this door closed," Bug added, tearing a couple of paper towels off a roll and stuffing them in the bullet hole in one of the door's window panes.

"We better stay inside," Scat added. "I don't want my flesh rotting off me, especially while I'm still alive."

"Now how do you know it does that?" Bug said.

"Saw it in a movie about nuclear war that Mr. Johnson showed. It's really gruesome what that stuff does to you. Your skin turns yellow and starts to melt off. Kinda like what paint remover does to paint... you know, bubble and drip."

"My God! How does it do that?" Bug said.

"You know what else it does?" Clancy said. "I saw one of those documentaries and they were talking about mutations. In the forest near that Russian nuke that blew up, those poor people over there were seeing all kinds of hideous things coming out of the woods."

Scat eyes widened. "Mutants. I've heard of them. What were they like?"

"I don't want to know," Bug said. He thought about putting his hands over his ears.

Clancy loved telling horror stories. "They were hideous things, you know, like deer with two heads, and there was this shapeless sort of thing that engulfed this farmer's wife. It ate her! I mean just dissolved her screaming body until all that was left was bones."

"Could that happen here?" Scat said.

Bug cautiously looked out the window.

"I don't know," Clancy said, "but the worst of all was the mutant squirrels. My God them little buggers were fast, and there were a lot of them, and they could eat into anywhere with these huge, glowing teeth."

"I don't see nothing yet. Let's listen to the radio," Bug said to change the subject, and turned it on before Clancy could tell them any more about mutants.

After listening to the portable radio for a half hour, Bug suggested the best thing to do was to turn in and then check the radiation in the morning. So they rolled out the sleeping bags on the racks.

After about ten minutes of rest in the dark, Bug heard Clancy swear and jump out of his rack. A small flashlight came on and Bug rolled over to see Clancy whacking his bed frame with one of his boots.

"What the hell are you doing?" Scat said.

Bug, groping for his pistol in the dark, said, "Is it a mutant squirrel?"

"Dang nest of spiders. They was crawling all over me," Clancy said and continued to whack in the dark. Finally he must have gotten them all because he shut off the light, got back in his sleeping bag, and shelter was quiet once again.

The next morning Bug woke to find Scat cursing by the window.

"What's the problem, partner?" Bug said sleepily.

"I found out where that gun of yours shot when you went and stepped on it. My right front tire is flatter than a pancake."

"You're kidding," Bug said, as he rose and walked to the door.

Sure enough, the truck had a pronounced flat tilt.

"Dang, Bug. That piece of yours has wiped out two of our three vehicles," Clancy said, eyeing his bike.

"What's done is done," Bug offered philosophically. "Let me stir up some breakfast for you boys. You check the radiation." He proceeded to fire up the stove.

The little radiation instrument set up a buzz that was angrier than it had been the night before just as soon as the Geiger tube was stuck out the door. Scat whisked it back into the shelter and closed the door.

"I hope you guys don't mind cold food. We forgot to turn the propane on," Bug said. "The propane tank is outside."

"We ain't gonna get any breakfast?" Scat said with disdain. Then when realization hit, he yelled, "You blockheads left the food and water in the back of my truck!"

Bug and Clancy ran to the door and looked. Sure enough, they could see a tarp still stretched over the pickup's bed.

"It's your truck," Clancy said. "You never unloaded it."

"My truck!" Scat yelled. "If you two hadn't been shooting at that vicious piece of rope we wouldn't be in this predicament!"

"Don't yell at me!" Clancy yelled back. "All I did was run for cover. I dang near got killed by John Bug Wayne here!" He pointed at Bug.

"You two squirrels calm down," Bug said. "This is my shelter and if you'd rather leave, be my guest." He made a sweeping ceremonious gesture with an upward-turned palm swung gracefully toward the door.

Clancy and Scat looked at the door and calmed down.

"Okay, okay," Scat reasoned. "Somehow we have got to get that food."

"We can't eat it if we get it," Clancy argued. "By now it has been gotten by that radiation. I sure don't want that stuff inside me!'

"Clancy's right," Bug said. "Everything out there is radioactive by now. Even the water."

Mentioning the water made them all thirsty, so they sat down and finished off the six warm beers that remained.

A few minutes later Scat spoke up. "We got another problem, boys. There ain't no bathroom in here."

"It's been two days," Bug said, "And we haven't had drink or food and the inside of this shelter smells like a dang porta-potty. We got to figure something out."

"No need," said Scat at his perch by the door. Come here, quick." Scat licked his cracked lips. "It's Bear in his patrol car... and you will not guess who he has with him." They rushed the door and peered out the tiny window.

Bug couldn't believe it. County Deputy "Bear" Severnson was pulling up to a stop in his patrol car with Candy in the passenger seat. They both got out.

"Looks like a war been going on here," Bear said to Candy, cocking his trooper hat back on his head.

"That's Bug's bike, or was," Candy said. She was decked out in a ponytail, tight blue jeans, and a red and black checkered, flannel, lumberjack's shirt that could not hide her gender. She spotted the three men looking out the shelter's window and walked up to it.

"Come on out," Bear said, sensing something wrong.

The door came open and Scat yelled. "Get in here quick before you get too much of that radioactivity."

"What radioactivity?" Candy said, and then said, "Puweee! Did one of you boys dump a load in your britches?" She wrinkled up her nose and backed away.

"You three really make a pair," Deputy Severnson said, shaking his head and grinning from ear to ear.

"What's he mean by that, Bug?" Clancy said.

"I think we done been insulted," Bug replied.

Analysis of Chapter 22

The author hopes a little humor amid such a difficult subject will not be seen as offensive. The intent in this scenario is to make the point that areas not directly under the path of the mushroom cloud may also see a small rise in radioactivity. In this case we see three common folk... well, sort of common folk, caught up in an event about which they have little understanding.

These three have an overblown sense of their ability to survive major disasters, but do not have the requisite knowledge to pull it off well. They are like many of us. We don't store food for emergencies because there has always been food available at the nearest store. We don't fill storage tanks or bottles with clean water because clean water has always been available. The medical clinic is just down the street so we keep the minimum amount of adhesive bandages, sunburn spray, and antibiotic ointment somewhere in the house. The phones always work so we don't bother to get a radio license or purchase extra communication equipment. Unless we live in hurricane alley, we probably don't have portable generators. Who needs it? Electricity is always available. So somewhere in the back of our minds we think we are prepared enough. Nothing could be further from the truth.

We have to give Bug credit for his shelter. He built it well and had read enough civil defense literature to adequately bury it to shield its occupants from radiation. Three feet of earth on heavy logs or concrete provide pretty good radiation reduction. There are several nuances that Bug missed, however, so let's look at a shelter you might expect to stay in for several days to ride out a radioactive fallout event. Here are some of the necessities of that shelter. We will list them and then discuss each of them.

1.   Shielding
2.   Folded entrance
3.   Space
4.   Ventilation
5.   Sanitary facilities
6.   Light
7.   Radio
8.   Mind stuff
9.   First-aid kit
10.   Food and water
11.   Air
12.   Contamination control

1. Shielding

One of the three factors in radiation protection is shielding.[67] The denser a material is, the better it stops gamma rays. Just as a piece of tin will stop a BB but not stop a high-powered rifle bullet, a brick wall will stop some gamma rays, but a three-foot-thick wall of earth will stop most gamma rays.

Bug built his shelter of wooden logs and earth. With the walls and ceiling at least three feet thick, his shelter can adequately protect him from dangerous radiation. His problem is he did not cover the front, as well. He left the front made only of wood to accommodate a door and window. He should have used the folded entrance design (see the shelter design graphic on the next page).

2. Folded Entrance

Remember that nuclear radiation travels in a straight line once it leaves the radioactive material. Bug's shelter's design allows radiation from in front of the shelter to come right in through the relatively thin front wall, window, and door, with little reduction.

A good shelter entrance will permit easy access but will not allow radiation an easy line-of-sight path to the people inside. Consider the two simple sketches below. On the left is a poor design. Radioactive fallout at position "A" can easily

---

[67] The other two are time of exposure and distance from the radioactive sources.

irradiate someone in the shelter at position "B." On the right is a folded entrance design. Radiation coming from "A" cannot reach "B" without passing through shielding, which reduces its intensity.

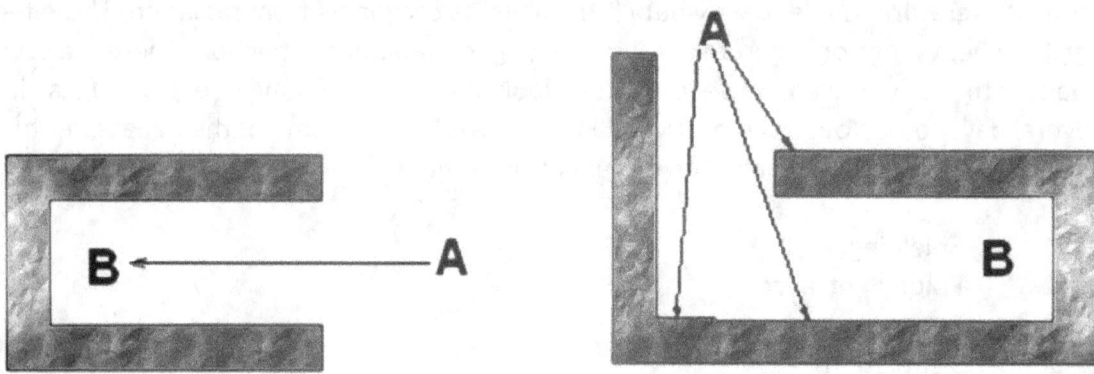

Simple Shelter Details

The folded design at the right assumes the entire entrance is covered with a barrier so that no radioactive material can blow in.

3. Space

When designing a shelter space, consider how many people will occupy the space. If the shelter is for one, the time of stay is short (a day or two), and comfort is not an issue, the shelter can be very simple. Something like a concrete pipe buried under three feet of earth might do.

It is more likely that several folks will be in the shelter. Thus there will be a need for restroom privacy (minimal – like a curtain), food preparation and storage, sleeping accommodations, and a place to pass the time (books, games, cards, etc.) waiting for outside radiation levels to decrease.

Ingenuity can lead to clever ways to use space so that less square footage is needed. Rather than beds or cots on the floor, for example, cots can be secured horizontally on the walls, one above the other. These can be folded up against the walls when no one is using them. Likewise, chair seats arranged along a wall, so they can fold up, will allow seating for several and can be quickly gotten out of the way. Use your imagination, or better yet, don't reinvent the wheel. Go to your public library or internet and see what has already been thought out.

4. Ventilation

You will want your shelter to be dust tight so that radioactive dust cannot filter in. At the same time, there should be provision for circulating fresh air in and old air out. There are several ways to do this. The most common is a simple hand crank blower (the folks in the shelter need something to do!) Fifteen minutes of cranking when the shelter gets stuffy will suffice. The blower should suck in fresh air from outside through a filter that remains outside the shelter. (Outside the shelter because radioactive dust will collect on the filter and it will become a concentrated source of radiation.) Exhausted air should travel out of the shelter through a pipe that is opened only when fresh air is being brought in by the crank blower. A pipe with a rag stuffed in it will do. When someone cranks in fresh air, the rag stopper is removed. When cranking stops, in goes the rag plug. Both the inlet and outlet air passage ways should be screened to prevent insect and small animal intrusion.

5. Sanitary facilities

Is there a chance someone might have to use the restroom while in the shelter? Plan on it. Provide a curtain around a small camping-type porta-potty and a cache of toilet paper. Smells can be controlled by having the ventilation exit pipe behind the curtain, and team members coordinating the use of the blower at appropriate times. You will need to dump the waste material outside from time to time. Short trips outside are generally not a danger to you even in strong radiation. But such trips should be short trips, and that also means those coming back into the shelter must not bring radioactive contamination with them (see item 10 in the coming pages). Keep in mind that not dumping this material outside generally will not kill anyone or even make them sick. The shelter is not supposed to be a five-star hotel.

6. Light

Bug's window was a bad idea. A couple of panes of window glass do not stop gamma rays. So your shelter will be very dark without some sort of interior lighting. You could wire it for utility power, but don't count on that power being available. Flashlight and battery-powered lanterns will do well, especially if you buy the LED type, which will make the batteries last longer. Rechargeable batteries with an external solar cell power supply are ideal, but a bit more expensive.

Plan ahead for the maximum length of time you expect to use the shelter, and remember that loss of light in the shelter will drive you outside.

7. Radio

How will you keep in touch with the outside world? Your cell phone will probably not work inside the shelter, which will shield the cell's radio transmissions to the local cell tower.

A land-line phone would be good since it may continue to work when the power is off.

A portable radio is a must, and for really nasty radiation problems (like general nuclear war) a shortwave radio might be needed. Like the cell phone, the radios may not work well in a buried shelter, but you can correct this by placing an antenna outside the shelter and running a shielded antenna wire inside to your radio.

Citizens Band radios will allow you two-way communications for some distance around you, and if you are in a city, the local emergency services personnel may also have CB radios.

Finally, store the batteries separate from the flashlights and radio. They will last longer this way, and if they leak, as batteries sometimes do, they will not ruin the device they are to be installed in.

8. First-aid kit

Plan for a simple first-aid kit in your shelter. You can buy a prepared kit at your local mart or pharmacy, or just throw one together yourself. Be prepared to treat cuts and abrasions, minor infections, fevers, headaches, etc.

If you live in a big city, and are sheltering after a nuclear terror attack, you might consider other kinds of medical supplies to treat more severe injuries you would want to stabilize prior to running for a safe hospital.

9. Food and water

Keep it simple, and consider how long a stay you want to plan for, and how many people will need to eat and drink.

Emergency food rations that do not require cooking are preferred. That reduces the garbage waste control problem and the need to cook and clean up. Remember that radiation cannot harm food and water in sealed containers. An open bag of cookies on the shelf could get contaminated. Keep it closed and the food will be okay to eat.

Clean water is more important than food. Be sure you store enough for human use and for decontamination (see 10).

A word of warning: Do not try to use charcoal, propane, or other fuels to cook inside the shelter. Bug had a propane tank outside his shelter, and a small stove inside. It is probably a good thing that, in their haste to escape the radiation, they forgot to turn on the supply valve at the tank. There are hidden, subtle dangers involved that could kill you while you try to stay safe from radiation. The carbon monoxide produced by the cooking flame is one of these.

10. Contamination control

The shelter protects its occupants from gamma rays emanating from the dust and dirt that falls near the shelter from the nuclear explosion. The shelter becomes less protective if you allow that dust and dirt to be tracked into it. You will be hiding inside right next to what you are trying to avoid, and the gamma rays from the dirt you bring into the shelter will get to you.

This means once the fallout from the bomb has landed outside the shelter, those who venture outside and come back in must be cleaned up before they reenter. If all they did was walk around outside, then it is likely that only their shoes are contaminated. If they touched anything or handled something outside, then their hands may carry the radioactive material. If they brushed up against something, like foliage or a fence, then their clothing may carry the radioactive dust.

How do you keep it out? There is a way that has been developed and used at nuclear power plants for years. It requires understanding the technique and self-discipline while performing it to make it effective.

Here is how it works. Place a bench seat across the shelter entrance so that it must be stepped over to enter. The floor outside the bench is considered radioactive. The floor inside is considered clean. No one ever steps over the bench.

<u>Coming in</u>, you enter by sitting down on the bench with your feet on the radioactive side (assuming your clothes are still clean). You remove your dirty shoes and leave them on the dirty floor. You do not touch the dirty floor with your feet, and you rotate your body on the seat to place your clean feet on the clean floor, put on clean shoes, and then stand up. All the radioactive contamination remains on your shoes (it won't hurt them) and you can walk around in the shelter.

<u>Going out</u> reverses the process. You sit on the boundary bench facing inward and remove your clean shoes, rotate to face outward and put on your dirty shoes. You may have to place one clean foot on top of the bench, but this is allowed.

If hands are contaminated, you will need to wash them with soap and water before removing your shoes at the bench. You'll have to figure out how to work that, but it can be as simple as a wash basin and a supply of soap and water near the entrance.

Contaminated clothing is a bit more complicated. At a nuclear plant, employees put on disposable paper shoe covers and a suit that completely covers their street clothing and enter the contaminated area. When they return to the bench, they peel off the paper suit from shoulders to shoes, sit on the bench, and then remove the rest of the paper suit and shoe covers before moving to the clean side of the bench.

You will not have the paper shoe covers and suit, so just do the best you can. Have a rack where clothing can be hung just outside the shelter and put contaminated clothing there. Just change clothing at the bench, both going in and coming out.

This all sounds like a hassle, and it is. In most cases you will not need to exit the shelter for the two or three days it takes for the radiation level to decrease to the point where you can leave and drive or walk out of the badly contaminated zone. But plan ahead; something may require an exit and reentering during your stay in the shelter.

Keep in mind that you cannot see, smell, touch, taste, or hear radiation, so there is some value in owning a portable radiation detection instrument.

11. Radiation instruments

These devices are simple to use and relatively inexpensive. You can easily find them on the internet. The trick is to buy the ones most effective for your use.

First, you need to decide if you want to monitor gamma radiation only, and if so, what ranges of radiation intensity you want to be able to watch for.

Second, you will have to decide if you want to be able to detect and locate beta and alpha ray emitters.[68] These generally will not hurt you unless they get inside you if you ingest contaminated food or water. You might be able to scan the food or water before you eat or drink it to assure yourself that it is not contaminated. Once inside you, the alpha and beta ray emitters will constantly irradiate the living tissue near them.

12. Mind stuff

You should plan on spending many hours in the shelter. A radio, games, and books can make the time pass quicker. Store these in the shelter ahead of time. That way you will not have to remember them, and they will be clean.   Don't count on electronic or cell phone games, as batteries will last only so long..

The kids will drive you crazy ("Can we go out now, Dad?") if you do not plan something to occupy those young minds. A small DVD player and lots of movies will help; just don't forget to provide lots of batteries or purchase a solar battery recharger.

Bug, Scat, and Clancy were written into this chapter for your entertainment, as well-meaning goofballs with guns. They are not NRA members and have not been trained in weapon safety.

You will have to decide whether you want a weapon in your shelter (read chapter 21 "Gentle as a Lamb" to get a sense of the value of a weapon in a shelter). This is a decision not to be taken lightly, because with that decision comes responsibilities and liabilities you need to be aware of.

If you decide you will have a weapon, then you have a responsibility to get training on firearm safety, to practice using your weapon, and to know the legal ramifications of the possession and use of a weapon.

Just having a shelter puts you in a sticky situation that you'd better think out ahead of time. How will you handle sharing your shelter with others who come to you after the attack and are fearful of the radiation that is coming? Are you thinking of having a weapon to keep people out? Would you use a weapon to stop people from coming into your shelter? Think this situation out ahead of time so you will not have to decide under a stressful survival situation.

One good way of working out what you would do is to consider the after effects. Suppose you have survived the terror attack and are now safe in a radiation-free zone, but you are in court being sued by the family of someone you kept out of your shelter, who died of radiation exposure. How will the judge or jury see your case? Or perhaps the lawyers are arguing that you shot and killed someone to keep him or her out of the safety of your shelter. How will the judge or jury see that?

---

[68] All radioactive materials are "emitters" because they "emit" radiation. Alpha and beta emitters emit alpha rays and beta rays. These will not hurt you if they stay outside your body. Read Appendix B1: "Radiation and Radioactivity" (in Part 1 of this handbook) for a complete description.

You want to make a decision you can defend, or won't have to defend, later. The author recommends you always choose to help people.

The rope being taken for a snake might be funny, but critters like snakes and spiders will take a liking to your shelter. Be aware of this hazard, and take precautions.

If there was radiation outside Bug's shelter, why did the Deputy and Candy drive around in it? The answer is the amount of radiation within twenty miles of Bug's shelter was only slightly above background, or natural, radiation levels. If a nuclear bomb is set off, it will cause some areas downwind to be highly radioactive, so dangerous that you can be made sick or die from exposure to the fallout. That said, the general background level of radiation for hundreds of miles around the attacked city, and downwind of that city, but not under the drifting mushroom cloud, will increase a little, but will be harmless. The Geiger counter Scat brought to the shelter is a very sensitive instrument. The fact that it clicked so fast it sounded like a buzz just means there were many atomic particles shooting through the detector. But this amount was not harmful.

Note that Scat had fallen prey to believing the Hollywood nuclear horror stories contain truth, and this clouded the thinking of everyone in Bug's shelter. He and the boys had several serious errors in their knowledge about radioactive materials and radiation. See if you believe any of the following nonsense:

1. They thought if the door was shut, radiation could not get in.
   Truth: Radiation flies through solid materials. Less gets through thicker and heavier materials. Radioactive dirt can get in wherever there is a hole or a crack. It can even be carried in on someone's shoe. Be careful to not confuse radiation and radioactive materials. A door with good seals can keep radioactive materials (like dust) out, but it cannot stop gamma radiation.

2. They were afraid radiation would melt their skin off.
   Truth: It doesn't do that. If it did, we would all be skinless since radiation from outer space pours out of the sky on us all day and all night.

3. They believed the food on the truck was ruined by the radiation and was probably radioactive itself.
   Truth: Their food was perfectly good. Alpha, beta, and gamma radiation does not make anything radioactive. But radioactive dirt can contaminate food and water if you let it. So keep your food and water sealed and clean.

4. They thought there is no difference between the amount of radiation and the presence of radiation.
   Truth: Radiation is everywhere and is always with us. The amount is important. The amount of radiation from the Yorksberg bomb outside Bug's shelter was harmless. There is radiation hitting you where you are even while you are reading

this book. Some of it is natural and some of it is in from nuclear testing. It is harmless.

5. They thought even short excursions from the shelter would doom them to some horrible consequence.
    Truth: You can go into intense radiation and not be significantly harmed if you keep the time short. Remember it is the total accumulated dose of radiation that is important. And remember that our bodies will heal themselves. If you get a little radiation damage, it will heal.

6. They believed the radiation would mutate some of the forest creatures, which would then try to harm them.
    Truth: Sorry, there are no mutant squirrels with glowing buckteeth. Radiation does not do that. Such nonsense should be reserved for old black-and-white sci-fi movies; however, beware of radioactive parasitic wasps with stingers that can inject radioactivity into you.[69] (Read the footnote at the bottom of this page.)

Quiz on Chapter 22
(Answers are in Appendix A2)

1. List as many aspects of a well-prepared shelter you can think of.
2. Why is a "folded entrance" to a shelter important?
3. If air is filtered for a shelter, why not put the filter inside the shelter where it can be changed without going outside?
4. What are some common misconceptions people have about radiation?
5. True or False: Small amounts of radiation will be detectable almost everywhere in the surrounding countryside after a nuclear attack on a nearby city.

---

[69] Hah! Gotcha! Radiation doesn't do that either. Radioactive parasitic wasps that inject radiation do not exist.

Wrap-up

If you have carefully read Part 1 and Part 2 of the *Nuclear Terror Survival Handbook*, you are now better prepared to survive a nuclear attack on your city.

Your best bet is to get away from the area until authorities determine it is safe for you to return. Leave everything. Just grab your emergency "go-pack" and leave. And remember it is dust and dirt that contain the radiation-emitting materials. Avoid breathing the dust, clean off the dust and dirt, wash and take care not to eat contaminated food, and keep your wounds as clean as possible, and you will do well. Work with others. We will all need each other in times like this.

Finally, your homework assignment is to...

1. Prepare a "bug-out kit," "go-pack," or "Get Out Of Dodge pack" for each member of your family. To start, find an army surplus store and buy a backpack for each family member (the kind where the weight of the backpack sits on your hips, not your shoulders). Take the backpacks home and pack them. (You can find lists of go-pack recommended contents on the internet.) Don't put this off. You may need it for more than just a nuclear attack. Remember that water is more important than food and that for a few bucks you can buy a hand-held water bottle that can filter ditch water and make it safe to drink.[70] Make sure there is one in each go-pack.

2. Work on your government officials to get prepared shelters set up in your city and to set emergency equipment out of nuclear harm's way.

3. Ask your local hospital's administrators whether they are prepared to accept patients from a nuclear attack. Can they perform decontamination and control radioactive materials from coming into their emergency room? Have your hospital administrators coordinated with other hospitals in the county or state in the case of a nuclear attack?

4. Get some good maps, and plot your escape from the city using back roads as much as possible. Don't forget to include all family members, because there is no telling where each person will be when the big boom comes.

5. Establish a distant point of contact (your sister in Kalamazoo, etc.) and give out that person's phone number so that those in your family who escape nuclear death can call from wherever they end up. That way you can know others in the family are alive and can make plans to bring the family back together.

---

[70] Search the internet for "survival water bottles," etc. Note that these bottles may not remove chemicals, so do not use water contaminated by oil, gasoline, antifreeze, or other dangerous chemical substances.

6.   Locate all the hospitals within 200 miles of your location. You will be surprised how easy this is using the internet. Google Maps is a good start. Enter "hospitals" in the search, and then pan around the state.   Print out and save this information, with routes to the hospitals, in your go-pack. Then if you are injured and have to leave your city to get help at a distant hospital you will know where to go.

7.   Consider that following a nuclear attack on your city the criminal element may go wild until order is reestablished. Police in some areas may be nonexistent. You have a responsibility to protect all family members from lawless thugs until authority returns. Buy and learn to handle a sidearm. Take an NRA firearm safety class. Your local gun shop or the NRA can help you. Obtain a carry permit so you can carry the weapon in your go-pack. Learn the laws pertaining to the handling, carrying, and use of weapons for self-defense. This use of a sidearm is one of the two reasons our nation's founders gave us the Second Amendment to the U.S. Constitution.[71]

8.   Learn how to pray. If the bad guys drop the big one on your city, you can't go wrong if the Lord can hear you and you can hear Him.

End
Part 2
The Nuclear Terror Survival Handbook

---

[71] Believe it or not, the second reason our forefathers gave us the Second Amendment is so the people can overthrow the federal government should it turn tyrannical. We are a nation born out of a revolution against a tyrannical government and our founders wanted to be sure we could do it again if necessary. We were formed to be a nation with a government ruled by the people (us), not a nation where government rules the people.

Appendix A2: Part 2 Answers to the Quizzes

Chapter 12

1. Yes, because the number of walking wounded will be enormous. In a city of 3 million people, there may be tens of thousands of burned and injured folks looking for a way out, looking for help. Many of these will die if help is not found within 24 hours. Many of these could be saved if those running our big cities would provide below-ground emergency shelters.

2. Yes, and so can their passengers. If you fly, stay away. Your aircraft does not have to fly through the mushroom cloud to become so contaminated the authorities will have to bury it. Remember also that hours after the explosion, the smoke of continuing fires will lift radioactive materials up into the air above and downwind of the city.

3. Local governments tend to place the high-reach hook-and-ladder trucks and main police stations downtown. This makes sense in terms of public service, but it can mean the loss of all high-reach equipment and loss of police central command if the terrorists explode the bomb downtown.

4. The wind gust (blast wave) from a 19-kt bomb at a distance of 1 mile is about 120 mph. That instant impulse is plenty strong to throw a man into a ditch.

5. His burns were from radiant heat from the white-hot rising mushroom cloud. Radiant heat is like the heat you feel near the stove and it is not nuclear radiation. It cannot make your burns radioactive. The answer is yes, however, because radioactive dust from the bomb's fallout eventually got into Lamar's damaged skin. Much of this was removed when his wounds were cleaned up.

Chapter 13

1. Yes, if they want to live. Nothing you have is worth getting sick from excessive radiation exposure. Note: Locking up before leaving would be proper if it can be done quickly, but in many cases the blast wave may have damaged the building such that it cannot be secured (broken windows, etc.).

2. That depends on timing. There will be a lot of confusion with many people seeking to leave the city right after the bomb goes off. The explosion in Yorksberg occurred at 2:30 p.m. Nick awoke and came out into the streets at about 5 p.m., near the end of daylight for a clear December day. In those few hours, word of the danger of radiation had spread via radio and police, and those who heard it left the city. The ones who did not leave are mostly inside. They would be sick and dying from excessive radiation exposure unless they were in a shelter with adequate shielding from radiation. So yes, it is plausible that our clueless, drunk Nick would find the streets mostly deserted.

3. The area of Yorksberg where Nick lived was directly downwind from the point of the explosion. Considerable radioactive fallout fell around Nick's neighborhood; the park with the restroom, the liquor store, the apartment where he found the baby, and even at the church where Rabbit was sitting. Nick basically wandered around in a death zone, accumulating more and more radiation damage to his body.

4. Unlikely, impaired by alcohol as he was. If he had left his boiler room and walked directly to the hospital he would have received a large dose of radiation damage, but might have survived depending on how quickly he traveled.

5. A go pack, sometimes referred to as a "Get Out Of Dodge Pack" (GOOD pack), is a backpack or suitcase prepared ahead of time for a quick escape from your home. It contains a collection of things you would take with you if you ever had to leave your home in such a hurry that you did not have time to pack. With radiation falling around you, you have zero time to pack, and you will be so rattled and scared you probably will not be able to think of everything you would really need to take. Plan your pack's contents ahead of time, pack it, and then grab the pack and run if a nuclear bomb is ever exploded in a city near you.

    Basics might include a change of clothes, including shoes; food for three days; a water-purifying bottle; sunscreen; a simple first-aid kit; medicines you need; and paperwork (passport, bank account numbers, house lot information if you're a home owner, photocopy of your driver's license, school records, marriage certificate, etc.) Search the internet for "go pack lists" to see lists others have assembled.

Chapter 14

1. There may be other answers, but these three stand out above the non-nuclear mass-casualty incidents:

    A. A huge influx of casualties that will quickly swamp the facility. Hospitals will need to have pre-arranged with local officials to set up triage stations in places with parking and a large habitation area, such as schools and gymnasiums.

    B. Extensive radioactive contamination on patients. Hospitals should have pre-arranged locations and facilities with showers/washing areas where a large number of casualties can be cleaned and the contaminated waste water controlled as much as possible.

    C. Thousands of contaminated vehicles transporting casualties to the hospital. A plan must be prepared ahead of time and coordinated with local police and fire to direct this contaminated traffic to a parking area away from people. If this is not done, you will have desperate people parking the radioactive vehicles along city streets, subjecting anyone who walks by them to high radiation.

2.	Newly arriving patients must be sent to hospitals in non-contaminated areas of the county and wholesale evacuation of in-house patients should be started immediately.

3.	Gamma and alpha/beta radiation survey instruments should be stored in the hospital.
	a.	Replace batteries periodically, and do not store them in the instruments.
	b.	Calibrate the instruments periodically per the manufacturer's recommendations.
	c.	Train the staff on the use of these instruments, and periodically put the staff through retraining.

4.	Work this out ahead of time. Talk this over with the staff. Workers will have families they need to help get to a safe location. This is not a time to be shorthanded because nobody thought about planning what to do.

5.	False, except for the presence of radioactive contamination. Expect cuts, contusions, broken bones, burns, etc., all injuries you have seen before but with the complication of possible radioactive contamination.

Chapter 15

1.	Education of the general public and intelligent placement of resources prior to the explosion. Well-equipped "shelters" means having supplies of drinking water, an air filtration system, food, sanitary facilities, medical supplies, and places for people to sleep, prearranged and sufficient for several days.

2.	True. Take, for example, a man who misses his airplane, only to learn later that it crashed.

3.	Yes, but less likely the deeper the line runs and the farther away from the point of explosion it is.

4.	It is possible. Consider a contaminated train running underground out to the suburbs, or the subway ventilation system pulling contaminated, dust-laden air down the tracks to the various exhaust ports miles away.

5.	Prepare local shelters throughout the city and educate the people so they know where they can shelter until radiation levels drop.

Chapter 16

1.	Yes, if they have not read this book. Many will be enjoying the excitement and will be taking pictures of the huge cloud and the ruined cityscape when they should be leaving to escape radiation exposure.

2.	Across our country our schools' teachers and staff are not trained to respond to a nearby nuclear attack. They do not have plans for evacuating the kids from the city, without parental permission, to unknown locations. Buses may not be at the school when evacuation is ordered. On top of this, there may be many casualties among the students and no doctors or ambulances available.

3.   Driving into the site of the explosion with her son, and then carrying contamination to a restaurant and to her sister's home. She had no right to risk her son's health, and could be charged with child endangerment. In her ignorance, her visit to the restaurant put that establishment out of business, and contaminated other families. She caused untold damage to her sister's home, which was not covered by insurance because the damage was due to radiation due to terrorist action.

4.   Primary fallout consists of larger particles that fall shortly after the explosion from the mushroom cloud within a mile or two of the point of the explosion. Secondary fallout is the smaller particles that fall far from the point of the explosion, sometimes many hours after the event.

5.   The zone of survivable destruction is an annulus-shaped area centered on the explosion point within which survivable injuries will occur when a nuclear weapon is exploded in a city. The size of the inner edge of this annulus (r) where a few people survive, and the outer edge of the ring (R) where everybody survives, depends upon the energy released by the weapon used.

        In a very large city there will be hundreds of thousands of survivors no matter how big the bomb is. In fact, because the area of an annulus increases as its diameters increase, a larger explosion can result in more survivors and more people needing medical care.

The area (A) of an annulus is given by $A = \pi(R^2 - r^2)$.

The shaded area (zone 2), the shape of an annulus, is the zone of survivable destruction. In this zone there will be much destruction, but surviving is possible. Almost everyone dies inside the white area (zone 1, radius r). Almost everyone survives outside the shaded area (zone 3, beyond radius R) because there is little destruction there.

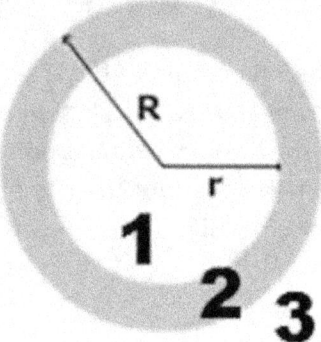

Chapter 17

1.   0.000006 seconds (6 millionths of a second).
2.   One hundredth of a second.
3.   They are not important to your survival, just interesting to some people.
4.   No, her skin and every part of her were instantly vaporized when the bomb exploded. She could not feel pain. Her molecular disassociation happened so

fast that nerve impulses could not reach her brain before her nerves and brain were gone.

5.   A huge amount of soft X-rays. The production of these soft X-rays is how the hot core of the early nuclear fireball radiates heat.

Chapter 18

1.   If your Emergency Operations Center (EOC) is located in the heart of the city, why? It will be rendered useless in the event the nuclear terrorists strike downtown. Think – if you were a terrorist, where would you put the bomb?

2.   No, as you see from Rob Oberfelt's story. The wind carried high radiation to the airport and the EOC staff had to run. Having a mobile EOC command center, or several EOC locations, is a wise choice.

3.   This should be done. The bad guy's bomb will likely take out anything downtown in the city, and they will probably shoot it off when the most folks can be affected. You may lose all your leadership in a white-hot instant just when you will need them the most.

4.   A. Contamination – most borrowed equipment will become so contaminated it will have to be disposed of when it is no longer needed in your city. This financial impact may inhibit willingness to supply emergency equipment.
B. Local Needs – surrounding areas will need to retain some equipment for their own use.
C. Distance – some equipment may take days or weeks to arrive.

5.   Yes. Remember that radiation is not being washed off. Radioactive materials such as dirt, dust, and sand are being washed off. They are radiation sources and when they are gone, the radiation dose rate coming from the mobile unit will be reduced. Remember also that running water may not be available unless you plan to make it happen.

Chapter 19

1.   Hard-line phones and the internet. It is possible cell phones may also continue to work, at least until your cell phone battery goes dead. This is why you should have a car adapter for your phone or a solar-cell charger.

2.   Here are four; you may think of more.

    a.   Damage and obstacles that may be in your way. As they slow you down, you get more radiation exposure.

    b.   You have no radiation instrumentation and may be going into a lethal field of radiation.

    c.   The person you are looking for may have already evacuated. It would be better to stay out and contact some distant, beforehand-agreed relative as an emergency contact point.

    d.   You could get trapped in the traffic trying to exit the city and be killed by radiation exposure.

3.   True. You may be bussing them to their deaths. Get out of the city crosswind or upwind of the path of the mushroom cloud and wait for the authorities to tell you it is safe to go home.

4.   You will have to decide this. If you stay to help, you both may live or you both may die. A radiation instrument would shed some light on this dilemma.

5.   False. A Geiger counter is a very sensitive device used to read tiny amounts of radiation, like when prospecting for uranium. It will be saturated (overwhelmed) by the radiation levels from an atomic bomb explosion and be useless.

Chapter 20

1.   About 40 seconds (5 seconds per mile X 8 miles)

2.   Yes. It is best not to look directly at an exploding nuclear bomb the instant it goes off, at any distance. The initial flash can hurt your eyes. Watching the rising mushroom cloud will not hurt your eyes unless you are so close you are exposed to intense heat from the glowing cloud.

3.   The blast wave moving across the surface of the water. You can't see the blast wave, but you can see its effect on the water's surface.

4.   If you are far from the city it is probably not necessary. It might be a conservative move to make until you know for sure your home is safe. It will take the authorities some time to map out the dangerous radiation zones. Keep in mind if you evacuate with little knowledge of fallout patterns, you may inadvertently travel out of one zone into a more dangerous radiation zone.

5.   That you can survive if you move fast and make the right choices.

Chapter 21

1.   Reasons include opportunity, few people to see them, willingness to risk their health and lives on a chance for a quick profit, and absence of the police from contaminated areas.

2.   A. Energy yield of the bomb – a larger explosion will loft more radioactive materials.
B. Bomb placement – an explosion high in the air will result in much less radioactive fallout.
C. Wind direction – the wind may blow fallout away from your home, or toward it.
D. Wind speed – if fallout is headed your way, a higher wind speed will bring it over you more quickly.
E. Precipitation – rain will tend to clean the air, but can create new hazards; for example, rain may wash fallout into ditches, your rain gutters, or storm drains, making these areas radioactive hazards.
F. Orders from authorities – pay attention to these folks. They should have radiation-measuring equipment that will help you know what to do.

3.   Follow the recommendations of state and federal authorities. If you have to leave and if you have time you might want to tape and seal all windows and doors so that radioactive dust entry into your home is minimized. The outside of the house can be washed when you return.

4.   They can be, but knives, rat poison, swimming pools, and plastic bags are dangerous to children too. With training of the kids and proper locked storage of the weapons, guns will be safer than the knives and poisons you now live with. Keep in mind that statistically an automobile probably has the greatest chance of causing your children injury or death.

5.   True. If you listen to what the experts say following the explosion, you will be okay. But if you choose to ride it out at home, the instruments would be a good idea. Remember that the fallout patterns can be unpredictable.

Chapter 22

1.   Here are some aspects of a well-prepared shelter:

    a.   Shielding.
    b.   Folded entrance.
    c.   Space enough.
    d.   Ventilation.
    e.   Sanitary facilities.
    f.   Lights.
    g.   Radio.
    h.   Mind stuff. Games, reading, art...
    i.   First-aid kit.
    j.   Food and water.
    k.   Air.
    l.   Contamination control.
    m.   Radiation instrumentation.

2.   Radiation flies in a straight line. By folding the entrance, people are placed out of line-of-sight of contamination outside the shelter. Radiation cannot go around corners to get to those who are sheltering. (Radioactive dust can go around corners.)

3.   The filter will catch and concentrate radioactive dust from the air. The filter element will become very radioactive, so you don't want it inside the shelter with you. The dirty filter is something to stay far away from.[72] If need be, you can run out and change the filter and not receive much radiation damage to your body. Just be quick about it and wear gloves if you have them (leave them outside).

---

[72] If you bring a Geiger counter near your furnace air filter you will see a rise in the radioactive count rate. This is because your filters are catching radioactive materials from nuclear testing that happened long ago. (These filters are not dangerous because the amount of radiation is so low. Just don't lick them.)

4. There are many misconceptions, but chief among them are…
   a. Radiation never goes away.
   b. Radiation causes huge outbreaks of cancer and mutations.
   c. If a door is shut, radiation can't get in.
   d. Radiation will melt your skin.
   e. Food is ruined by radiation passing through it.
   f. Any radiation is bad for you. This can be considered true, but small amounts of radiation won't generally be harmful.
5. True. Authorities will cordon off areas where there is a health risk. These areas may change in time, so keep current on where the seriously contaminated areas are.

A month <u>after</u> you survive the explosion, will you still be alive?

Appendix B2: What is an Explosion?

We have been describing the effects of nuclear explosions, but what exactly is an explosion?

An explosion is the result of a rapid release of energy. How rapid is rapid? A lit match is a release of energy. We sense the energy being released as heat and light and even the motion of the smoke and sparks. We might even hear sounds. The match is a good example because when it first ignites, a fuel on the tip is burned to get the wood or paper stem lit. This fuel burns fast enough to make a "shishing" sound you can hear, but once the wood in the match is burning steadily you hear nothing. This is because the slower release of energy in the lit match makes little noise.

In a real explosion there is a release of energy so fast that pressure is built up as the exploding material moves outward. This pressure build up creates a pressure wave in the air that expands outward from the origin of the explosion as a sound wave. Thus you hear the pop of a firecracker when the sound wave from the exploding gunpowder reaches your ear. On the 4th of July, when a big flash bomb firework goes off high overhead, you may even feel a thump on your clothing and body when its stronger sound wave reaches you. The sound wave is very strong at the point of the explosion, and decreases in intensity (strength) as the wave moves away from the point of the explosion.

Important concept: The air pressure wave created by an explosion decreases in strength as it moves away from the point of the explosion.

In Chapter 1, "How Close is Safe?" Mindy saw this fact demonstrated by the decrease in the damage done by the blast wave the farther away she moved from ground zero.

If we increase the amount of fuel (gunpowder, or in dynamite, nitroglycerin), then the pressure wave (sound wave) that comes from the explosion is even stronger. It can be strong enough to damage things; for example, you may have read or heard about a newspaper article about a child who lost a finger because he or she was holding a cherry bomb or an M80 firework in his or her hand when it exploded. The sound wave it emitted was intense enough to blow the child's hand apart.

So explosions can do damage, and that, in fact, makes them useful. Mountain sides can be moved, coal can be mined, and old buildings safely demolished, all using the power of the destructive force of explosives. Powerful explosives can even save lives, such as in times of war.[73]

---

[73] During the battle to capture Saddam Hussein's sons in Mosul Iraq in July 2003, the U.S. forces were reported to have entered the first floor of the villa. The occupants barricaded themselves on the second floor and the ensuing fight would have claimed many more American lives. So the troops withdrew and allowed a highly explosive missile (Tow missile) to be fired from an Apache helicopter to end the fight. For details Google "battle Saddam Hussein's sons" or see http://www.cnn.com/2003/WORLD/meast/07/22/sprj.irq.sons/ . The

In an automobile engine, the gasoline and air are mixed and compressed by the cylinders to cause a burn rate (explosion rate) that is slow enough that we cannot hear the explosion. Sometimes, however, if the fuel mixture is not quite right we will hear a tapping sound from the engine. We say the engine is knocking or pinging. Actually what we are hearing is the gasoline-air mixture burning too fast. It is exploding too rapidly and we are hearing the expanding hot gases in the cylinder slapping the cylinder walls. This is not good for the engine, but it is a good example of how the rate of release of energy affects what we hear.

Chemical Explosives

At the core of any explosion is the production of heat. Recall from your science class that heat in matter exists as the motion of the molecules or atoms in that material. The faster the atoms or molecules vibrate the higher the temperature. Cool down the material and the vibrations of the molecules decrease. To make a chemical explosion we need only to find a chemical that can quickly make the vibration of its atoms and molecules increase enormously.

How does a chemical change or chemical reaction cause heat? We can visualize this if we consider springs for a moment. You have seen springs, the little metal coils of wire, usually steel, that can be squeezed together to shorten their lengths, or stretched to make them longer. If you pick up a springs and pull it at each end, the spring will grow longer, but as it grows longer you will find it harder and harder to pull it farther. Why? Because the spring metal is storing the "pull apart" energy your hands have added to it when they stretched it. If you let go of one end, the spring will snap back into its original shape *giving up the energy your hands added to it.* You can tell the energy came out because the ends of the spring rapidly move toward each other and you can feel a solid "whap" on the hand still holding the spring.

The key point here is that the spring stored energy, and when it gave that energy back there was a shaking, a disturbance of both the spring and whatever was holding it (in this example, your hand).

Now put on your imagination again and look down into a highly explosive chemical material. We will go so far down into the material that we can actually see the individual molecules of the explosive. We can visualize each of these molecules as being shaped in such a way that they, like the spring, can be compressed and hold stored-up energy. If we can get all those little molecules to suddenly "snap" just like when we released one end of the spring, the resulting vibrational energy in the material caused by the "snap" will be huge. Remember that vibration of atoms and molecules in a material is the same thing as heat. So "snap" all these special molecules at the same time and the material is filled with heat. Its temperature actually rises from 70 degrees to 5,000 °C (9,000 °F)[74] in an instant

---

example of the use of two atomic bombs on Japan in World War II is also often cited as a case where hundreds of thousands of American lives were saved by using those explosions.

[74] *The Effects of Nuclear Weapons*, 1977, Samuel Glasstone and Philip J. Dolan, 2.03.

and you have an explosion when the explosive material becomes a white-hot gas and rapidly expands outward.

The above description is simple. Please understand there are not tiny metal springs in the molecules, but there is a "spring" of another sort. Scientists call it "chemical binding energy." The change in the binding energy when the molecules "snap" to a lower energy shape is a measure of the amount of stretch of these molecular "springs." The molecules have an attraction to each other that wants to tear them apart and recombine them into other molecules that have a lower binding energy. It is like letting a spring snap to a lower energy position, and when this happens in an explosion the molecules are torn apart and rearranged.

The molecules in explosive materials are stable, which means they do not "snap" to the lower energy state by themselves. There must be a trigger. In the next sections we will talk about two types of triggers.

1. Deflagration – Triggered by a spreading flame front.

The first type of trigger is a flame, or the leading edge of zone of burning material passing through a material rapidly, heating the material and triggering the molecules to come apart and recombine in a lower binding state. Exploding gasoline vapor is an example of an explosion caused by a spreading flame front. This kind of combustion driving an explosion is called a deflagration, which just means the burn proceeds through the material slower than the speed of sound. This limits the rate at which energy (heat) can be released and therefore limits the power of the explosion.

Gasoline burning normally in a car engine is undergoing deflagration. When the spark plug ignites the gasoline vapor in an engine's cylinder, the burning fuel ignites the vapor next to it, which ignites the vapor next to it, and so on. The place in the fuel air mixture where the burning occurs is called the flame front and can be visualized as a surface of rapid heat-releasing chemical reaction that moves through the fuel at a speed never faster than the speed of sound in that mixture. This is actually a slow process as far as nature is concerned, even though it occurs in the blink of an eye.

To see why this is "slow," suppose you created a ball of gasoline vapor in air two miles in diameter and then used a remote spark plug to light it in the center of the ball of vapor – that would be 1 mile from the outer edge of this ball of vapor. Sound travels about 1 mile in 5 seconds. So in our big ball of gasoline vapors it would take the burning vapor at the middle of this ball about 5 seconds to expand the flame front outward to the edge of the ball. That would be one huge "boom," but it is relatively slow when it comes to explosions. And you can see that to build up higher explosive pressures we would have to increase the amount of fuel or make it burn faster. Adding more fuel is clearly an impossible task if we want to use it in a controlled manner like for demolishing a building or breaking apart an iceberg. And we cannot easily make it burn faster. For more power and higher explosive pressures we need another method of triggering a material's molecules to suddenly "snap" like a spring and release energy.

2.   **Detonation – supersonic combustion.**

In certain chemical explosives, enough energy is released that the temperature rises so fast that the expansion it produces creates a high-pressure shockwave in the material. This shockwave actually sets off combustion in the adjacent material much faster than a speed-of-sound flame-front could. This is called a "detonation."   In this "detonation" the supersonic (above the speed of sound) shockwave travels through the explosive material, triggering it to release its energy, constantly reinforcing the shockwave. This results in a much faster reaction rate, higher temperatures, and more explosive force. This is the process used in industrial or military high explosives.

Summary: The chemical explosion

To summarize, a chemical explosion is the rapid release of heat and light caused by the change of the molecular state of a special material called an explosive. The more heat and the faster it is created the bigger the bang. The heated material expands outward, compressing the air around it, and creating a shockwave that travels outward at the speed of sound, about a mile every 5 seconds. This shockwave can be very destructive if it contains a large overpressure or it may just be sensed as "boom" noise if its overpressure is small. The farther from the source of the explosion the weaker the blast wave is. The byproducts of the explosion are small amounts of burnt material, often just carbon dioxide, nitrous oxides, water vapor, and the shattered pieces of the explosive container.

Appendix C2: The Anatomy of a Nuclear Explosion

In this appendix we will give a description of how the atomic bomb works. This information is available from any library in the United States and on many sites on the internet. We will describe it in general terms that ceased being a top secret long ago.

Bomb Basics

At the heart of an atomic bomb is an isotope of uranium that is fissionable. Fissionable means the nuclei in the atoms in this material can be split by impact with a neutron, and when the atoms are split, two or more neutrons are released. These new neutrons cause more atoms to split, releasing even more neutrons. This process is called a "chain reaction" because it progresses in a step-by-step, chain-like fashion. On the internet you can find several examples of this type of chain reaction.[75]

Chain Reaction

The "step-by-step" progress of this nuclear reaction is important to understanding how the fission proceeds. Assume for a moment that we have a special clock that ticks off tenths of a millisecond. Each tick is a very small amount of time. This clock divides a millionth of a second into ten parts and ticks for each of those tiny parts of a second. The atomic reaction starts when the first neutron hits a uranium atom, so that is when we start our special clock. Scientists call that the "first generation" of neutrons. The atom splits, releasing two or more neutrons, which each strike uranium atoms. That completes the second tick and the second generation. Ten ticks later only a millionth of a second has passed and ten generations of nuclear reactions have taken place. The number of neutrons released (which equals the number of atomic fissions if we assume none escape) grows something like this for the first ten generations.[76]

Generation	Time passed	Number of fissions
1	.0000001 of a second	3
2	.0000002 of a second	7
3	.0000003 of a second	20
4	.0000004 of a second	55
5	.0000005 of a second	149
6	.0000006 of a second	406
7	.0000007 of a second	1105
8	.0000008 of a second	3008

[75] To see a mousetrap and ping pong ball chain reaction, go to http://www.archive.org/details/The_Atom (A Disney movie). Google "nuclear chain reaction" and you can find many more examples.

[76] We are assuming two new neutrons are created for each fission. The actual number is larger, following the growth rule $N = N_0 10^{n/2.3}$ where N_0 is the initial number of neutrons and n is the generation. Reference http://undergroundbombshelter.com/radiation-fallout.htm.

| 9 | .0000009 of a second | 8185 |
| 10 | .0000010 of a second | 22275 |

Fission Energy Released

The energy released by each fission is tiny, so small in fact that it would take 70,000,000,000,000,000 fissions to light a 60-watt light bulb for one second. So how can an atomic bomb make such a big explosion? The answer lies in the huge number of atoms of uranium in the core of the bomb. If the core contains 25 lbs (11.34 kg of uranium) there would be approximately 2.86×10^{25} atoms available for fission.

The actual energy output from a nuclear bomb is so large it is usually spoken of in terms of the equivalent thousands of tons of TNT required to make that big of an explosion. Thus a 10-kt (kiloton) bomb produces the energy of 10,000 tons of TNT.

What is a Critical Mass?

Small amounts of uranium will not work as the core of an atomic bomb because most of the neutrons produced by splitting atoms escape out of the uranium and do not cause additional fissions. This is called a "subcritical" mass of uranium. If we increase the amount of uranium or compress it to pack the atoms closer together we can reach the point where exactly the same number of neutrons is created as are lost. This is called a critical mass. It might get warm or even melt if the reaction rate is high enough. If we put even more uranium together or compress it past the critical point we create a supercritical mass. You do not want to do this in your kitchen.

The Supercritical Mass

When the mass of uranium becomes supercritical, an amazing thing happens. More neutrons are produced (as each unit of time passes) and the number of neutrons grows unbounded. This means the reaction will grow without limit, as fast as nature allows, until something stops it. To see the amazing part of this, consider the following table[77] showing the increase in the number of fissions after one neutron is let loose in a supercritical piece of uranium.

---

[77] Some of you mathematical geniuses may question the accuracy of the numbers presented in this table. These numbers were derived largely from section 1 of Glasstone and Dolan's book, *The Effects of Nuclear Weapons*, using an Excel spreadsheet. We do not claim these numbers are extremely accurate but we have endeavored to use them to make the text interesting and to make a point: unbounded nuclear chain reactions are very fast.

TABLE OF FISSIONS AS TIME PASSES

Generation	Time (seconds)	Number of fissions	Number of fissions in scientific notation	Equivalent energy in kt of TNT
1	0.0000001	3	3.00E+00	
2	0.0000002	7	7.41E+00	
3	0.0000003	20	2.02E+01	
4	0.0000004	55	5.48E+01	
5	0.0000005	149	1.49E+02	
6	0.0000006	406	4.06E+02	
7	0.0000007	1105	1.11E+03	
8	0.0000008	3008	3.01E+03	
9	0.0000009	8185	8.19E+03	
10	0.0000010	22275	2.23E+04	
11	0.0000011	60619	6.06E+04	
12	0.0000012	164965	1.65E+05	
13	0.0000013	448925	4.49E+05	
14	0.0000014	1221677	1.22E+06	
15	0.0000015	3324598	3.32E+06	
16	0.0000016	9047357	9.05E+06	
17	0.0000017	24620924	2.46E+07	
18	0.0000018	67001875	6.70E+07	
19	0.0000019	182334800	1.82E+08	
20	0.0000020	496194760	4.96E+08	
21	0.0000021	1350314038	1.35E+09	
22	0.0000022	3674661941	3.67E+09	
23	0.0000023	10000000000	1.00E+10	
24	0.0000024	27213387684	2.72E+10	
25	0.0000025	74056846923	7.41E+10	
26	0.0000026	201533768594	2.02E+11	
27	0.0000027	548441657612	5.48E+11	BULB[78]
28	0.0000028	1492495545052	1.49E+12	
29	0.0000029	4061585988377	4.06E+12	
30	0.0000030	11052951411260	1.11E+13	
31	0.0000031	30078825180431	3.01E+13	
32	0.0000032	81854673070691	8.19E+13	
33	0.0000033	222754295199958	2.23E+14	
34	0.0000034	606189899349762	6.06E+14	
35	0.0000035	1649648074098030	1.65E+15	
36	0.0000036	4489251258218650	4.49E+15	
37	0.0000037	12216773489968000	1.22E+16	

[78] This number of fissions produces enough heat energy to light a 60-watt bulb.

38	0.0000038	33245979322709800	3.32E+16	
39	0.0000039	90473572423493900	9.05E+16	
40	0.0000040	246209240149464000	2.46E+17	
41	0.0000041	670018750350967000	6.70E+17	
42	0.0000042	1823348000868460000	1.82E+18	
43	0.0000043	4961947603002940000	4.96E+18	
44	0.0000044	13503140378698900000	1.35E+19	
45	0.0000045	36746619407367000000	3.67E+19	
46	0.0000046	100000000000000000000	1.00E+20	
47	0.0000047	272133876837532000000	2.72E+20	
48	0.0000048	740568469226246000000	7.41E+20	
49	0.0000049	2015337685941750000000	2.02E+21	
50	0.0000050	5484416576121050000000	5.48E+21	
51	0.0000051	14924955450518300000000	1.49E+22	0.1
52	0.0000052	40615859883770100000000	4.06E+22	
53	0.0000053	110529514112603000000000	1.11E+23	
54	0.0000054	300788251804313000000000	3.01E+23	
55	0.0000055	818546730706910000000000	8.19E+23	
56	0.0000056	2227542951999570000000000	2.23E+24	
57	0.0000057	6061898993497640000000000	6.06E+24	
58	0.0000058	16496480740980300000000000	1.65E+25	100
59	0.0000059	44892512582186700000000000	4.49E+25	
60	0.0000060	122167734899681000000000000	1.22E+26	

Notice in the above table, it takes 51 generations, or about 5.1 millionths of a second, to produce enough fissions to release 0.1 kt (or 100 tons) of TNT explosive power. But notice that 6 generations later, 100,000 tons of TNT-equivalent power has been released. It is amazing that most of the explosive power of an atomic bomb is released in the last 7 generations of the unbounded fission reaction, an extremely short time. Imagine a mountain of high explosives weighing 100,000 TONS compressed into a chunk of material the size of a softball and then have the whole heat-producing reaction over in 7 ten millionths of one second. The temperature produced in the core of the atomic bomb by this rapid release of energy is truly astounding.

This brings us to the question, what stops the chain reaction? After all, if the reaction proceeds without limits the power output should go up high enough to consume the whole earth. This idea occurred to some scientists who made and exploded the first bomb. They asked the question, would the bomb start a chain reaction in the earth and turn our planet into another star?

When they exploded the first bomb, they were really not concerned because they knew three things that would guarantee the reaction would not "run away" and destroy everything. First, they knew there are only three elements that fission. These are listed in the following table.

Fissionable Elements (special nuclear materials)

Uranium 235
Uranium 233
Plutonium 239

The silica and other minerals that make up the earth's surface and the steel and copper in the bomb's case are made of atoms that will not fission and release more neutrons. So the atomic explosion's energy source is limited to the bomb core material.

The second reason is there is a limited amount of uranium in the bomb. It would eventually get used up.

Third, and the most limiting reason the explosion cannot go on forever, has to do with the effect of heat on materials. Remember that only a supercritical piece of uranium can undergo a chain reaction and explode. As the fissions occur during the initiation of a nuclear explosion, heat is produced. Heated materials expand. So as the nuclear bomb's core heats up, it expands in size, moving the individual uranium atoms farther apart. This allows more neutrons to leak out without causing more fissions. As soon as the expansion is sufficient to make the fissionable material sub-critical the reaction rapidly stops.

Can you see that there is a little competition here? The bomb is making heat very quickly and the material is trying to blow apart from the high temperature being created inside the core. But to make a bigger "bang" the material has to stay together long enough for enough generations to pass. Thus one of the factors that determine the total "bang" from any particular atomic bomb is how long you can hold it together.

There have been "criticality accidents" at facilities and labs that handle these special nuclear materials. A "criticality accident" is when something goes wrong and fissionable material goes super-critical and the chain reaction begins. These accidents vividly demonstrate how sensitive the reactivity of the fissionable material is.

Most of these accidents involve the unexpected change in the geometry (shape) of a concentrated solution of uranium or plutonium from a sub-critical to a super-critical shape. Sometimes the accident is due to carelessness. The following story gives you an idea of how sensitive this issue of criticality is. Incidentally, the use of beryllium in this example is because beryllium acts as a neutron reflector. If beryllium is placed around a fissionable material, it reflects escaping neutrons back into the fissionable material effectively, increasing the material's reactivity.[79]

In May of 1946 a scientist was demonstrating how surrounding a fissionable material with beryllium could make the material more reactive. A sphere of fissionable material was sitting in a half sphere shell of beryllium while another half

---

[79] Reactivity is a mathematical expression of the criticality of a fissionable material. A reactivity less than 1 is sub-critical, a reactivity of 1 is critical, and a reactivity greater than 1 is super-critical.

sphere shell of beryllium was slowly lowered over the fissionable material. One-inch spacers that acted as a safety feature kept the upper beryllium half-sphere shell from getting too close to the fissionable material to keep it from reflecting too many neutrons back into the fissionable material. During the demonstration these safety spacers were removed to allow one edge of the upper beryllium half-sphere shell to rest on the edge of the lower beryllium half-sphere shell. The other edge of the upper beryllium piece was kept from dropping in place by the tip of a screwdriver. At some point in the demonstration the screwdriver slipped and the upper beryllium shell fell into position around the fissionable material. Instantly a "blue glow" was seen and a sensation of heat was perceived by personnel in the lab. The scientist doing the demonstration died several days later from the radiation he received, and several others received significant radiation exposure.

You can read more about these sorts of incidents by going to your favorite search engine and searching the three words "criticality safety incidents" or "demon core".

How the Bomb Works

You can see that all that is required to make a fissionable material explode is to change the shape or amount of the material until it becomes super-critical. The material spontaneously initiates a chain reaction within itself when this happens. Historically there have been two different approaches to making an atomic bomb: the gun-barrel bomb and the implosion bomb.

The gun-barrel bomb

In the gun-barrel design two sub-critical pieces of uranium are fashioned such that when they are brought together to make a sphere, the final shape is significantly super-critical. These two pieces are placed several feet apart in a steel tube (the "gun-barrel"). One piece cannot move and the other is free to slide down the tube to mate with the immobile part. Conventional high explosives are placed behind the movable piece. When the explosives are set off, the blast from the explosion drives the movable half of the fissionable material down the "gun barrel," ramming it into the stationary piece at high velocity, forming a super-critical hunk of uranium. In about 5.8 millionths of a second, the temperature in this fissionable material reaches approximately 10 million degrees and the reaction is stopped when the hot core material begins to fly apart.

The implosion bomb

When something blows apart outward we say it explodes. When something experiences a blast inward we call it an implosion. In the implosion bomb a piece of fissionable material, perhaps spherical in shape, is fashioned with a crushable filler material mixed with the fissionable material. This is surrounded with conventional high explosives that have multiple igniters. When all these igniters are set of simultaneously, the sphere is imploded or blown inward with tremendous pressure. This crushes the crushable filler and jams the non-critical uranium into a super-critical shape in a very short time. About 5.8 millionths of a second later... well, you know the rest of the story.

The Thermonuclear Bomb

There is a bomb much more powerful than a fission-type bomb; this is the fusion bomb, or as it is often called, the hydrogen or thermonuclear bomb. We will just mention it in passing because it is larger and more complicated than the fission bomb to the extent that your average run-of-the-mill terrorist wouldn't bother with it. In a fusion bomb the energy comes from the fusion, or the joining together of two heavy hydrogen atoms to form helium atoms. Each fusion releases much more energy than a fission; however, getting hydrogen to undergo fusion into helium is much more difficult to cause than simple fission. Basically one has to use atomic fission bombs to cause enough heat and pressure to initiate the fusion in hydrogen. The thermonuclear bomb yields megatons of TNT equivalent, some of the testing done in the South Pacific having been done at the 5 to 100 MT levels.

Appendix D2: Watch as a Nuclear Bomb Explodes

Okay, so from previous appendices you now know where a nuclear bomb gets its bang. What we would like to do now is to slow the explosion down and talk you through the whole process. Read on if interested.

We count down to zero and press the button. The high explosives in our bomb drive our fissionable material together, making it go super-critical. Almost instantly, in less than a tenth of a millisecond, enough fissions occur to liberate the equivalent of approximately 2 billion KWH of energy. The bomb's core, the fission material, the bomb's casing, and other parts are raised to temperatures similar to that found at the center of the sun (i.e., between 10 & 40 million degrees).[80] All the materials used in the bomb are vaporized into gaseous form at enormous pressure, perhaps as much as millions of pounds per square inch. This vaporization is due to the intense X-ray radiation coming out of the hot core even before the core expands. The bomb and core are so hot that the ionized atoms emit thermal energy as X-ray radiation. In fact, the X-rays are so intense, and because they are largely absorbed by air, the air within a few feet of the bomb is heated to incandescence (glowing a brilliant blue-white).

The Fireball
This "fireball" is spherical in shape, consisting of a hot mass of air surrounding the even hotter bomb residue inside, and is formed within less than a millionth of a second of the peak of the fusion power release. This is the early stage of the fireball. From 40 miles away this fireball will appear to be brighter than the noon-day sun, and at night it can be commonly seen at distances of more than 400 miles. Within a few miles of ground zero those looking directly at it when the bomb goes off will be permanently blinded before they can blink or avert their eyes. People within a few miles and not looking at ground zero may be temporarily flash blinded as the super-intense light saturates the light-detecting chemicals in their eyes. Think of the bright after image of a flash camera that you see for a minute or two after someone takes your photograph. Picture that effect spread over the whole eye and you get the idea. Those folks affected this way will find their vision slowly returning over the next few minutes.

---

[80] Conventional explosives produce temperatures of perhaps 5,000 °C or 9,000 °F.

Read only if you want deeper technical knowledge

> "Immediately after the explosion starts, the temperature of the weapon material is several tens of millions of degrees and the pressures are estimated to be many million atmospheres. As a result of numerous inelastic collisions, part of the kinetic energy of the fission fragments is converted into internal and radiation energy. Some of the electrons are removed entirely from the atoms, thus causing ionization; others are raised to higher energy (or excited) states while still remaining attached to the nuclei. Within an extremely short time, perhaps a hundredth of a microsecond or so, the weapon residues consist essentially of completely and partially stripped (ionized) atoms, many of the latter being in excited states, together with the corresponding free electrons. The system then immediately emits electromagnetic (thermal) radiation, the nature of which is determined by the temperature. Since this is of the order of several times 10^7 degrees, most of the energy emitted within a microsecond or so is in the soft X-ray region."[81]

The Transition to a Shockwave

The intense X-rays heat the surrounding few meters of air so hot they effectively ionize the air around the hot bomb material. Air at this temperature is opaque to light, so the light emitted by the vaporized bomb parts actually cannot get out. This X-ray heated air is heated so fast, within a microsecond, it literally begins to explode outward, initiating compression of the air around it and thus creating the beginning of the blast wave. The expanding hot gases from what was the bomb and its casing move outward at supersonic velocity and for a 20-kt weapon catch up to the sonic shockwave caused by the intense X-ray heating when the debris temperature drops to about 300,000 °C. This occurs when the fireball is about 12 meters (roughly 40 ft) in diameter about a tenth of millisecond after the bomb is set off.

---

[81] *The Effects of Nuclear Weapons*, Samuel Glasstone and Philip J. Dolan, United States Department of Defense, 1977, 2.107.

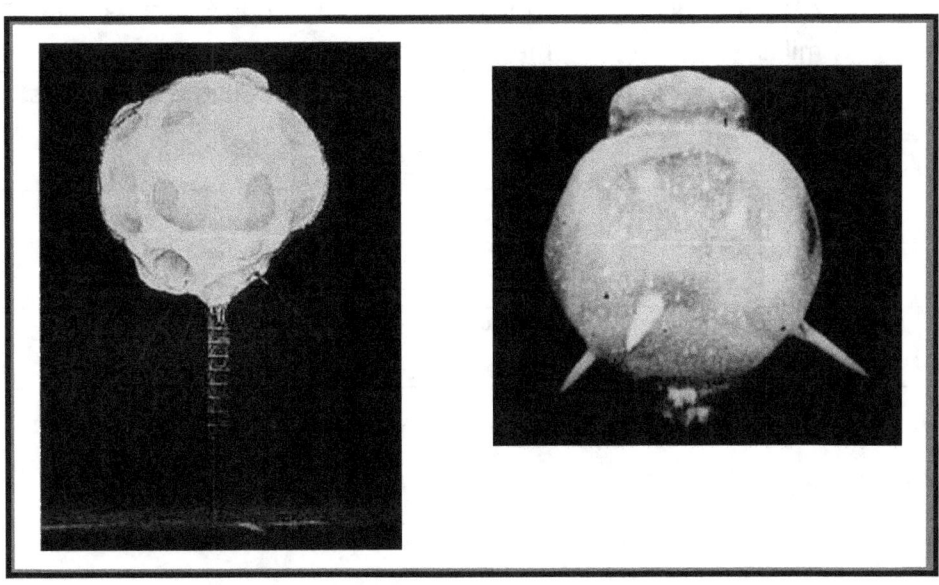

Rapatronic Photographs of Nuclear Fireballs[82]

These photos show two different fireballs photographed with a special device called a Rapatronic camera and capable of exposures as short as 10 billionths of a second. You are looking at the glowing sphere of air around the bomb explosion. Observers suggest the mottled appearance of this sphere is due to the hotter, higher-speed bomb debris catching up to the outer surface of the glowing sphere of air. Note that in one of the photos the intense invisible X-ray flux extends out beyond the fireball and has begun the vaporization of the metal guy wires that are (were) holding up the tower supporting the bomb. This produces the three spikes extending out of the fireball.

This fireball grows very rapidly due to the enormous pressure within. In .01 of a second the nuclear fireball is the size of a football field and slowing down. It begins rising and lifts smoke and debris into the classical shape of a mushroom cloud.

As the fireball expands, it compresses the air, creating the blast wave. As the blast wave moves outward, its strength (measured in overpressure) decreases as shown in the following table. Data represents an approximately 19-kiloton explosion.

Overpressure	19 kt		1 mt
10	2268 ft or .51 miles	813 meters	10000 ft or 1.89 miles
5	4003 ft or .76 miles	1220 meters	15000 ft or 2.84 miles

[82] National Archives and World War II historical archives. To see more of these fascinating photos use Goggle Images and search for "Rapatronic photographs".

4	4269 ft or .81 miles	1301 meters	16000 ft or 3.03 miles
3	5870 ft or 1.11 miles	1789 meters	22000 ft or 4.17 miles
2	6671 ft or 1.26 miles	2923 meters	25000 ft or 4.73 miles
1	10007 ft or 1.9 miles	3959 meters	37500 ft or 7.10 miles

Appendix E2: Nuclear Devices

How big is a nuclear bomb, and could someone really sneak one of these into a city? The original nuclear bombs were much too large for an individual to carry into a country in a suitcase. "Little Boy," the first bomb, weighed 9,000 lbs, and was dropped on Hiroshima.

Little Boy being loaded on B-29 in WWII[83]

"Fat Man," the second bomb, weighed 10,000 lbs and was dropped on Nagasaki. As nuclear weapons technology improved over the years it became possible to produce smaller devices.

---

[83] Little Boy and Fat Man bomb images courtesy of National Archives

"Fat Man" being prepared for delivery to Nagasaki, Japan, in World War II. [84]

In the United States these smaller devices were called Special Nuclear Demolition Munitions (SADM), which measured approximately two feet by two feet by three feet and weighed about 150 lbs.[85] These demolition munitions were apparently intended to be used to destroy bridgeheads, dams, factories, or ports during times of war. They were convenient ways to transport the equivalent destructive power of thousands of tons of TNT without having to actually transport that much explosive material. The media, and particularly the genre of cold war spy-thriller fiction, coined the phrase "suitcase nuke" for a nuclear device small enough for a man to carry.

You can search for "suitcase nuke" to chase this rabbit.[86]

Why Use a Nuclear Bomb?

The key word is terror. During 9/11, for example, a small group of men captured the media for months (arguably for years) simply by crashing jet aircraft into the New York City World Trade Center towers. Most people can still picture in their minds some of the images from that attack; hordes of dust-covered people retreating from the destruction, a weeping fireman holding the limp body of a small child, the dust-covered, blood-streaked, distraught

---

[84] Little Boy and Fat Man bomb images courtesy of National Archives – 31 declassified photos of the final preparations for atomic bombings on Hiroshima and Nagasaki.

[85] *Wall Street Journal* article, October 31, 2005, by Richard Miniter.

[86] Rabbit trails in the wild run everywhere. The phrase "chasing a rabbit" just means leaving this handbook and taking off into cyberspace after other information.

woman being comforted on the curb by two policemen, and the smashed fire and police vehicles amid the dust and destruction. The terror was evident. We all felt it.[87]

Ask yourself, what would have been different if the 9/11 terrorists had used a nuclear bomb at the World Trade Center instead of those airplanes? Here are just some of the differences:

- People as far away as New Jersey would have suffered eye injuries, including blindness, from the intense light given off at the moment of explosion.
- Many more buildings would have come down.
- The explosion would have started fires all over the city.
- The dust and smoke hazards would have been much larger.
- Many more people would have died, some as far away as two miles from the detonation point.
- The blast area would be contaminated with radioactive materials.
- Large areas of the city otherwise not affected by the explosion would have received a shower of radioactive fallout. Many of the people in these areas might have died over the following weeks.
- Much of the city would have to be evacuated, with the evacuees having the potential to spread the radioactivity.
- It is likely that no one would have been able to live in selected areas of the city for several years.

---

[87] Search for "9/11 attack." See http://www.washingtonpost.com/wp-srv/photo/attack/newyork/1.htm for example.

References

1.	*The Effects of Nuclear Weapons*, Samuel Glasstone and Philip J. Dolan, United States Department of Defense, 1977.

2.	*Hibakusha. Survivors of Hiroshima and Nagasaki.* Translated by Gaynor Sekimori. Kōsei Publishing Co., Tokyo.

3.	Jamestown Foundation Publication: *Terrorism Monitor,* Volume 2, Issue 6, March 24, 2004. By Scott Atran.

Disclaimer

This handbook, Part 1 and Part 2, examines the effects of a nuclear explosion in a fictional city called Yorksberg. The effects of the Yorksberg bomb have been carefully described to be as close as possible to effects seen in nuclear testing and in the two cities bombed to bring World War II to a conclusion.

The reader should remember there has never been a nuclear bomb set off at ground level in a metropolitan city where many very large structures will interfere with the propagation of both the thermal radiation and the blast wave. *The effects of the nuclear explosion woven into the fictional short stories and factual analyses in this handbook may be either less severe or more severe than the effects of an actual weapon used in a real city.*

The terrorist organization we have chosen to call the PPF is an invention based on the accounts of the characteristics of terrorist groups in the media, modern novels, technical analyses, and in recent world news reports. No relationship to any particular terrorist group is either known or implied.

The names used for the characters in the short stories were selected at random, and any similarity to real persons, living or dead, anywhere in the world is purely coincidental. The city name, Yorksberg, is also pure invention. To Yorksberg, if you really exist, our apologies. Yorksberg has a nice English-American, historical sound to it and we had to let the bad guys blow up a city to make our points. The author hopes this never happens to you or any other city in the world.

INDEX

ABOUT THE AUTHOR

Vern Blanchette is a graduate of the University of Alabama (B.S. – Physics/Mathematics) and the University of Texas at Austin (M.Ed.). He has taught in public schools, community colleges, and for General Electric Company in the commercial nuclear power industry. He recently retired as an engineer with URS Corporation at the Kennedy Space Center.

Mr. Blanchette, married with six children, has been writing for more than thirty years, and is an alumnus of the Christian Writer's Conference at Lake Yale, Florida. His unpublished works include several science fiction stories, and a historical romance novel wherein love reaches across the centuries to reveal a treasure hidden for hundreds of years.

Published Works

Safe Schools Now – Arming America's Teachers, begun October 6, 2011, Dog Ear Publishing, 2013. Written after the Sandy Hook massacre, this book uses facts and four fictional stories to demonstrate the only way to truly protect school children from murderers is to train and arm the school teachers and staff.

An Encounter with the Honey Island Swamp Monster. Createspace, 2016. This is a true story of a strange encounter with something in a dark, Mississippi swamp. Exactly what was that thing?

Why You are Alive on Earth – Why do You Exist? Createspace, 2016. This book answers that question with some amazing revelations. Do you know why you are here, and who you really are?

Comments to the author may be sent to Survive@CFL.RR.COM.

NOTES

NOTES

Cover: Special thanks to my daughter for her help on the design of the cover for both Part 1 and Part 2 of this book.

This book was published through Createspace.com and is available from any decent book store.